EFFICIENT ALGORITHMS
FOR LISTING COMBINATORIAL STRUCTURES

Distinguished Dissertations in Computer Science

Edited by
C.J. van Rijsbergen, University of Glasgow

The Conference of Professors of Computer Science (CPCS) in conjunction
with the British Computer Society (BCS), selects annually for publication up
to four of the best British Ph.D. dissertations in computer science. The scheme
began in 1990. Its aim is to make more visible the significant contribution
made by Britain - in particular by students - to computer science, and to
provide a model for future students. Dissertations are selected on behalf of
CPCS by a panel whose members are:

M. Clint, Queen's University, Belfast
R.J.M. Hughes, University of Glasgow
R. Milner, University of Edinburgh (Chairman)
K. Moody, University of Cambridge
M.S. Paterson, University of Warwick
S. Shrivastava, University of Newcastle upon Tyne
A. Sloman, University of Birmingham
F. Sumner, University of Manchester

EFFICIENT ALGORITHMS FOR LISTING COMBINATORIAL STRUCTURES

Leslie Ann Goldberg
Sandia National Laboratories

CAMBRIDGE UNIVERSITY PRESS
Cambridge, New York, Melbourne, Madrid, Cape Town, Singapore, São Paulo, Delhi

Cambridge University Press
The Edinburgh Building, Cambridge CB2 8RU, UK

Published in the United States of America by Cambridge University Press, New York

www.cambridge.org
Information on this title: www.cambridge.org/9780521117883

First published 1993
This digitally printed version 2009

A catalogue record for this publication is available from the British Library

ISBN 978-0-521-45021-8 hardback
ISBN 978-0-521-11788-3 paperback

Table of Contents

Abstract

This thesis studies the problem of designing efficient algorithms for listing combinatorial structures. The main notion of efficiency that we use is due to Johnson, Yannakakis, and Papadimitriou. It is called *polynomial delay.* A listing algorithm is said to have *delay d* if and only if it satisfies the following conditions whenever it is run with any input *p*:

1. It executes at most $d(p)$ machine instructions before either producing the first output or halting.

2. After any output it executes at most $d(p)$ machine instructions before either producing the next output or halting.

An algorithm is said to have *polynomial delay* if its delay is bounded from above by a polynomial in the length of the input. In the thesis we also define a weaker notion of efficiency which we call *cumulative polynomial delay.*

There are some families of combinatorial structures for which it is easy to design a polynomial delay listing algorithm. For example, it is easy to design a polynomial delay algorithm that takes as input a unary integer *n* and lists all *n*-vertex graphs. In this thesis we focus on more difficult problems such as the following.

Problem 1 — Listing unlabeled graphs

Design a polynomial delay algorithm that takes as input a unary integer *n* and lists exactly one representative from each isomorphism class in the set of *n*-vertex graphs.

Problem 2 — Listing Hamiltonian graphs

Design a polynomial delay algorithm that takes as input a unary integer *n* and lists all Hamiltonian *n*-vertex graphs.

We start the thesis by developing general methods for solving listing problems such as 1 and 2. Then we apply the methods to specific combinatorial families obtaining various listing algorithms including the following.

1. A polynomial space polynomial delay listing algorithm for unlabeled graphs

2. A polynomial space polynomial delay listing algorithm for any first order one property†

---

† A first order graph property is called a *one property* if and only if it is the case that almost every graph has the property.

3. A polynomial delay listing algorithm for Hamiltonian graphs

4. A polynomial space polynomial delay listing algorithm for graphs with cliques of specified sizes

5. A polynomial space cumulative polynomial delay listing algorithm for k-colorable graphs

We conclude the thesis by presenting some related work. First, we compare the computational difficulty of listing with the difficulty of solving the existence problem, the construction problem, the random sampling problem, and the counting problem. Next, we consider a particular computational counting problem which is related to a listing problem described earlier in the thesis. The counting problem that we consider is the problem of evaluating Pólya's *cycle index polynomial*. We show that the problem of determining particular coefficients of the polynomial is #P-hard and we use this result to show that the evaluation problem is #P-hard except in certain special cases. We also show that in many cases it is NP-hard even to evaluate the cycle index polynomial *approximately*.

Acknowledgements

My advisor Mark Jerrum has made a significant contribution to the work described in this thesis and to my mathematical education. I am grateful to him for suggesting the topic of this thesis, for teaching me how to develop intuition about mathematical problems, for reading my work, and for making many helpful suggestions. I am also grateful to my second advisor, Alistair Sinclair, who has read much of my work and provided encouragement and useful suggestions. I am grateful to Bob Hiromoto and Olaf Lubeck of Los Alamos and to Corky Cartwright, Ken Kennedy, and other professors at Rice for helping me to develop the academic self-confidence that sustained me during difficult times. Finally, I am grateful to the Marshall Aid Commemoration Commission of the UK and to the National Science Foundation of the USA for providing the financial support for my PhD.

Declaration

This thesis was composed by me and the work described in the thesis is my own except where stated otherwise. Some of the material in chapter 2 has appeared in [Gol1 90] and some of the material in chapter 5 has appeared in [Gol2 90].

Leslie Ann Goldberg, December 1991

General References

Background material and definitions of standard terms and notation can be found in the following references.

Algorithms and Discrete Mathematics....................[AHU 74, CLR 90, Knu 73]

Complexity Theory .... [GJ 79, HU 79]

Graph Theory..[Gib 85, Bol 85, Hof 82]

Probability Theory .... [Fel 68, Bol 85]

Permutation Groups ....[Led 73, BW 79, Hof 82]

Pólya Theory (and Burnside's Lemma) ....[HP 73, DeB 64, PR 87]

Index of Notation and Terms

1. Introduction

This thesis studies the problem of designing listing algorithms for families of combinatorial structures. In particular, it studies the problem of designing listing algorithms whose implementations do not use overwhelming quantities of computational resources. The computational resources that are considered are running time and storage space. Using standard terminology from complexity theory, we indicate that the time and space requirements of an algorithm are small by saying that the algorithm is "efficient".

Section 1 of this chapter introduces our problem by defining the notion of a *family* of structures. It explains informally what we mean by a *listing algorithm* for a family of structures without discussing computational details. Section 1.2 motivates the study, describing three reasons that the problem deserves attention. Section 1.3 gives the phrase "listing algorithm" a precise meaning. In this section we specify a deterministic computational machine and a probabilistic machine. We discuss the process of implementing combinatorial listing algorithms on these machines. Section 1.4 establishes criteria which we will use to determine whether or not a given listing algorithm is efficient. The criteria will be sufficiently general that we will be able to change the computational machines that we consider (within a large class of "reasonable" machines) without changing the set of families of combinatorial structures that have efficient listing algorithms. Section 1.5 contains a synopsis of the thesis. Finally, section 1.6 contains some bibliographic remarks.

1.1. Families of Combinatorial Structures

A *simple family* of combinatorial structures is an infinite collection of finite sets of structures together with a specification of a parameter. Each set in the family is associated with a particular value of the parameter. Here are three examples of simple families of combinatorial structures.

Example 1 — The family $\mathcal{G}$
Every parameter value of $\mathcal{G}$ is a positive integer. The value n is associated with the set $\mathcal{G}(n)$ which contains all undirected graphs that have vertex set $V_n = \{v_1, \ldots, v_n\}$:

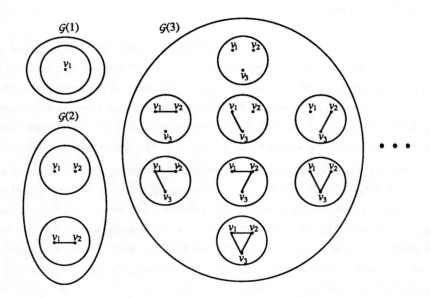

Example 2 — The family Pa

Every parameter value of Pa is an undirected graph. The value G is associated with the set $Pa(G)$ which contains all undirected simple paths in G. Suppose that the graphs G_1 and G_2 are defined as follows:

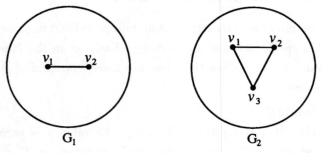

G_1 G_2

Then we have

$$Pa(G_1) = \{[v_1], [v_2], [v_1, v_2]\}$$

$$Pa(G_2) = \{[v_1], [v_2], [v_3], [v_1, v_2], [v_1, v_3], [v_2, v_3], [v_1, v_2, v_3], [v_1, v_3, v_2], [v_2, v_1, v_3]\}$$

Example 3 — The family SAT

Every parameter value of SAT is a boolean formula. The value F is associated with the set SAT(F) which contains all satisfying assignments of F. Suppose that F is the formula $F = x_1 \vee \overline{x_2}$. Then we have

$$\text{SAT}(F) = \{[x_1 = 1, x_2 = 1], [x_1 = 1, x_2 = 0], [x_1 = 0, x_2 = 0]\}.$$

We have said that these three families are *simple* because they treat each combinatorial structure (i.e. each graph, each path, and each assignment) as being distinct. In general, a *family* of combinatorial structures is an infinite collection of finite sets of *equivalence classes* of structures together with a specification of a parameter. Once again, each set in the family is associated with a particular value of the parameter. For example, one well-known equivalence relation on undirected graphs is graph isomorphism. Using this relation, we obtain an example of a non-simple family.

Example 3 — The family $\widetilde{\widetilde{\mathcal{G}}}$

Every parameter value of $\widetilde{\widetilde{\mathcal{G}}}$ is a positive integer. The value n is associated with the set $\widetilde{\widetilde{\mathcal{G}}}(n)$ which contains the isomorphism classes of $\mathcal{G}(n)$:

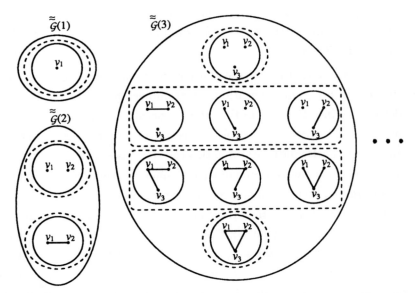

As the examples have demonstrated, we use the notation $S(p)$ to refer to the set of equivalence classes that is associated with parameter value p in family S. We say that a structure s is a *structure of S* if and only if there is a parameter value p of S such that s is a member of an equivalence class in $S(p)$.

A *simple* family can be viewed more generally as being a family in which the equivalence relation is the identity relation. We will view simple families in this way whenever it is convenient to do so.

In order to associate *computational* problems with families of combinatorial structures, we will specify a particular computational machine. A *listing algorithm* for a family S of structures is a program written in the language of our machine that takes as input a value p of the parameter of S and lists exactly one representative from each equivalence class in $S(p)$. In the next section, we describe three reasons for studying the problem of designing efficient listing algorithms for families of combinatorial structures.

1.2. Motivation

1.2.1. Designing Useful Algorithms

The most obvious reason for undertaking this study is that it produces useful algorithms. Algorithms for listing combinatorial structures have been used for solving a variety of practical problems from diverse fields such as chemistry, electrical engineering, and automatic program optimization (See, for example, the works that are referenced in [Chr 75, BvL 87, and CR1 79]).

Lists of combinatorial structures are also useful to computer programmers. Despite theoretical advances in program verification, programmers generally use some empirical testing in order to convince themselves that their programs are correct. Efficient listing algorithms can be used to provide valuable sources of test data. Listing algorithms for non-simple families are particularly useful in this case because the lists of structures that these algorithms produce do not contain numerous copies of structures that are essentially "the same". For example, there are many computer programs for solving graph-theoretic problems which have the property that their behavior is independent of the labeling of the vertices of the input graph. That is, if G_1 and G_2 are two isomorphic graphs then the behavior of such a program is the same when it is run with input G_1 as it is when it is run with input G_2. To test such a program one would only require one representative from each isomorphism class of graphs. Therefore a listing algorithm for $\widetilde{\widetilde{\mathcal{G}}}$ could be used to provide test data.

Lists of structures have also been used extensively by combinatorialists. Examining such a list can suggest conjectures and can provide counter-examples to existing conjectures. Furthermore, lists of combinatorial structures contain empirical information about questions that seem to be difficult to answer theoretically. The usefulness of lists of combinatorial structures is explained in [Rea 81, NW 78, and SW 86]. McKay and

Royle document some of the efforts that have been made by mathematicians to produce such lists [MR 86].

1.2.2. Discovering General Methods for Algorithm Design

A second reason for undertaking this study is that it yields general methods for designing algorithms.

It is true that there are already several well-known general techniques which can be used to obtain efficient algorithms for listing various simple families of combinatorial structures [NW 78, BvL 87]. However, the families to which the techniques apply all have the property that the structures of a given size are constructed by augmenting smaller structures – that is, the families have inductive definitions. It is not clear, however, how these general techniques should be applied to the problem of listing more complicated families of structures. For example, it is not clear how the techniques could be applied to the problem of designing listing algorithms for non-simple families of structures.

Despite the absence of general techniques, various researchers have discovered efficient listing algorithms for some non-simple families of structures (see for example the algorithms in [BH 80] and [WROM 86] which list unlabeled trees). Unfortunately, it seems difficult to modify these algorithms to come up with efficient listing algorithms for other more complicated families such as $\widetilde{\widetilde{\mathcal{G}}}$.

In this work, we devise general listing techniques which we use to obtain efficient listing algorithms for various non-simple families of combinatorial structures including the family $\widetilde{\widetilde{\mathcal{G}}}$.

1.2.3. Learning about Combinatorial Structures

A third reason for studying the problem of designing efficient algorithms for listing combinatorial structures is that such a study contributes directly to our knowledge about the structures themselves. In part, this contribution is due to the mathematical content of the algorithms. Efficient techniques for listing combinatorial structures often depend upon non-trivial properties of the structures. Therefore, the search for an efficient listing algorithm for a specific family of combinatorial structures can lead to interesting discoveries about the structures in the family.

More generally, we view the property of having an efficient listing algorithm as being a mathematical property of a family of structures and we study families of combinatorial structures by determining whether or not they have efficient listing algorithms. This thesis concentrates on positive results. That is, we concentrate on showing that particular families of structures *do* have efficient listing algorithms. A few negative results are discussed in the bibliographic note at the end of this chapter and in chapter 5.

Now that we have discussed several reasons for studying the problem of designing efficient listing algorithms for families of combinatorial structures, we proceed to set up the framework for the study.

1.3. Listing Algorithms

The machine that we take as our model of deterministic computation is the random access machine (see [AHU 74]). This machine consists of a read-only input tape, a write-only output tape, a finite program written in a very simple machine language, and a sequence of registers $r_0, r_1, \ldots$, each of which is capable of holding an integer of arbitrary size. Each square on a tape of a random access machine is capable of holding a single character from a finite input/output language such as the language $\{0, 1, -, [,], (,), , \}$ which is used in [GJ 79].

The machine that we take as our model of probabilistic computation is the probabilistic random access machine. This machine is identical to an ordinary random access machine except that it can execute an additional machine instruction that causes it to flip an unbiased coin [Gil 77].

In order to write a random access machine program for listing a family of combinatorial structures, we must encode the relevant parameter values and structures as strings in the language that the machine uses for input and output. We will measure the efficiency of our programs in terms of the computational resources that they use when they are given encoded parameter values of specified lengths. Therefore, the results that we obtain regarding efficiency will depend upon the encoding schemes that we use. In this section, we will describe a few criteria that we can apply to determine whether or not a given encoding scheme is "reasonable". As long as we restrict our attention to "reasonable" encoding schemes, the results that we obtain will not depend upon the specific scheme that we use. Therefore, this thesis will often blur the distinction between parameter values and encoded parameter values and the distinction between structures and encoded structures. In the course of this work, we will not spell out the encodings that we use but we will assume that they conform to our established criteria. We will explicitly describe any encoding schemes that we use that do not conform to the criteria.

The criteria that we will use are the following. First, we will restrict our attention to encoded families in which structures have concise encodings. That is, we will assume that each encoded family S that we consider can be associated with a polynomial r in such a way that for every pair (p, s) in which p is an encoded parameter value of S and s is an encoded structure whose equivalence class is in $S(p)$ we have $|s| \leq r(|p|)$†. Second, we will assume that encodings are "reasonable" in the sense of Garey and Johnson [GJ 79] unless such an assumption causes the first criterion to be violated.

In order to ensure that our model of computation is "realistic", we will not consider algorithms that use random access machine registers to store extremely large integers. In fact, any given run of any algorithm that we consider will only store integers whose binary representations are polynomially long in the number of tape cells that are used to store the encoded input parameter value.

We are now ready for the following definition. A deterministic *listing algorithm* for a family S of combinatorial structures is a random access machine program that takes as input an encoded value p of the parameter of S and lists exactly one encoded representative from each equivalence class in $S(p)$.

In most contexts, a *probabilistic* algorithm for performing a given task is defined to be a program running on a probabilistic machine that has the property that a given run of the program with any specific input is very likely to perform the task correctly, but may in fact fail to do so. In the context of listing combinatorial structures, we choose a fairly restrictive notion of a probabilistic algorithm. In particular, we require that when a probabilistic algorithm for listing a family of structures fails to list exactly one representative from each equivalence class in the appropriate set that it fails by leaving out some of the equivalence classes entirely. That is, we consider algorithms that sometimes omit some of the structures that should be output but we do not consider algorithms that produce outputs that are "wrong".

More formally, a *probabilistic listing algorithm* with *failure probability* ρ for a family S of combinatorial structures is a random access machine program that takes as input an encoded value of the parameter p and lists exactly one encoded representative from zero or more equivalence class in $S(p)$. We require that on a given run of the program with input p the probability that *all* of the classes in $S(p)$ are represented in the output is at least $1 - \rho(p)$. Furthermore, we require that for every parameter value p it is the case that $\rho(p) \leq 1/2$.

We say that the failure probability ρ of a probabilistic listing algorithm is *exponentially small* if there is a constant $c > 1$ such that for every parameter value p it is the case that $\rho(p) \leq c^{-|p|}$.

---

† The notation $|s|$ denotes the length of the string s.

Following Aho, Hopcroft, and Ullman, we will generally describe algorithms in a rather high-level language, relying on the fact that it is very easy to translate these algorithms to random access machine programs.

1.4. Efficient Listing Algorithms

Now that we have explained what we mean by a "listing algorithm" for a family of combinatorial structures, we can proceed to explain what we mean by an *efficient* algorithm for listing combinatorial structures.

We begin by considering running time. Intuitively, a listing algorithm is "fast" if it produces outputs in quick succession one after the other. There are several ways in which this idea can be formalized [JYP 88]. We will discuss two natural formalizations of the idea which we will refer to throughout the thesis.

We will need the following definition. An algorithm for listing a family of combinatorial structures is said to have *delay* d if and only if it satisfies the following conditions whenever it is run with any input p:

1. It executes at most $d(p)$ machine instructions† before either outputting the first structure or halting.

2. After any output it executes at most $d(p)$ machine instructions before either outputting the next structure or halting.

It is quite natural to say that a listing algorithm with small delay is a "fast" listing algorithm. Johnson, Yannakakis, and Papadimitriou refer to algorithms whose delay is bounded from above by a polynomial in the length of the input as *polynomial delay* algorithms. *Polynomial delay* is the strongest notion of "fast" that is considered in their paper [JYP 88] and is the strongest notion that will be considered in this thesis.

There is a sense, however, in which the notion of polynomial delay seems to be too strong to be a reasonable definition of "fast". Consider the following deterministic algorithms for listing a simple family S in which $|S(p)| = 2^{|p|}$. Algorithm $\mathcal{A}$ takes input p and produces an output from $S(p)$ after every sequence of $2|p|$ instructions. Algorithm $\mathcal{B}$ takes the same input p and produces an output from $S(p)$ after every sequence of $|p|$ instructions until there is just one structure remaining to be output. Then it takes $2^{|p|}$ instructions to produce the last structure. Clearly, algorithm $\mathcal{B}$ is always ahead of

---

† The amount of time needed to execute a single machine instruction is referred to as a "time step" or simply as a "step" of a computation.

algorithm $\mathcal{A}$. However, using our definition, we can easily see that algorithm $\mathcal{A}$ has polynomial delay and algorithm $\mathcal{B}$ does not.

In order to get around this difficulty, we provide a slightly weaker notion of "fast". We say that a listing algorithm has *cumulative delay d* if it is the case that at any point of time in any execution of the algorithm with any input p the total number of instructions that have been executed is at most $d(p)$ plus the product of $d(p)$ and the number of structures that have been output so far. While algorithm $\mathcal{B}$ does not have polynomial delay, its *cumulative delay* is bounded from above by $|p| + 1$, so we say that it has *cumulative polynomial delay*. It is easy to see that any algorithm that has delay d has cumulative delay d, so $\mathcal{A}$ also has cumulative polynomial delay.

Now that we have established criteria for determining whether or not a given listing algorithm is fast, we turn to the problem of determining whether or not it uses storage space efficiently.

We say that an algorithm has *space complexity r* if it is the case that whenever it is run with any input p it uses at most $r(p)$ random access machine registers†. We generally consider an algorithm to be space-efficient if and only if its space complexity is bounded from above by a polynomial in the length of the input. In this case, we say that the algorithm is a *polynomial space* algorithm.

It is easy to see that there are polynomial delay listing algorithms that do not have polynomially-bounded space complexity. Therefore, in the context of listing, we should consider the question of whether or not an algorithm is fast independently of the question of whether or not it is space-efficient‡

If we are only concerned with whether or not a given listing algorithm is fast and we are not concerned with the amount of storage space that it uses then it will not matter very much whether we take *polynomial delay* or *cumulative polynomial delay* as our notion of "fast". In fact, we could easily transform an algorithm with cumulative delay d to an algorithm with delay d. We would simply modify the algorithm so that it places structures in a large buffer rather than outputting them. We would then interrupt the execution of the algorithm with input p after every $d(p)$ steps in order to output from the buffer. We would need to use quite a lot of registers to store the buffer, however.

---

† For technical reasons, we assume that $r(p) \geq 1$.

‡ These two questions cannot be considered independently if our model of computation is the Turing Machine because the simulation of a *single* high-level instruction on a Turing Machine requires the machine to read its entire work tape. Therefore, we have chosen the random access machine as our model of computation.

In practice, one would probably prefer a cumulative polynomial delay algorithm that runs in polynomial space to the polynomial delay algorithm that could be obtained by applying this transformation.

1.5. Synopsis of the Thesis

Before giving a detailed synopsis of the thesis we first describe its general outline. Chapter 2 discusses general techniques for listing combinatorial structures. We illustrate the techniques by applying them to specific families of structures, but the primary purpose of the chapter is to explain the methods. More comprehensive applications are presented in chapter 3. The purpose of that chapter is to describe particular algorithms that we have developed and to describe what we have learned about combinatorial structures in the course of this work. Chapter 4 discusses open problems and directions for future work in listing. Finally, chapter 5 contains related results. In this chapter we compare the computational difficulty of the listing problem with the difficulty of other computational problems involving combinatorial structures. In addition, we consider a particular computational counting problem which is related to a listing problem described in chapter 4.

Now that we have described the general outline of the thesis, we present a more detailed synopsis. We start by describing chapter 2, which discusses general techniques for listing combinatorial structures.

In section 2.1 we focus our attention on certain *simple* families of structures. We consider two basic methods which can be used to design efficient listing algorithms for these families. First, in subsection 2.1.1, we consider the class of *recursively listable* families. We show how to use the inductive structure of these families to obtain efficient listing algorithms. There are many known listing algorithms that are based on the idea of exploiting inductive structure. Since this idea is well understood we do not really pursue it in this thesis. However, we consider recursively listable families in subsection 2.1.1 so that we can describe the recursive listing method which we will use as a building block when we design more powerful listing methods later in the thesis.

In subsection 2.1.2 we consider the class of simple families which have efficient random sampling algorithms. First, we show how to use an efficient random sampling algorithm for a simple family of structures to obtain a probabilistic polynomial delay listing algorithm for that family. The listing algorithms that we obtain using this method require exponential space. We use an information-theoretic argument to show that *any* uniform reduction from polynomial delay listing to efficient random sampling must produce exponential space algorithms. Finally, we show that we can trade delay for space in our reduction, obtaining listing algorithms which use less space and have longer delays.

In section 2.2 we describe two general methods which we will use in our design of listing algorithms. The first method is called the interleaving method and the second is called the filter method.

In section 2.3 we show how the techniques from the first two sections of chapter 2 can be used to design efficient listing algorithms for *non-simple* families of structures. We start by considering probabilistic listing algorithms in subsection 2.3.1. This subsection defines the notion of an efficient random sampling algorithm for a non-simple family and demonstrates the fact that random sampling can be used in the design of polynomial delay probabilistic listing algorithms for these families. The subsection contains two examples that demonstrate the ease with which known results about combinatorial structures can be combined with random sampling methods to yield efficient probabilistic listing algorithms for non-simple families. In particular, it contains a polynomial delay probabilistic algorithm for listing unlabeled graphs and a polynomial delay probabilistic algorithm which takes input n and lists the $k(n)$-colorable n-vertex graphs where k is any function from $\mathbf{N}$ to $\mathbf{N}$ which satisfies *Kučera's condition* (see p. 55.)

In subsection 2.3.2 we discuss the problem of designing *deterministic* listing algorithms for non-simple families. We present two approaches to solving the problem. One of the approaches is based on the filter method and the other is based on the interleaving method. We illustrate the approaches by using them to design two non-trivial listing algorithms. The first is a polynomial delay listing algorithm for a certain family of graphs whose members can be colored with a specified number of colors. The second is a polynomial space polynomial delay listing algorithm for the family $\widetilde{\widetilde{\mathcal{G}}}$.

Chapter 3 contains more comprehensive applications of our listing methods. The purpose of the chapter is to describe particular algorithms that we have developed and to describe what we have learned about combinatorial structures in the course of the work. The sections in chapter 3 are fairly independent of each other, although they are not completely independent.

In section 3.1 we consider the problem of listing first order graph properties. We distinguish between first order one properties and first order zero properties. We show that every first order one property has an efficient listing algorithm and we describe a general method that can be used to obtain a polynomial space polynomial delay listing algorithm for any first order one property.

In section 3.2 we consider the problem of listing Hamiltonian graphs. We present a polynomial delay algorithm for listing these graphs.

In section 3.3 we consider the problem of listing graphs with cliques of specified sizes. We obtain the following results. Suppose that j is a function from N to N such that $j(n) \leq n$ for every $n \in \mathsf{N}$. If there are positive constants ϵ and n_0 such that $j(n) \leq (1-\epsilon)\log(n)$† for every $n \geq n_0$ then we can use the interleaving method to design a polynomial space polynomial delay algorithm that takes input n and lists all n-vertex graphs that have a clique of size $j(n)$. If, on the other hand, there are positive constants ϵ and n_0 such that $j(n) \geq (2+\epsilon)\log(n)$ for every $n \geq n_0$ then we can use the filter method to design a polynomial delay algorithm that takes input n and lists all n-vertex graphs containing cliques of size $j(n)$. We discuss the problem of listing graphs with cliques whose sizes are between $\log(n)$ and $2\log(n)$.

In section 3.4 we consider the problem of listing graphs which can be colored with a specified number of colors. This problem turns out to be rather difficult, so the results that we obtain are incomplete. However, we do obtain the following results. Suppose that k is a function from N to N such that $k(n) \leq n$ for every $n \in \mathsf{N}$. If there is a positive constant n_0 such that $k(n) \leq \sqrt{n/28\log(n)}$ for every $n \geq n_0$ then we are able to design a deterministic polynomial delay algorithm that takes input n and lists the $k(n)$-colorable n-vertex graphs. If $k(n) = O(1)$ then we are able to design a deterministic *polynomial space* cumulative polynomial delay algorithm that takes input n and lists the $k(n)$-colorable n-vertex graphs. Finally, if there are positive constants ϵ and n_0 such that for every $n \geq n_0$ we have $k(n) \geq (1+\epsilon)n/\log(n)$ then we are able to design a probabilistic polynomial delay algorithm that takes input n and lists the $k(n)$-colorable n-vertex graphs.

In chapter 4 we discuss open problems and directions for future work on listing. We focus our attention on two particular problems — the problem of designing efficient listing algorithms for unlabeled graph properties and the problem of designing efficient listing algorithms for equivalence classes of functions.

In chapter 5 we describe some work which is related to the work contained in chapters 1–4. In section 5.1 we compare the computational difficulty of listing with the difficulty of solving four other computational problems involving combinatorial structures. In particular, we compare the difficulty of solving the listing problem with the difficulty of solving the *existence* problem, the *construction* problem, the *random sampling* problem, and the *counting* problem.

---

† All logarithms in this thesis are to the base 2.

In section 5.2 we consider a specific computational counting problem which is related to a listing problem which was described in chapter 4. In particular, we consider the computational difficulty of evaluating and approximately evaluating Pólya's *Cycle Index Polynomial*. We show that the problem of determining particular coefficients of the polynomial is #P-hard and we use this result to show that the evaluation problem is #P-hard except in certain special cases, which are discussed in chapter 5. Chapter 5 also contains a proof showing that in many cases it is NP-hard even to evaluate the cycle index polynomial *approximately*.

In subsection 5.2.1 we give some corollaries of our results which describe the difficulty of solving certain counting problems which are related to listing problems which were discussed in chapter 4.

1.6. Bibliographic Notes

It appears that the first person to study the difficulty of listing from the perspective of computational complexity was Paul Young [You 69]. Young was primarily concerned with the difficulty of listing infinite sets. The notion of polynomial enumerability which follows from Young's definitions is described in [HHSY 91]. It is similar to the notion of cumulative polynomial delay.

The notion of cumulative polynomial delay does not appear in any of the subsequent papers studying the difficulty of computational listing. This note surveys the alternatives which have been considered.

Hartmanis and Yesha's paper [HY 84] introduces the notion of *P-printability* which is commonly used as a notion of polynomial enumeration [HHSY 91]. A set S is said to be *P-printable* if and only if there is a polynomial time Turing machine that takes input n (in unary) and outputs all elements of S of length at most n. Hartmanis and Yesha point out that every P-printable set is sparse and in P. As one will see from the examples in this thesis and elsewhere, algorithm designers are often required to design fast listing algorithms for dense sets† (and, less often, for sets whose membership problem is not known to be in P‡). For these reasons we choose not to consider the notion of P-printability in this thesis.

A third notion of polynomial enumeration comes from the paper [HHSY 91] by Hemachandra, Hoene, Siefkes, and Young. Hemachandra et al. say that a set S is *polynomially*

---

† For example, one may want to list all permutations of $\{1, \ldots, n\}$.
‡ See, for example, the algorithm for listing Hamiltonian graphs in section 3.2.

enumerable by iteration if it is of the form $S = \{x, f(x), f(f(x)), \ldots\}$ for some polynomial time computable function f. Their definition is analogous to a recursion-theoretic characterization of recursive enumerability. From the perspective of algorithm design there seems to be no reason for restricting attention to algorithms which use an iterative technique. Therefore we have not considered the difficulty of enumeration by iteration in this thesis.

A fourth notion of polynomial enumeration was introduced in the paper [Tar 73] by Tarjan. The notion was later called *polynomial total time* by Johnson, Yannakakis, and Papadimitriou [JYP 88]. A listing algorithm for a family of combinatorial structures is said to run in *polynomial total time* if and only if its running time is bounded from above by a polynomial in the size of the input and the number of outputs.

It is easy to show that there are families of combinatorial structures which do not have polynomial total time listing algorithms. In order to describe one such family we will consider the EXPTIME-complete problem CHECKERS:

CHECKERS

Input: An $n \times n$ checkers board with some arrangement of black and white pieces

Question: Can white force a win?

Robson showed in [Rob 84] that there is no polynomial time algorithm for solving this problem although the problem can be solved in $p(n)\, 5^{n^2}$ time for some polynomial p since there are at most 5^{n^2} possible $n \times n$ checkers boards. We can now observe that the following family has no polynomial total time listing algorithm.

CHECKERS$_1$ — Every parameter value of CHECKERS$_1$ is a square checkers board with some arrangement of black and white pieces. The board B is associated with the set

$$\text{CHECKERS}_1(B) = \begin{cases} \{\text{``yes''}\} & \text{if white can force a win on } B \\ \{\text{``no''}\} & \text{otherwise.} \end{cases}$$

While there are families that have no polynomial total time listing algorithms it is still true that *polynomial total time* is a weaker criterion for efficiency than *cumulative polynomial delay*. To see this, observe that every cumulative polynomial delay algorithm runs in polynomial total time. On the other hand, the following family has a polynomial total time listing algorithm and does not have a cumulative polynomial delay listing algorithm.

CHECKERS$_2$ — Every parameter value of CHECKERS$_2$ is a square checkers board with some arrangement of black and white pieces. The $n \times n$ board B is associated with the set

$$\text{CHECKERS}_2(B) = \left\{ \langle x, y \rangle \; \middle| \; \begin{array}{l} x \text{ is an integer between 1 and } 5^{n^2} \text{ and} \\ y \text{ is a member of CHECKERS}_1(B) \end{array} \right\}.$$

Lawler, Lenstra, and Rinooy Kan's paper [LLR 80] describes a number of polynomial total time algorithms for listing combinatorial structures. Many of the algorithms described in their paper actually have polynomial delay. However, their listing algorithm for "on time sets of jobs" is a natural example of a polynomial total time algorithm for listing a combinatorial family which has no known cumulative polynomial delay listing algorithm.

The first paper to compare the notion of polynomial total time with other notions of polynomial enumerability is [JYP 88]. This paper discusses the notion of polynomial total time and introduces the notion of polynomial delay. It also introduces a new notion called *incremental polynomial time*. Listing in incremental polynomial time is more difficult than listing in polynomial total time and is easier than listing with cumulative polynomial delay. In particular, an incremental polynomial time algorithm for listing a family S is a polynomial time algorithm which takes as input a parameter value p and a subset S' of $S(p)$ and returns a member of $S(p) - S'$ or determines that $S(p) = S'$.

We conclude this bibliographic note by mentioning one more criterion for efficient listing which is being used by researchers. An algorithm for listing a combinatorial family S is said to run in *constant average time* [RH 77] if and only if there is a constant c such that whenever it is run with any parameter value p its *computation* time is bounded from above by $c|S(p)|$. (Note that more time will be needed for printing the output.) Constant average time algorithms are based on the idea of Gray codes. (See [RH 77], [NW 78], and [Wil 89]).

2. Techniques for Listing Combinatorial Structures

This chapter describes general techniques for listing combinatorial structures. Section 2.1 describes two basic methods for listing certain *simple* families of structures. Section 2.2 describes two methods that can be used when we have an efficient listing algorithm for a family S and we want to design an efficient listing algorithm for another family that is closely related to S. Finally, section 2.3 explains how the techniques from the first two sections of this chapter can be used to design efficient listing algorithms for *non-simple* families of structures. We conclude the chapter by using the methods that we have described to design two non-trivial listing algorithms. The first is a polynomial delay listing algorithm for a certain family of graphs whose members can be colored with a specified number of colors. The second is a polynomial space polynomial delay listing algorithm for the family $\widetilde{\widetilde{\mathcal{G}}}$.

2.1. Basic Building Blocks

In this section we describe two basic methods which can be used to design efficient listing algorithms for certain simple families of combinatorial structures. First, in subsection 2.1.1, we consider a class of families which we call *recursively listable* families. We show how to use the inductive structure of these families to obtain efficient listing algorithms. Next, in subsection 2.1.2, we consider a class of families whose members have efficient random sampling algorithms. We show how to use the random sampling algorithms to obtain efficient listing algorithms.

2.1.1. Recursive Listing

The introduction to this thesis points out that there are well-known efficient techniques for listing certain simple families of structures that have inductive definitions. We call these families *recursively listable* families. Since there are known methods for designing efficient listing algorithms for recursively-listable families we do not study these families in this thesis. However, we find it useful to discuss the concept of a "recursively listable" family. We discuss this concept in this subsection and we show how to use the inductive definitions of these families to obtain polynomial space polynomial delay listing algorithms.

There are two reasons for discussing recursively listable families in this subsection. First, the discussion enables us to recognize recursively listable families. When we come across such a family later in the thesis we will be able to use its inductive definition to obtain an efficient listing algorithm so we will not need to resort to complicated listing methods. Second, we will use the recursive method that we describe in this subsection as a building block when we design listing algorithms for more complicated families later in the thesis.

In order to explain the notion of a "recursively listable" family we start by considering a very elementary example. Let $\mathcal{G}$ be the simple family of graphs which we described in example 1. Every parameter value of $\mathcal{G}$ is a positive integer which is encoded in unary†. The value n is associated with the set $\mathcal{G}(n)$ which contains all undirected graphs with vertex set $V_n = \{v_1, \ldots, v_n\}$. We will show that $\mathcal{G}$ can be defined inductively and that the inductive definition can be used to obtain a polynomial space polynomial delay listing algorithm for $\mathcal{G}$.

For the base case we observe that the only graph in $\mathcal{G}(1)$ is $(V_1, \varnothing)$. For the inductive case we will establish a relationship between the members of $\mathcal{G}(n)$ and the members of $\mathcal{G}(n-1)$. Our method will be as follows. For every integer $n > 1$ and every graph $G \in \mathcal{G}(n)$ we will designate a particular member of $\mathcal{G}(n-1)$ which we will call the *truncation* of G. For every positive integer n and every graph $G \in \mathcal{G}(n)$ we will define the set of *augmentations* of G to be the set $\{G' \in \mathcal{G}(n+1) \mid G \text{ is the truncation of } G'\}$. We will define truncations in such a way that every graph $G \in \mathcal{G}(n)$ is guaranteed to have at least one augmentation. Then we will be able to use the following recursive listing strategy for $\mathcal{G}$:

```
Input n
If (n = 1)
      Output (V₁, ∅)
Else
      For Each graph G ∈ 𝒢(n−1)
            For Each augmentation G' of G
            Output G'
```

---

† The criteria that we established in chapter 1 imply that the parameter values of $\mathcal{G}$ must be encoded in unary. Otherwise, the number of tape cells needed to write down a structure would be exponential in the size of the input.

In order to turn this recursive strategy into a polynomial space polynomial delay listing algorithm for $\mathcal{G}$ we will need a polynomial space polynomial delay algorithm that takes as input a graph $G \in \mathcal{G}(n)$ and lists the augmentations of G.

Suppose that we define truncations in the following manner: For every integer $n > 1$ and every graph $G \in \mathcal{G}(n)$ the truncation of G is defined to be $G - \{v_n\}$. Then there is a polynomial space polynomial delay algorithm for listing augmentations so we obtain a polynomial space polynomial delay listing algorithm for $\mathcal{G}$. The algorithm for listing augmentations is the following:

Procedure *Augment*

Input $G = (V_n, E)$

For Each $W \subseteq V_n$

    (V_{n+1}, $E \cup \{(v_{n+1}, w) \,|\, w \in W\}$) is an augmentation of G

The process of listing the augmentations of a graph $G \in \mathcal{G}(n)$ is very straightforward. There are many interesting families of structures (for example, the *self-reducible* families, which will be discussed later) which have such simple augmentation algorithms. However, there are many recursively listable families which require much more complicated augmentation algorithms. To illustrate this point, we will consider the algorithm of Tsukiyama et al. [TIAS 77] which lists maximal independent sets.

We start with some definitions. Suppose that G is an undirected graph with vertex set V. A subset U of V is called an *independent set* of G if and only if every pair of vertices in U is a non-edge of G. An independent set U is called a *maximal* independent set if and only if every vertex in $V - U$ is adjacent to some vertex in U. Let MI be the simple family of structures with the following definition. Every parameter value of MI is an undirected graph. The value G is associated with the set $MI(G)$ which contains the maximal independent sets of G.

For convenience, we will assume that every n-vertex graph G has vertex set $V_n = \{v_1, \ldots, v_n\}$. We will consider the vertices in V_n to be ordered by index. That is, we will say that v_l is *smaller* than v_m if and only if $l < m$. We will say that a subset U of V_n is *lexicographically smaller* than another subset W of V_n (written $U < W$) if and only if the smallest vertex in $(U-W) \cup (W-U)$ is a member of U. Finally, we will use the notation $\Gamma_G(v_i)$ to denote the set of neighbors of vertex v_i in G.

Following Tsukiyama et al. we will show that MI can be defined inductively and that the inductive definition can be used to obtain a polynomial space polynomial delay listing algorithm for MI. For the base case note that $\{v_1\}$ is the only maximal independent set of the graph $(V_1, \varnothing)$. For the inductive case we will establish a relationship between the members of $MI(G)$ (for $G \in \mathcal{G}(n)$) and the members of $MI(G-\{v_n\})$.

We will define truncations as follows: Suppose that n is greater than 1, that G is a member of $\mathcal{G}(n)$, and that U is a maximal independent set of G. If v_n is a member of U then we define the truncation of U to be the lexicographically least superset of $U-\{v_n\}$ which is a maximal independent set of $G-\{v_n\}$. Otherwise, we define the truncation of U to be U. In either case, the truncation of U is a maximal independent set of $G-\{v_n\}$.

Suppose that n is greater than 1, that G is a member of $\mathcal{G}(n)$, and that U is a maximal independent set of $G-\{v_n\}$. We define the set of augmentations of U (with respect to G) to be the set $\{U' \in MI(G) \mid U \text{ is the truncation of } U'\}$. It is easy to see that if G is a member of $\mathcal{G}(n)$ (for $n > 1$) and U is a maximal independent set of $G-\{v_n\}$ then U has at least one augmentation with respect to G. Therefore, we can use the following recursive listing strategy for MI:

```
Input G = (Vₙ, E)
If G = (V₁, ∅)
    Output {v₁}
Else
    For Each maximal independent set U ∈ MI(G−{vₙ})
        For Each augmentation U′ of U with respect to G
        Output U′
```

In order to turn this recursive strategy into a polynomial space polynomial delay listing algorithm for MI we will need a polynomial space polynomial delay algorithm that takes as input a graph $G \in \mathcal{G}(n)$ (for $n > 1$) and a maximal independent set U of $G-\{v_n\}$ and outputs the augmentations of U with respect to G. It can be shown by case analysis that the following algorithm suffices:

Procedure *Augment*

Input $G \in \mathcal{G}(n)$

Input a maximal independent set U of $G - \{v_n\}$

If $U \cap \Gamma_G(v_n) = \varnothing$

    $U \cup \{v_n\}$ is an augmentation of U

Else

    U is an augmentation of itself

    If $U - \Gamma_G(v_n) \cup \{v_n\}$ is a *maximal* independent set of G

        If U is the lexicographically least superset of $U - \Gamma_G(v_n)$

        which is a maximal independent set of $G - \{v_n\}$

            $U - \Gamma_G(v_n) \cup \{v_n\}$ is an augmentation of U

In order to describe the common features of the two inductive definitions that we have given let S stand for an arbitrary family of combinatorial structures and let c be a positive integer. The inductive definitions have the following form: If p is a parameter value of S such that $|p| < c$ then $S(p)$ is defined directly. Otherwise, we define the structures in $S(p)$ by choosing a shorter parameter value p_1 and defining truncations and augmentations in such a way that $S(p)$ is equal to the set of augmentations (with respect to p) of structures in $S(p_1)$.

In general, there is no reason why we should have to limit ourselves to a *single* shorter parameter value p_1. Suppose that p is an arbitrary parameter value of S and that $|p| \geq c$. Let $p_1, \ldots, p_m$ be some parameter values of S such that each p_i is shorter than p and $S(p_i)$ is non-empty for each i. We can define $S(p)$ inductively in terms of $S(p_1), \ldots, S(p_m)$. (In such a definition we will refer to $p_1, \ldots, p_m$ as the *shorter parameter values* of p.)

Our method will be as follows. For each structure $s \in S(p)$ we designate a particular parameter value p_i which we call the *shorter parameter value* for s. Similarly, we designate a particular structure $s_t \in S(p_i)$ to be the *truncation* of s. As one would expect, we define the set of *augmentations* of a structure $s_t \in S(p_i)$ with respect to p to be the set $\{s'_t \in S(p) \mid s_t \text{ is the truncation of } s'_t\}$.

Suppose that we provide an inductive definition for S and that at least one of the following conditions is satisfied for every parameter value p of S:

1. $|p| < c$

2. For every shorter parameter value p_i of p and every structure $s_t \in S(p_i)$ it is the case that s_t has at least one augmentation with respect to p

Then we can use the following recursive listing strategy for S:

```
Input p
If (|p| < c)
    Output every structure in S(p)
Else
    For Each shorter parameter value pᵢ of p
        For Each structure sₜ ∈ S(pᵢ)
            For Each augmentation s′ₜ of sₜ with respect to p
                Output s′ₜ
```

In order to turn the recursive strategy into a polynomial space polynomial delay listing algorithm for S we will need a polynomial space polynomial delay algorithm which takes as input a parameter value p and lists the shorter parameter values of p. In addition, we will need a polynomial space polynomial delay algorithm that takes as input a parameter value p, a shorter parameter value p_i of p, and a structure $s_t \in S(p_i)$ and outputs the augmentations of s_t with respect to p.

In many cases it is easy to design these algorithms. For example, suppose that S is a simple family of structures which is *self-reducible* [Sch 76]. Suppose further that there is a polynomial time algorithm that takes as input a parameter value p of S and determines whether or not $S(p) = \emptyset$. The self-reducibility of S can be used to construct an inductive definition of S. Furthermore, it is easy to design polynomial space polynomial delay algorithms for listing shorter parameter values and augmentations. Therefore, we obtain a polynomial space polynomial delay listing algorithm for S†

We will conclude this subsection with a final example of an inductive definition for a recursively listable family. We start by defining some terms. Suppose that G is a connected graph with edge set E. A set $C \subseteq E$ is a *cutset* of G if and only if $G - C$ is

---

† Valiant [Val 79] was the first to observe that a simple recursive strategy yields polynomial delay listing algorithms in this case.

disconnected. C is a *minimal* cutset of G if and only if every proper subset of C fails to be a cutset of G. It is easy to see that every minimal cutset of G divides G into exactly two connected components. That is, if G is a connected graph and C is a minimal cutset of G then $G-C$ has two connected components. Let MC be the simple family of structures with the following definition. Every parameter value of MC is a connected graph. The value G is associated with the set $MC(G)$ which contains the minimal cutsets of G.

There are several known polynomial space polynomial delay listing algorithms for MC (see [TSOA 80]). In this subsection we show that MC has an inductive definition and that we can use the inductive definition to obtain a new recursive listing algorithm for MC which runs in polynomial space with polynomial delay.

For the base case we observe that a graph must have at least two vertices to have a cutset. So if G consists of a singleton vertex then $MC(G) = \varnothing$. For the inductive case we will need some notation. Suppose that n is greater than 1 and that G is an n-vertex graph. Let v be the largest vertex of G (recall that vertices are ordered by index) and let $G_1, \ldots, G_m$ be the connected components of $G-\{v\}$. let S_i be the set of edges connecting v to the vertices of G_i.

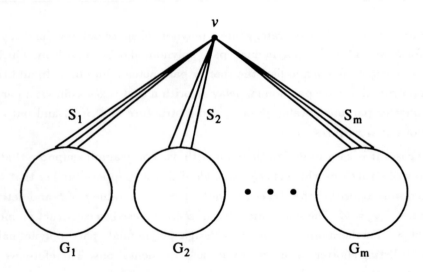

The sets $S_1, \ldots, S_m$ are minimal cutsets of G. Since these minimal cutsets are easy to list in polynomial time we will list them directly†. We will establish a relationship between the other members of $MC(G)$ and the members of $MC(G_1), \ldots, MC(G_m)$.

Suppose that C is a minimal cutset of G and that C is not one of $S_1, \ldots, S_m$. It is fairly easy to see that there must be some integer i in the range $1 \leq i \leq m$ such that C is wholly contained in the subgraph $G_i \cup S_i$. We will designate G_i as the shorter parameter value for C. It is not difficult to see that $C - S_i$ is a minimal cutset of G_i. We define the truncation of C to be $C - S_i$. Suppose that C_t is a minimal cutset of G_i. Following our general recursive strategy we define the set of augmentations of C_t with respect to G to be the set $\{C_t' \in MC(G) \mid C_t \text{ is the truncation of } C_t'\}$. It is easy to see that for every shorter parameter value G_i of G every minimal cutset of G_i has at least one augmentation. Therefore, we can use the following recursive strategy for listing MC:

```
Input G
If G has only one vertex
     Return without output
Else
     /* let v be the largest vertex of G */
     /* let G₁,...,Gₘ be the connected components of G−{v} */
     /* let Sᵢ be the set of edges of G connecting v to the vertices of Gᵢ */
     For i ⟵ 1 To m
          Output Sᵢ
          For Each Cₜ ∈ MC(Gᵢ)
               For Each augmentation Cₜ′ of Cₜ
               Output Cₜ′
```

It is easy to see that there is a polynomial time algorithm which takes input G and lists the shorter parameter values of G. In order to turn our recursive strategy into a polynomial space polynomial delay listing algorithm for MC, we need a polynomial

---

† We have treated the sets $S_1, \ldots, S_m$ as being "special" in order to make the presentation of the recursive strategy on this page simpler. It is possible to re-write the strategy to make it adhere strictly to the general strategy described on page 21.

space polynomial delay algorithm that takes as input a graph G (with largest vertex v), a connected component G_i of $G-\{v\}$, and a minimal cutset C_t of G_i and outputs the augmentations of C_t with respect to G. There is a simple polynomial time algorithm for performing this task. We conclude this subsection by giving an informal description of the algorithm.

Suppose that G_i is a connected component of $G-\{v\}$ and that C_t is a minimal cutset of G_i. Let $H_{i,1}$ and $H_{i,2}$ be the two connected components of G_i-C_t. Let $S_{i,1}$ be the set of edges of G connecting v to vertices in $H_{i,1}$ and let $S_{i,2}$ be the set of edges of G connecting v to vertices in $H_{i,2}$. There are two cases. If $S_{i,2}$ is the empty set (or $S_{i,1}$ is the empty set) then C_t is a minimal cutset of G and C_t is an augmentation of itself:

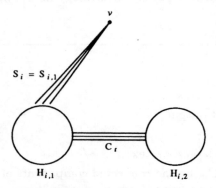

Otherwise, the augmentations of C_t are $C_t \cup S_{i,1}$ and $C_t \cup S_{i,2}$:

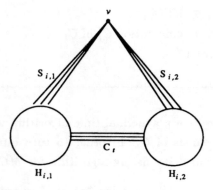

We have now seen several examples of recursively listable families and we have shown how to use the inductive structure of these families to obtain polynomial space polynomial delay listing algorithms. In the remainder of the thesis we will not discuss recursively listable families but we will use the recursive method as a building block when we design listing algorithms for more complicated families of structures.

2.1.2. Random Sampling

This subsection describes another basic technique for listing certain simple families of combinatorial structures. The families to which this technique applies are simple families that have efficient random sampling algorithms.

A *random sampling* algorithm for a simple family S is a probabilistic random access machine program that takes as input a value p of the parameter, halts if $S(p) = \varnothing$, and returns a randomly chosen member of $S(p)$ otherwise. We say that the algorithm has *bias factor* b if, on any given run of the algorithm with any input p such that $S(p)$ is non-empty, the probability that any given member of $S(p)$ is selected is at least $(b(p) \times |S(p)|)^{-1}$. We say that a random sampling algorithm is *efficient* if its expected running time and its bias factor are bounded from above by a polynomial in the length of its input.

There are many known random sampling algorithms for families of combinatorial structures. For example, Nijenhuis and Wilf's book [NW 78] contains random sampling algorithms for quite a few recursively listable families. Random sampling algorithms for more complicated families are found in works such as [CDN 89] and [JS 90]. (We will mention examples of random sampling algorithms from these works later in the thesis.)

In this subsection we will show that efficient probabilistic listing is at least as easy as efficient random sampling. In fact, we will describe a *uniform reduction* from (probabilistic) polynomial delay listing to efficient random sampling.

We start by defining the terms. A *uniform reducer* from probabilistic listing to efficient random sampling is a listing program which contains calls to an external single-parameter function, $S\text{-}Sample$. The reducer must have the property that whenever it is combined with any efficient random sampling algorithm $S\text{-}Sample$ for any simple family S it becomes a probabilistic listing algorithm for S. (In addition to calling $S\text{-}Sample$, the reducer may call three external subroutines to obtain information about $S\text{-}Sample$. In particular, the reducer may call external routines to evaluate three functions, which we will call g, b, and u. g will be a function which is bounded from above by a polynomial in the length of its input and is an upper bound on the expected running time of $S\text{-}Sample$. b will be a function which is bounded from above by a polynomial in the length of its input and is an upper bound on the bias factor of $S\text{-}Sample$. u will be a function which is bounded from above by a polynomial in the length of its input and satisfies two related conditions. First, $u(p)$ is an upper bound on the size of the encoded structures that are output by *S-Sample* when it is run with input p†. Second, $u(p)$ is an upper bound on $\log(|S(p)|)$‡.

We will describe a uniform reducer from probabilistic listing to efficient random sampling and we will show that whenever it is combined with any efficient random sampling algorithm *S-Sample* for any simple family S it becomes a probabilistic *polynomial delay* listing algorithm for S which has o(1) failure probability. Then we will show how to modify the reducer so that whenever it is combined with any efficient random sampling algorithm *S-Sample* for any simple family S it becomes a probabilistic polynomial delay listing algorithm for S which has exponentially small failure probability.

Since there are many interesting families of structures for which efficient random sampling algorithms are known there are many cases in which we can use the reducer to obtain probabilistic polynomial delay listing algorithms which have exponentially small failure probability.

The reducer itself is straightforward. It repeatedly calls *S-Sample* to generate random structures. It maintains a queue which it uses to store structures that have not yet been output. In addition, it maintains a dictionary which it uses to keep track of the structures that have been put on the queue. As it makes calls to *S-Sample*, it puts new structures on the queue. After every sequence of $q(p)$ machine instructions (for a function q which will be defined below) it interrupts itself to output a structure from the queue.

---

† We have stated in chapter 1 that we are only considering families that have concise encodings so we can assume that the length of each encoded structure in $S(p)$ is bounded from above by a polynomial in $|p|$.

‡ The second condition can be satisfied by making $u(p)$ sufficiently large relative to the size of encoded structures in $S(p)$ and the size of the alphabet in which structures are encoded. For example, it suffices to set $u(p) = (c + 1)(\ell(p) + 1)$ where $\ell(p)$ denotes the length of the largest encoded structure in $S(p)$ and c denotes the base 2 logarithm of the size of the alphabet.

Uniform Reducer 1

Input p

$z(p) \longleftarrow \max(\, u(p),\, \lceil \log(b(p)) \rceil \,)$

$q(p) \longleftarrow b(p) \times g(p) \times z(p)^3$

While true Do

    simulate $q(p)$ steps of procedure *Build_Queue(p)*

    If the queue is empty **Then Halt**

    Else Output a structure from the queue

Procedure *Build_Queue(p)*

While true Do

    $s \longleftarrow$ *S-Sample(p)* †

    If (s is not already in the dictionary) **Then**

        put s in the dictionary

        put s on the queue

The proof of the following theorem establishes the claims that we have made about *Uniform Reducer 1*.

Theorem 1. Whenever *Uniform Reducer 1* is combined with any efficient random sampling algorithm *S-Sample* for any simple family S it becomes a probabilistic polynomial delay listing algorithm for S which has o(1) failure probability.

Proof: Suppose that *Uniform Reducer 1* is combined with an efficient random sampling algorithm *S-Sample* for a simple family S. Let g, b, and u be the functions associated with *S-Sample* and let z and q be the functions defined in the algorithm. To avoid trivialities we will assume that g and u are $\omega(1)$. It is easy to see that when *Uniform Reducer 1* is run with input p it outputs only members of $S(p)$ and the structures that are output are output without duplication. Furthermore, the delay between outputs is at most $q(p)$, which is bounded from above by a polynomial in $|p|$. We would like to

---

† If *S*-Sample halts without returning a structure then *Uniform Reducer 1* halts immediately.

show that on a given run of *Uniform Reducer 1* with input p the probability that *every* member of $S(p)$ is output is $1-o(1)$.

On a given run of *Uniform Reducer 1* with input p every member of $S(p)$ will be output *unless* for some integer j in the range $1 \leq j \leq |S(p)|$ the simulation of $j \times q(p)$ steps of procedure *Build_Queue(p)* yields fewer than j distinct members of $S(p)$.

Let r be the function defined by the equation $r(p) = 5\,b(p)\,z(p)$. On a given run of *Uniform Reducer 1* with input p every member of $S(p)$ will be output *unless either*

1. For some integer j in the range $1 \leq j \leq |S(p)|$ the simulation of $j \times q(p)$ steps of procedure *Build_Queue(p)* completes fewer than $j \times r(p)$ iterations of the while loop

   or

2. For some integer j in the range $1 \leq j \leq |S(p)|$ fewer than j distinct members of $S(p)$ are produced by $j \times r(p)$ calls to *S-Sample*.

We will use the notation ρ_1 to denote the probability of the first event occurring and ρ_2 to denote the probability of the second event occurring on a given run of *Uniform Reducer 1* with input p. We will show that both ρ_1 and ρ_2 are $o(1)$.

First, consider event 1. If the dictionary in *Uniform Reducer 1* is implemented using a data structure such as a 2–3 tree (see [AHU 74]) then the running time of an iteration of the while loop in procedure *Build_Queue(p)* (apart from the time spent in *S-Sample(p)*) is $O(u(p)^2)$. We conclude that there is a positive constant c such that event 1 only occurs if there is an integer j in the range $1 \leq j \leq |S(p)|$ such that $j \times r(p)$ calls to *S-Sample(p)* take more than $j \times q(p) - j \times r(p) \times c\,u(p)^2$ time steps. Let ℓ be the function defined by the equation $\ell(p) = g(p)\,z(p)^{3/2}$. Using the facts that $g(p) = \omega(1)$ and $u(p) = \omega(1)$ and performing some algebraic manipulation we observe that $j \times q(p) - j \times r(p) \times c\,u(p)^2$ is greater than or equal to $j \times r(p) \times \ell(p)$. Therefore, event 1 only occurs if there is an integer j in the range $1 \leq j \leq |S(p)|$ such that $j \times r(p)$ calls to *S-Sample(p)* take more than $j \times r(p) \times \ell(p)$ time steps.

So ρ_1 is less than or equal to the probability that for some integer j in the range $1 \leq j \leq r(p) \times |S(p)|$ it is the case that j calls to *S-Sample(p)* take more than $j\,\ell(p)$ time steps. Therefore, ρ_1 is at most

$$\sum_{i=1}^{\lceil \log(\,r(p)\,|S(p)|\,)\rceil} \Pr(\ 2^i \text{ calls to } S\text{-}Sample(p) \text{ take more than } 2^{i-1}\ell(p) \text{ steps}).$$

We conclude that

$$\rho_1 \leq \sum_{i=1}^{\lceil \log(\, r(p)\,|S(p)|\,) \rceil} \frac{2^i g(p)}{2^{i-1}\ell(p)} \leq \frac{2\,\lceil \log(\, r(p)\,|S(p)|\,) \rceil}{z(p)^{3/2}} = o(1).$$

Now consider event 2. We've defined ρ_2 to be the probability that for some integer j in the range $1 \leq j \leq |S(p)|$ fewer than j distinct members of $S(p)$ are produced by $j \times r(p)$ calls to *S-Sample*. We wish to show that ρ_2 is $o(1)$.

We will start by considering $j \leq \lceil |S(p)|/2 \rceil$. Consider the phase during the execution of the algorithm in which the size of the dictionary is less than $|S(p)|/2$. During this phase, the probability that a given sample is not in the dictionary is at least $1/2b(p)$. Therefore, the probability that a set of $r(p)$ samples contains no new structure is at most $(1 - 1/2b(p))^{r(p)}$. We conclude that the probability that for some integer j in the range $1 \leq j \leq \lceil |S(p)|/2 \rceil$ fewer than j distinct members of $S(p)$ are produced by $j \times r(p)$ calls to *S-Sample* is at most $\lceil |S(p)|/2 \rceil (1 - 1/2b(p))^{r(p)}$ which is at most $\lceil |S(p)|/2 \rceil \exp(\, -r(p)\, /\, 2b(p)\,)$. Using the definition of r we can show that this probability is $o(1)$.

We will conclude the proof by showing that the probability that fewer than $|S(p)|$ distinct members of $S(p)$ are produced by $\lceil |S(p)|/2 \rceil \times r(p)$ calls to *S-Sample* is $o(1)$. We will use the *coupon collector* argument [DW 83, Fel 68]. This argument says that the probability that a set of m samples which are chosen uniformly at random from a set S contains every element of S is at least $1 - |S| \exp(-m\, /\, |S|)$. Applying the argument, we find that the probability that a set of $\lceil |S(p)|/2 \rceil \times r(p)$ samples which are generated by calls to *S-Sample* fails to include every member of $S(p)$ is at most $b(p)|S(p)| \exp(\, -r(p)\, /\, 2b(p)\,)$. Using the definition of r we can show that this probability is $o(1)$. We conclude that ρ_2 is $o(1)$, which proves the theorem. □

In theorem 1 we showed that whenever *Uniform Reducer 1* is combined with any efficient random sampling algorithm for any simple family S it becomes a probabilistic polynomial delay listing algorithm for S. Furthermore, we showed that the failure probability of the resulting listing algorithm is $o(1)$. We can make the failure probability exponentially small by making a simple modification to *Uniform Reducer 1*. The modified algorithm simulates multiple copies of procedure *Build_Queue*, sharing the dictionary and the queue between all copies. In particular, suppose that l is a polynomial and consider the following uniform reducer:

Uniform Reducer 2

Input p

$z(p) \longleftarrow \max(u(p), \lceil \log(b(p)) \rceil)$

$q(p) \longleftarrow b(p) \times g(p) \times z(p)^3$

While true Do

    For $j \longleftarrow 1$ **To** $l(|p|)$

        simulate $q(p)$ steps of the jth copy of procedure *Build_Queue(p)*

    If the queue is empty **Then Halt**

    Else Output a structure from the queue

Procedure *Build_Queue(p)*

While true Do

    $s \longleftarrow S\text{-}Sample(p)$ †

    If (s is not already in the dictionary) **Then**

        put s in the dictionary

        put s on the queue

Observing that the different copies of procedure *Build_Queue* run independently and that the probability that any given copy fails to produce enough outputs is less than $1/2$, we obtain the following theorem.

Theorem 2. Whenever *Uniform Reducer 2* is combined with any efficient random sampling algorithm *S-Sample* for any simple family S it becomes a probabilistic polynomial delay listing algorithm for S. The listing algorithm has failure probability $2^{-l(|p|)}$.

As we mentioned in the introduction to this subsection, there are many families of combinatorial structures for which efficient random sampling algorithms are already known. Theorem 2 shows that we can use *Uniform Reducer 2* to obtain probabilistic polynomial delay listing algorithms for these families. The listing algorithms that we obtain using this method have exponentially small failure probability. Unfortunately, however, they require quite a lot of space. In particular, when *Uniform Reducer 2* is combined with a

---

† If S-Sample halts without returning a structure then *Uniform Reducer 2* halts immediately.

random sampling algorithm *S-Sample* and run with input p the dictionary can contain up to $|S(p)|$ structures.

In the remainder of this subsection we will show that there is a sense in which the high space complexity of these listing algorithms is inevitable. In particular, we will show that for any uniform reducer $\mathcal{U}$ from probabilistic listing to efficient random sampling there is an efficient random sampling algorithm *S-Sample* for a simple family S which has the property that when $\mathcal{U}$ is combined with *S-Sample* the product of its delay and its space complexity is within a factor of a polynomial in $|p|$ of $|S(p)|$ (and is therefore exponentially large). We will conclude the subsection by showing how to trade delay for space to obtain uniform reducers which have larger delay and smaller space requirements. We start, then, by proving the following theorem.

Theorem 3. Let $\mathcal{U}$ be any uniform reducer from probabilistic listing to efficient random sampling. There is an efficient random sampling algorithm *S-Sample* for a simple family S such that for some polynomial q we have $d(p)\,r(p)\,q(|p|) = \Omega(|S(p)|) = \Omega(2^{|p|})$ where d is the cumulative delay of the listing algorithm that we get by combining $\mathcal{U}$ with *S-Sample* and r is the space complexity of the same listing algorithm.

Proof: We begin the proof by proving a lemma about space-bounded probabilistic listing algorithms. In order to state the lemma we need some definitions. Suppose that $\mathcal{A}$ is a probabilistic listing algorithm for a simple family S and that p is a parameter value of S. We say that a set $M \subseteq S(p)$ is the $|M|$-element *starting set* of a particular run of $\mathcal{A}$ with input p iff the run outputs at least $|M|$ structures and the first $|M|$ structures that get output during the run are members of M. We can now state and prove the lemma.

Lemma 1. Suppose that $\mathcal{A}$ is a probabilistic listing algorithm for a simple family S and that $\mathcal{A}$ has space complexity r. Then there is a polynomial q such that for every function m satisfying $1 \le m(p) \le |S(p)|$ and for every parameter value p there is a set $\Psi(p)$ that satisfies the following requirements.

1. The members of $\Psi(p)$ are $m(p)$-element subsets of $S(p)$.

2. $|\Psi(p)| \le 2^{q(|p|)r(p)}$.

3. The probability that a given run of $\mathcal{A}$ with input p has an $m(p)$-element starting set that is a member of $\Psi(p)$ is at least $1/3$.

Proof: The proof of the lemma is straightforward but it requires a slightly formal view of random access machine computation. Let $\mathcal{A}$ be the probabilistic random access machine program that is described in the statement of the lemma. We can describe the state of a given run of $\mathcal{A}$ at any point in time by constructing an *instantaneous description* which includes the input p, the position of the tape head on the input tape, the machine instruction that will be executed next, and the contents of the $r(p)$ registers. We use the notation $ID(p)$ to denote the set of instantaneous descriptions that describe states of runs of $\mathcal{A}$ with input p. The restriction that we have placed on the size of integers that can be stored in random access machine registers ensures that there is a polynomial q such that $4\,|ID(p)| \leq 2^{q(|p|)\,r(p)}$ for every parameter value p.

Let m be a function satisfying $1 \leq m(p) \leq |S(p)|$. We will construct the set $\Psi(p)$ as follows. An $m(p)$-element set $U \subseteq S(p)$ is a member of $\Psi(p)$ if and only if the probability that a given run of $\mathcal{A}$ with input p lists *all* of the structures in $S(p)$ conditioned on the fact that U is the $m(p)$-element starting set of the run is at least $1/4$.

The probability that a given run of $\mathcal{A}$ with input p lists all of the structures in $S(p)$ is at least $1/2$. Therefore, the probability that a given run with input p has an $m(p)$-element starting set that is a member of $\Psi(p)$ is at least $1/3$.

We will show that $|\Psi(p)| \leq 4\,|ID(p)|$, which proves the lemma. Let $\rho(i,p,U)$ denote the probability that the computation described by the ith instantaneous description in $ID(p)$ outputs the structures in U and then halts. If U is a member of $\Psi(p)$ then it must be the case that the sum over all instantaneous descriptions $i \in ID(p)$ of $\rho(i,p,S(p)-U)$ is at least $1/4$. Therefore

$$\sum_{i \in ID(p)} \sum_{U \in \Psi(p)} \rho(i,p,S(p)-U) \geq |\Psi(p)|/4.$$

It follows that $|\Psi(p)| \leq 4\,|ID(p)|$, which proves the lemma. □

Having proved lemma 1, we can now prove the theorem. Let $\mathcal{U}$ be any uniform reducer from probabilistic listing to efficient random sampling. We wish to exhibit a simple family S, an efficient random sampling algorithm $S\text{-}Sample$ for S, and a polynomial q such that $d(p)\,r(p)\,q(|p|) = \Omega(|S(p)|) = \Omega(2^{|p|})$ where d is the cumulative delay of the listing algorithm that we get by combining $\mathcal{U}$ with $S\text{-}Sample$ and r is the space complexity of the same listing algorithm.

We will define S to be the simple family in which every parameter value is a unary integer and the value p is associated with the set $S(p)$ which contains all binary integers of length p.

It is easy to see how to write a probabilistic polynomial time algorithm which takes as input a unary integer p and returns a binary integer of length p in such a way that each binary integer of length p is equally likely to be output on any given run with input p. Let $S\text{-}Sample$ be such an algorithm.

We will now define the functions g, b, and u which will be associated with S-$Sample$. For reasons which will become clear later we will define g to be a function which is *larger* than the expected running time of S-$Sample$. In particular, we will define g to be a function which is bounded from above by a polynomial in the length of its input and is an upper bound on the expected running time of an algorithm called S'-$Sample$, which we will describe shortly. Similarly, we will define the function b by the equation $b(p) = 3/2$ even though S-$Sample$ has bias factor 1. We will define the function u by the equation $u(p) = |p|$.

Let $\mathcal{A}$ be the algorithm that we get by combining $\mathcal{U}$ with S-$Sample$. Let d denote the delay of $\mathcal{A}$ and let r denote the space complexity of $\mathcal{A}$. We wish to show that there is a polynomial q such that $d(p)\, r(p)\, q(|p|) = \Omega(|S(p)|)$.

We will start by proving the following claim:

Claim 1.   When algorithm $\mathcal{A}$ is run with input p it only outputs structures which have been generated by calling S-$Sample(p)$.

We will prove the claim by contradiction. Suppose that for some parameter value p' of S there is a run of $\mathcal{A}$ with input p' in which $\mathcal{A}$ outputs a structure $s' \in S(p')$ even though s' has not been generated by calling S-$Sample(p')$.

Let S' be the simple family with the following definition. Every parameter value of S' is a unary integer. The sets in S' are defined as follows.

$$S'(p) = \begin{cases} S(p) - \{s'\} & \text{if } p = p' \\ S(p) & \text{otherwise} \end{cases}$$

Let S'-$Sample$ be the following random sampling algorithm for S':

```
Function S'-Sample(p)
s  ⟵  S-Sample(p)
If (p = p')
    If (s = s')
        s  ⟵  s - 1  (mod 2^p)
Return s
```

We assumed earlier that the function g which is associated with S-$Sample$ is sufficiently large that for every fixed parameter value p' the expected running time of S'-$Sample$ is bounded from above by g†. It is easy to see that the bias factor of S'-$Sample$ is bounded from above by b. The encoded structures which are output by calls to S'-$Sample(p)$ are no longer than the structures which are output by calls to S-$Sample(p)$. Therefore, we can associate the functions g, b, and u with S'-$Sample$.

Let $\mathcal{A}'$ be the algorithm that we get by combining $\mathcal{U}$ with S'-$Sample$. Since there is a run of $\mathcal{A}$ with input p' in which $\mathcal{A}$ outputs s' even though s' has not been generated by calling S-$Sample(p')$ there must be a run of $\mathcal{A}'$ with input p' in which $\mathcal{A}'$ outputs s'. But s' is not a member of $S'(p')$. Therefore $\mathcal{A}'$ is not a listing algorithm for S'. We conclude that $\mathcal{U}$ is not a uniform reducer, which is a contradiction. Therefore, the claim must be correct.

Having proved lemma 1 and claim 1 we are now ready to prove the theorem. Consider algorithm $\mathcal{A}$ with space complexity r and let q be the polynomial whose existence is guaranteed by lemma 1. Let $m(p)$ denote $q(|p|)r(p)$. If $m(p) = \Omega(|S(p)|)$ then the theorem is true. Otherwise, let $\Psi(p)$ denote the set described in the lemma‡. The lemma establishes the fact that the probability that a given run of $\mathcal{A}$ with input p has an $m(p)$-element starting set that is a member of $\Psi(p)$ is at least $1/3$.

Since $\mathcal{A}$ has cumulative delay d we know that every run of $\mathcal{A}$ that outputs $m(p)$ structures does so after executing at most $d(p)m(p)$ machine instructions. Therefore every run of $\mathcal{A}$ that has an $m(p)$-element starting set from $\Psi(p)$ outputs all of the elements from some set in $\Psi(p)$ before the random sampler has produced more than $d(p)m(p)$ samples from $S(p)$. Furthermore, by claim 1 every element which is output is produced by a call to S-$Sample(p)$. The probability that a set of $d(p)m(p)$ (or fewer) samples produced by S-$Sample(p)$ contains some member of $\Psi(p)$ is at most

$$|\Psi(p)| \binom{|S(p)| - m(p)}{d(p)m(p) - m(p)} \binom{|S(p)|}{d(p)m(p)}^{-1} \leq \left(\frac{2\, d(p)\, m(p)}{|S(p)| - m(p) + 1} \right)^{m(p)}$$

The theorem follows from the fact that this probability is at least $1/3$. □

---

† The running time of S'-$Sample$ does not depend on the value of p' since at most $p+1$ bits of p' will ever be accessed.

‡ The lemma only applies if $1 \leq m(p) \leq |S(p)|$ for every parameter value p. Technically this condition may not be satisfied even though $m(p) = o(|S(p)|)$. If the condition is not satisfied then let m be some function satisfying $1 \leq m(p) \leq |S(p)|$ such that for every large enough parameter value p we have $m(p) = q(|p|)r(p)$.

Remark 1. In order to prove theorem 3 we carefully defined the family S, the sampler *S-Sample,* and the associated functions g, b, and u. However, the proof itself only made very limited use of our definitions. In particular, we used only two facts:

1. The functions g and b are large enough that they can be associated with a modified random sampling algorithm, S'-Sample.

2. *S-Sample* has bias factor 1. (We call a random sampling algorithm *unbiased* if its bias factor is 1. We used the fact that *S-Sample* is unbiased when we calculated the probability at the end of the proof.)

Using the same arguments that we used to prove theorem 3 we could prove the following stronger theorem.

Theorem 3 (strengthened). Let $\mathcal{U}$ be any uniform reducer from probabilistic listing to efficient random sampling. Let *S-Sample* be any unbiased efficient random sampling algorithm for any simple family S. There are functions g, b, u, and q satisfying the following conditions. Each of g, b, and u is bounded from above by a polynomial in the length of its input. q is a polynomial. Whenever g, b and u are associated with *S-Sample* we have $d(p)\,r(p)\,q(|p|) = \Omega(|S(p)|)$ where d is the cumulative delay of the listing algorithm that we get by combining $\mathcal{U}$ with *S-Sample* and r is the space complexity of the same listing algorithm.

We could strengthen the theorem further by observing that *S-Sample* doesn't really have to be unbiased (for example, it would suffice to require that on any given run of *S-Sample* with any input p the probability that any given member of $S(p)$ is selected is at most $\ell(|p|)|S(p)|^{-1}$ for some polynomial ℓ.) The calculations at the end of the proof would have to be modified slightly to account for the bias of *S-Sample*, however.

Remark 2. The statement of theorem 3 demonstrates a sense in which the high space complexity of the listing algorithms discussed in this subsection is inevitable. In addition, the proof of the theorem points to a different but related reason that the high space complexity is inevitable.

In order to explain the reason we need the following definition. A probabilistic listing algorithm for a simple family S is said to *uniformly sample S without replacement* if it is the case that on any given run of the listing algorithm with any input p the members of $S(p)$ are equally likely to be output in any order.

The proof of theorem 3 can easily be modified to prove the following theorem about sampling without replacement.

Theorem 4.　Suppose that S is a simple family of structures and that $\mathcal{A}$ is a probabilistic listing algorithm that uniformly samples S without replacement. There is a polynomial q such that the space complexity of $\mathcal{A}$ is $\Omega(|S(p)| / q(|p|))$.

Whenever we combine *Uniform Reducer 2* with an unbiased efficient random sampling algorithm *S-Sample* we obtain a probabilistic listing algorithm which uniformly samples without replacement. By theorem 4 we must end up with a listing algorithm with exponential space complexity.

Remark 3.　Let S be the simple family of structures which was defined in the proof of theorem 3. Let *S-Sample* be the random sampling algorithm for S which we defined previously. Let $\mathcal{A}$ be the listing algorithm that we get by combining *Uniform Reducer 2* with *S-Sample*. Let d denote the delay of $\mathcal{A}$ and let r denote the space complexity of $\mathcal{A}$. We know from the proof of theorem 2 that d is bounded from above by a polynomial in $|p|$ and that there is a polynomial q such that $r(p) = O(q(|p|) \times |S(p)|)$. We know from theorem 3 that there is a polynomial q' such that $d(p)\,r(p) = \Omega(|S(p)| / q'(|p|))$. Therefore, the space complexity of algorithm $\mathcal{A}$ could only be improved by a polynomial factor without increasing the delay. If we are willing to increase the delay, however, we can improve the space complexity to within a polynomial factor of the limit imposed by theorem 3. We will conclude this subsection by showing how to trade delay for space in uniform reductions, obtaining listing algorithms with larger delay and smaller space requirements.

We start with the following definition. A *space bounded uniform reducer* from probabilistic listing to efficient random sampling is a listing program which contains calls to an external function *S-Sample,* to external subroutines for evaluating the functions which are associated with *S-Sample,* and to an external subroutine for evaluating the space function λ. The reducer must satisfy the following condition: Suppose that *S-Sample* is any efficient random sampling algorithm for any simple family S. Suppose that λ is any function such that $1 \le \lambda(p) \le |S(p)|$. Suppose that there is a polynomial q such that the space complexity of *S-Sample* is $O(q(|p|) \times \lambda(p))$. If the reducer is combined with *S-Sample* and λ it becomes a probabilistic listing algorithm for S. Furthermore, there is a polynomial q' such that the space complexity of the resulting algorithm is $O(q'(|p|) \times \lambda(p))$.

We will describe a space bounded uniform reducer from probabilistic listing to efficient random sampling. We will show that it satisfies the following condition. Suppose that *S-Sample* is any efficient random sampling algorithm for any simple family S. Suppose that λ is any function such that $1 \le \lambda(p) \le |S(p)|$. Suppose that there is a polynomial q such that the space complexity of *S-Sample* is $O(q(|p|) \times \lambda(p))$. If the uniform reducer is combined with *S-Sample* and λ it becomes a probabilistic listing algorithm for S. Furthermore, there are polynomials q_1 and q_2 such that the space complexity of the resulting algorithm is $O(q_1(|p|) \times \lambda(p))$, the delay of the algorithm is $O(q_2(|p|)|S(p)| / \lambda(p))$, and the failure probability of the algorithm is exponentially small.

The basic idea behind the reducer is to divide $S(p)$ into $\lceil |S(p)| / \lambda(p) \rceil$ blocks $B_1(p), B_2(p), \ldots$, each of which contains $\lambda(p)$ structures except for the last block, which contains up to $\lambda(p)$ structures. The blocks will be ordered lexicographically, so the structures in $B_1(p)$ will be the lexicographically smallest encoded structures in $S(p)$ and the structures in $B_2(p)$ will be the lexicographically smallest encoded structures in $S(p) - B_1(p)$, and so on.

The reducer consists of a while loop in which the kth iteration outputs the members of $B_k(p)$ in an arbitrary order, using the dictionary and the queue to store the members of $B_k(p)$ and the members of $B_{k+1}(p)$:

Uniform Reducer 3

Input p

$z(p) \longleftarrow \max(u(p), \lceil \log(b(p)) \rceil)$

$q(p) \longleftarrow b(p) \times g(p) \times z(p)^3$

max_so_far $\longleftarrow$ a structure x such that $\forall s \in S(p) . x < s$

While true Do   /* The kth iteration outputs $B_k(p)$ */

    $i \longleftarrow 0$

    max_prev $\longleftarrow$ *max_so_far*   /* *max_prev* is the maximum structure */

                                          /* that was output */

                                          /* during the previous iteration */

  While $i < \lambda(p)$

    For $j \longleftarrow 1$ **To** $u(p) + |p|$

      simulate $q(p)\lceil |S(p)| / \lambda(p) \rceil$ steps

        of the jth copy of proc *Build_Queue*(p)

    If the queue is empty then **Halt**

    Else

      Output s, the smallest structure in the queue

      max_so_far $\longleftarrow$ maximum(*max_so_far*,s)

      $i \longleftarrow i + 1$

Procedure *Build_Queue*(p)

While true Do

    $s \longleftarrow$ *S-Sample*(p) †

    If $(s \leq max\_prev)$

        /* ignore s because it is too small to be in $B_k(p)$ */

    Else If s is in the dictionary

        /* ignore s because it is not new */

    Else If the dictionary contains fewer than $2\,\lambda(p)$ structures

        put s in the dictionary and on the queue

    Else If the minimum member of the dictionary is $\leq max\_prev$

        /* The dictionary contains a structure that is "left over" */

        /* from block $B_{k-1}(p)$. It will be removed to make room for s */

        let s' be the minimum member of the dictionary

        remove s' from the dictionary and from the queue if it is there

        put s in the dictionary and on the queue

    Else If the maximum member of the dictionary is smaller than s

        /* ignore s because it is too big to be in $B_k(p)$ or in $B_{k+1}(p)$ */

    Else

        /* the dictionary contains some structure that is too big */

        /* to be in $B_k(p)$ or in $B_{k+1}(p)$ */

        let s' be the maximum member of the dictionary

        remove s' from the dictionary and from the queue if it is there

        put s in the dictionary and on the queue

The proof of the following theorem verifies the claims that we have made about *Uniform Reducer 3*.

---

† If *S*-Sample halts without returning a structure then *Uniform Reducer 3* halts immediately.

Theorem 5. Suppose that *S-Sample* is an efficient random sampling algorithm for a simple family S. Suppose that λ is a function such that $1 \leq \lambda(p) \leq |S(p)|$. Suppose that there is a polynomial q such that the space complexity of *S-Sample* is $O(q(|p|) \times \lambda(p))$. If *Uniform Reducer 3* is combined with *S-Sample* and λ it becomes a probabilistic listing algorithm for S. Furthermore, there are polynomials q_1 and q_2 such that the space complexity of the resulting algorithm is $O(q_1(|p|) \times \lambda(p))$, the delay of the algorithm is $O(q_2(|p|)|S(p)|/\lambda(p))$, and the failure probability of the algorithm is exponentially small.

Proof: Suppose that *S-Sample* is an efficient random sampling algorithm for a simple family S. Suppose that λ is a function such that $1 \leq \lambda(p) \leq |S(p)|$. Suppose that q is a polynomial such that the space complexity of *S-Sample* is $O(q(|p|) \times \lambda(p))$. Let $\mathcal{A}$ denote the listing algorithm that we get by combining *Uniform Reducer 3* with *S-Sample* and λ.

It is easy to see that when $\mathcal{A}$ is run with input p it outputs only members of $S(p)$. It is more time-consuming to verify that the structures that are output are output without duplication but verifying this fact is straightforward. Furthermore, it is straightforward to verify that there are polynomials q_1 and q_2 such that the space complexity of $\mathcal{A}$ is $O(q_1(|p|)\lambda(p))$ and the delay between outputs is bounded from above by $O(q_2(|p|)|S(p)|/\lambda(p))$. We would like to show that on a given run of $\mathcal{A}$ with input p the probability that *every* member of $S(p)$ is output is at least $1 - 2^{-|p|}$.

Let ρ_k denote the probability that a given run of $\mathcal{A}$ with input p fails to output all of the structures in $B_k(p)$ conditioned on the fact that it did output all of the structures in $B_1(p), \ldots, B_{k-1}(p)$. We wish to show that $\sum_{k=1}^{\lceil |S(p)|/\lambda(p) \rceil} \rho_k \leq 2^{-|p|}$. It suffices, therefore, to prove that for every k in the range $1 \leq k \leq \lceil |S(p)|/\lambda(p) \rceil$ we have $\lceil |S(p)|/\lambda(p) \rceil \times \rho_k \leq 2^{-|p|}$.

We start by proving that $\lceil |S(p)|/\lambda(p) \rceil \times \rho_1 \leq 2^{-|p|}$. To do so we mimic the proofs of theorems 1 and 2, showing that $\rho_1 \leq 2^{-(u(p)+|p|)}$. (In the proof of theorem 1 we showed that with high probability the queue did not become empty before every member of $S(p)$ was output. This is analogous to showing that in this case with high probability the queue does not run out of members of $B_1(p)$ until every member of $B_1(p)$ has been output.) We use the fact that if the dictionary and the queue in *Uniform Reducer 3* are implemented using 2-3 trees with ordered leaves (see [AHU 74]) then the running time of an iteration of the while loop in procedure *Build_Queue(p)* (apart from the time spent in *S-Sample(p)*) is $O(u(p)^2)$.

To prove that $\lceil |S(p)|/\lambda(p) \rceil \times \rho_k \leq 2^{-|p|}$ for $k > 1$ we use the coupon collector argument to show that all of the members of a given block $B_k(p)$ are very likely to be found during iteration $k-1$ of the while loop. □

In this subsection we have described several uniform reducers. The first two uniform reducers which we have described provide a very simple and straightforward method for converting "off the shelf" random sampling algorithms into polynomial delay listing algorithms. We will mention some applications in which these uniform reducers can be used later in the thesis. In general, however, the thesis will focus on developing listing algorithms which have both small delay and small space complexity. In light of theorem 3, it will be necessary to develop different listing methods.

2.2. Using Listing Algorithms for Closely Related Families

In this short section we describe two methods for designing listing algorithms. The methods can be used when we have an efficient listing algorithm for a family S' and we want to design an efficient listing algorithm for another family that is closely related to S'. For example, suppose that we want to design an efficient listing algorithm for a family S. If S is closely related to a recursively listable family or to a simple family that has an efficient random sampling algorithm then we can combine the techniques from section 2.1 with the techniques described in this section to obtain an efficient listing algorithm for S. We will see further applications of the techniques described in this section when we consider the problem of listing non-simple families in section 2.3.

We start by defining the terms. (The following definitions will apply to non-simple families of structures as well as to simple families of structures.) We say that two families of combinatorial structures are *related* if and only if they have the same parameter specification. We say that two related families, S and S', are *polynomially related* if and only if there is a polynomial q which satisfies $|S(p)| \leq q(|p|)\,|S'(p)|$ and $|S'(p)| \leq q(|p|)\,|S(p)|$. Suppose that S and S' are related families and that $S'(p)$ is a subset of $S(p)$ for every parameter value p. In this case we say that S' is a *sub-family* of S and that S is a *super-family* of S'. We use the notation $S-S'$ to stand for the family that is defined by $(S-S')(p) = S(p) - S'(p)$.

We will describe two methods in this section. The *interleaving method* can be used to design an efficient listing algorithm for a family S if we have an efficient listing algorithm for a polynomially related *sub*-family of S. The *filter method,* on the other hand, can be used to design an efficient listing algorithm for a family S if we have an efficient listing algorithm for a polynomially related *super*-family of S. First, we describe the interleaving method.

2.2.1. The Interleaving Method

Suppose that we want to design a polynomial delay listing algorithm for a family S and that we have a polynomial delay listing algorithm for S', which is a sub-family of S that is polynomially related to S. Suppose further that we have a listing algorithm for $S - S'$ and that there is a polynomial ℓ such that this algorithm executes at most $\ell(|p|) \times (|S(p)| + 1)$ machine instructions when it is run with input p. Then we can interleave the listing algorithm for S' with the listing algorithm for $S - S'$ to obtain a polynomial delay listing algorithm for S.

This simple idea turns out to be very powerful and we use it repeatedly in section 3 of this chapter and in chapter 3. We make the idea more precise in the following observation.

Observation 1. Suppose that S is a family of combinatorial structures and that S' is a sub-family of S. Suppose further that there is a polynomial q satisfying the equation $|S(p)| \leq q(|p|)\, |S'(p)|$. Suppose that there is a listing algorithm $\mathcal{A}'$ for S' and that the delay of $\mathcal{A}'$ is d'. Suppose further that there is a listing algorithm $\mathcal{A}''$ for $S - S'$ and that ℓ is a function such that this algorithm executes at most $\ell(|p|) \times (|S(p)| + 1)$ machine instructions when it is run with input p. Then there is a listing algorithm for S whose delay, d, satisfies $d(p) \leq c_s\, \ell(|p|)\, q(|p|) + d'(p) + c_s$, where c_s is a positive constant representing the cost of doing the simulation in the following algorithm.

Proof: It is easy to see that the following algorithm is a listing algorithm for S and that its delay is sufficiently small.

Algorithm *Interleave*

Input p

While true Do

    simulate $\ell(|p|)\, q(|p|)$ steps of $\mathcal{A}''(p)$

    simulate $\mathcal{A}'(p)$ until it outputs or halts

    If $\mathcal{A}'(p)$ halted Then Halt

Remark 1. Suppose that $\mathcal{A}'$ and $\mathcal{A}''$ are *probabilistic* listing algorithms for S' and $S - S'$ and that they have failure probabilities ρ_1 and ρ_2 respectively. If $\rho_1(p)$ and $\rho_2(p)$ are each less than or equal to $1/4$ for every parameter value p then algorithm *Interleave* is a probabilistic listing algorithm for S with failure probability $\rho_1 + \rho_2$.

Remark 2.   If $\mathcal{A}'$ and $\mathcal{A}''$ are polynomial space algorithms then so is algorithm *Interleave*.

Remark 3.   Observation 1 remains true if we replace the word "delay" with "cumulative delay".

Application.   Recall the family $\mathcal{G}$, which was defined in the introduction to this thesis. A sub-family of $\mathcal{G}$ is called a *graph property*. Many of the combinatorial families that we consider in chapter 3 are graph properties. Therefore, we find it useful to state general conditions under which the interleaving method yields polynomial delay listing algorithms for graph properties.

Suppose that S is a graph property. We say that a listing algorithm for S is a *standard graph listing algorithm* if it is of the following form.

```
Algorithm Standard
Input n
For Each G ∈ 𝒢(n)
    If G ∈ S(n)
        Output G
```

Using the notion of a standard graph listing algorithm, we make the following observation.

Observation 2.   Suppose that S is a graph property and that S has a sub-family E. Suppose that there is a polynomial q such that the following conditions are satisfied.

1. $q(n)\,|E(n)| \geq 2^{\binom{n}{2}}$ for every large enough integer n.

2. There is a polynomial delay listing algorithm for E.

3. There is a polynomial expected time algorithm that takes as input a graph $G \in \mathcal{G}(n)$ and determines whether or not G is a member of $S(n) - E(n)$.

Then the interleaving method can be used to obtain a polynomial delay listing algorithm for S. When the listing algorithm is given an input n satisfying $q(n)\,|E(n)| \geq 2^{\binom{n}{2}}$ it interleaves the listing algorithm for E with a standard graph listing algorithm for $S - E$. If the listing algorithms for E and $S - E$ run in polynomial space then so does the listing algorithm for S.

2.2.2. The Filter Method

Suppose that we have a cumulative polynomial delay listing algorithm *List_S* for some family S and that we are interested in designing an efficient listing algorithm for S', which is a sub-family of S that is polynomially related to S. The method that we use to solve this problem is called the *filter method*. It is very straightforward. Essentially, we write a program called *Filter* which takes as input a parameter value p of S and a structure s which belongs to an equivalence class in $S(p)$. *Filter*(p, s) returns "yes" if s belongs to an equivalence class in $S'(p)$ and "no" otherwise. We combine the algorithm *List_S* with subroutine *Filter* to obtain a listing algorithm for S'.

We will see later in the thesis that this simple method leads to efficient listing algorithms for interesting families of combinatorial structures. In the remainder of this subsection we will derive general conditions under which the method can be used to obtain efficient listing algorithms.

In order to describe the conditions we will need some notation for describing lists of combinatorial structures. If $\mathcal{L}$ is a list of structures we will use the notation $|\mathcal{L}|$ to denote the length of $\mathcal{L}$. We will use the notation $\mathcal{L}[i]$ to denote the ith structure on $\mathcal{L}$ and the notation $\mathcal{L}[i, j]$ to denote the sub-list $\mathcal{L}[i], \dots, \mathcal{L}[j]$. If C is a set of equivalence classes of structures we will use the notation $\mathcal{L} / C$ to denote the sub-list consisting of all structures on $\mathcal{L}$ which belong to equivalence classes in C.

So suppose that S and S' are families of structures as described above and that *List_S* is a cumulative polynomial delay listing algorithm for S. Suppose that *Filter* is a subroutine behaving as described above. We will use the notation S_p to denote the list of structures that are output when algorithm *List_S* is run with input p. We will use the symbol T to denote the time complexity of *Filter*. We will consider the efficiency of the following listing algorithm for S':

```
Algorithm List_S'
Input p
For j  ⟵  1 To |S(p)|
    continue simulating List_S(p) to obtain Sₚ[j]
    If Filter (p, Sₚ[j]) = "yes"
        Output Sₚ[j]
```

We start with the following observation which follows directly from the definition of cumulative polynomial delay and from the fact that algorithm *List_S* has cumulative polynomial delay.

Observation 3.   If there exists a polynomial r such that for every integer i in the range $1 \leq i \leq |S(p)|$ we have

$$\sum_{j=1}^{i} T(p, S_p[j]) \leq r(|p|) \times |S_p[1, i] / S'(p)|$$

then algorithm *List_S'* has cumulative polynomial delay.

While the statement of observation 3 is very straightforward, we can make the observation easier to use by re-writing it in a slightly different form. In particular, it is useful to consider the list S_p as being broken up into "chunks". Suppose that $m(p)$ is a positive integer (the number of "chunks") and that S_p is the concatenation of the $m(p)$ lists $S_{p,1}, \ldots, S_{p,m(p)}$. The following observation follows easily from observation 3.

Observation 4.   If there exists a polynomial r such that the following conditions are satisfied then algorithm *List_S'* has cumulative polynomial delay.

Condition 1.   For every integer i in the range $1 \leq i \leq |S_{p,1}|$ we have

$$\sum_{j=1}^{i} T(p, S_p[j]) \leq r(|p|) \times |S_p[1, i] / S'(p)|$$

Condition 2.   For every integer l in the range range $1 \leq l < m(p)$ we have

$$\sum_{j=1}^{|S_{p,l+1}|} T(p, S_{p,l+1}[j]) \leq r(|p|) \times |S_{p,l} / S'(p)|$$

Condition 2 of observation 4 bounds the time needed to filter the structures in the $l+1^{\text{st}}$ "chunk" of S_p in terms of the number of structures that are output in the lth "chunk".

When we use the filter method in this thesis we will be able to define the "chunks" of S_p in such a way that every member of $S_{p,1}$ is a member of $S'(p)$. Therefore, it is not necessary to filter the structures on $S_{p,1}$. In practice, we may want to run subroutine *Filter* on these structures in order to obtain side-effects (such as putting the structures into a dictionary). However, it is not too restrictive to require that *Filter* run in polynomial time on these inputs. We can simplify condition 1 of observation 4 by making this requirement. We do so in the following observation, which follows directly from observation 4.

Observation 5. If every member of $S_{p,1}$ is a member of $S'(p)$ and there exists a polynomial r such that the following conditions are satisfied then algorithm *List_S'* has cumulative polynomial delay.

Condition 1. For every integer i in the range $1 \leq i \leq |S_{p,1}|$ we have

$$T(p, S_p[i]) \leq r(|p|)$$

Condition 2. For every integer l in the range range $1 \leq l < m(p)$ we have

$$\sum_{j=1}^{|S_{p,l+1}|} T(p, S_{p,l+1}[j]) \leq r(|p|) \times |S_{p,l} / S'(p)|$$

The statement of observation 5 seems rather technical but we will see that it is easy to use in section 2.3 and in chapter 3. We conclude this section with a few remarks.

Remark 1. If algorithm *List_S* and algorithm *Filter* run in polynomial space then so does algorithm *List_S'*.

Remark 2. Our description of the filter method assumes that algorithm *List_S* is a deterministic algorithm. We could instead assume that *List_S* is a *probabilistic* listing algorithm and we could make an observation similar to observation 5. However, all of the probabilistic listing algorithms that are studied in this thesis involve random sampling. When random sampling is involved, it is generally easiest to apply the filtering directly to the sampler. We conclude this subsection by showing how to design efficient listing algorithms by filtering existing random sampling algorithms and using the techniques from section 2.1. We start by proving the following lemma.

Lemma 2. Suppose that S is a simple family of combinatorial structures which has an efficient random sampling algorithm *S-Sample*. Suppose that S' is a sub-family of S that is polynomially related to S. Suppose further that there is a polynomial expected-time algorithm *Filter* that takes as input a parameter value p of S and an output s of *S-Sample(p)* and returns "yes" if and only if s is a member of $S'(p)$. Then S' has an efficient random sampling algorithm.

Proof: The algorithm is as follows:

```
Algorithm S'-Sample
Input p
Do forever
    s ⟵   S-Sample(p) †
    If (Filter(p, s) = "yes")
        Return s
```

In order to prove that S'-*Sample* is efficient we need some notation. Let b be the bias factor of S-*Sample* and let g be the expected running time of S-*Sample*. Let q be a polynomial such that $|S(p)| \leq q(|p|) \times |S'(p)|$. Let $t(p)$ denote the expected running time of *Filter*(p, s) when s is an output of S-*Sample*(p). Let $\rho(p)$ denote the probability that *Filter*$(p, s) =$ "yes" when s is an output of S-*Sample*(p) and let $x(p) = 1 - \rho(p)$.

Since the bias factor of S-*Sample* is b we know that $\rho(p) \geq |S'(p)| \, / \, b(p) \, |S(p)|$. There-fore, since $|S(p)| \leq q(|p|) \times |S'(p)|$ we have $x(p) \leq 1 - 1/b(p) \, q(|p|)$.

The expected running time of S'-*Sample* is

$$
O\left((g(p) + t(p)) \, (1 + x(p) + x(p)^2 + \cdots) \right) = O\left((g(p) + t(p)) \, \frac{1}{1 - x(p)} \right)
$$

$$
= O\left((g(p) + t(p)) \, b(p) \, q(|p|) \right)
$$

The probability that any given member of $S'(p)$ is selected is at least $1/b(p) \, |S(p)|$ which is at least $1/b(p) \, q(|p|) \, |S'(p)|$. So S'-*Sample* has bias factor b' where $b'(p) = b(p) \, q(|p|)$.

We conclude that S'-*Sample* is efficient. □

We now show how to use lemma 2 to design efficient listing algorithms. Suppose that S is a simple family of combinatorial structures which has an efficient random sampling algorithm S-*Sample*. Suppose that S' is a sub-family of S that is polynomially related to S. Suppose further that there is a polynomial expected-time algorithm *Filter* that

---

† If S-Sample halts without returning a structure then S'-*Sample* halts immediately without returning a structure.

takes as input a parameter value p of S and an output s of S-$Sample(p)$ and returns "yes" if and only if s is a member of $S'(p)$. Then we can use the method described in the proof of lemma 2 to obtain an efficient random sampling algorithm for S'. Having done so, we can use the methods from subsection 2.1.2 to obtain a probabilistic listing algorithm for S' that has polynomial delay and exponentially small failure probability.

Application. It is easy to see that there is an efficient random sampling algorithm for $\mathcal{G}$. Therefore, we obtain the following observation concerning graph properties.

Observation 6. Suppose that S is a graph property and that the following conditions are satisfied.

1. There is a polynomial q such that $q(n)|S(n)| \geq 2^{\binom{n}{2}}$ for every positive integer n.

2. There is a polynomial expected time algorithm that takes as input a graph $G \in \mathcal{G}(n)$ and determines whether or not G is a member of $S(n)$.

Then there is a probabilistic polynomial delay listing algorithm for S that has exponentially small failure probability.

Remark 3. In remark 2 we assume that S is a simple family of combinatorial structures. This assumption is not necessary — in section 2.3 we will extend the definition of a random sampling algorithm so that it applies to *non-simple* families of combinatorial structures.

2.3. Avoiding Duplicates

Section 2.1 introduced two basic techniques that can be used to design efficient listing algorithms for certain simple families of combinatorial structures. Section 2.2 extended these techniques by describing two methods that can be used when we have an efficient listing algorithm for a family S and we want to design an efficient listing algorithm for another family that is closely related to S. In the present section we further extend the techniques that we have developed by applying them to the problem of designing listing algorithms for families of structures that are not simple. We begin by discussing methods for designing probabilistic listing algorithms for non-simple families and then we consider the design of deterministic algorithms.

2.3.1. Probabilistic Algorithms

In subsection 2.1.2 we restricted our attention to simple families of combinatorial structures and we showed that for these families we could reduce polynomial delay probabilistic listing to efficient random sampling. In this subsection we show that the reductions still work even if we consider non-simple families of structures.

We start by defining the notion of an *efficient random sampling algorithm* for a non-simple family of structures. The definitions are similar to the corresponding definitions in the simple case except that a random sampling algorithm for a simple family takes as input a parameter value and returns a structure whereas a random sampling algorithm for a non-simple family takes as input a parameter value and returns a structure *along with the name of its equivalence class.*

Before formalizing the notion of a random sampling algorithm for a non-simple family we formalize the notion of an *equivalence class naming function.* Suppose that S is a non-simple family of structures. The relevant domain is the set of pairs (p, s) in which p is a parameter value of S and s is a member of an equivalence class in $S(p)$. The relevant range is the set of strings in the language in which structures of S are encoded. A function $\mathcal{N}$ from the specified domain to the specified range is called an *equivalence class naming function* for S if and only if the following conditions are satisfied.

1. For every parameter value p of S and every pair (s_1, s_2) of structures of S it is the case that $\mathcal{N}(p, s_1) = \mathcal{N}(p, s_2)$ if and only if s_1 and s_2 are members of the same equivalence class in $S(p)$.

2. There is a polynomial q such that $|\mathcal{N}(p, s)| \leq q(|p|)$ for every domain element (p, s).

If $\mathcal{N}$ is an equivalence class naming function for S we refer to $\mathcal{N}(p, s)$ as the "name" of the equivalence class of s in $S(p)$. Every family of combinatorial structures that we consider has an equivalence class naming function since the size of the encoded structures in the family (and therefore the number of equivalence classes in any given set) is restricted in chapter 1.

We are now ready to continue with our definitions. A *random sampling algorithm* for a family S of combinatorial structures is a probabilistic random access machine program satisfying the following conditions:

1. The program is associated with a function $\mathcal{N}$ which is an equivalence class naming function for S.

2. The program takes as input a value p of the parameter of S, halts if $S(p) = \varnothing$, and returns a randomly chosen pair $(s, \mathcal{N}(p, s))$ otherwise, where s is a member of an equivalence class in $S(p)$.

We say that the algorithm has *bias factor* b if, on any given run of the algorithm with any input p such that $S(p)$ is non-empty, the probability that any given equivalence class in $S(p)$ is represented in the output is at least $(b(p) \times |S(p)|)^{-1}$. We say that a random sampling algorithm for a non-simple family is *efficient* if its expected running time and its bias factor are bounded from above by a polynomial in the length of its input.

We could easily modify the uniform reducers described in subsection 2.1.2 to make them list non-simple families of structures as well as simple families. The modified reducers would store names of equivalence classes in their dictionaries rather than storing structures. For example, the modified version of *Uniform Reducer 2* is the following:

Uniform Reducer 4

Input p

$z(p) \longleftarrow \max(u(p), \lceil \log(b(p)) \rceil)$

$q(p) \longleftarrow b(p) \times g(p) \times z(p)^3$

While true Do

    For $j \longleftarrow$ 1 **To** $l(|p|)$

        simulate $q(p)$ steps of the jth copy of procedure *Build_Queue(p)*

    If the queue is empty **Then Halt**

    Else Output a structure from the queue

Procedure *Build_Queue(p)*

While true Do

    $(s, \nu) \longleftarrow$ *S-Sample(p)* †

    If (ν is not already in the dictionary) **Then**

        put ν in the dictionary

        put s on the queue

We could easily prove the following theorem by mimicking the proof of theorem 2.

Theorem 6. Whenever *Uniform Reducer 4* is combined with any efficient random sampling algorithm *S-Sample* for any family S it becomes a probabilistic polynomial delay listing algorithm for S. The listing algorithm has failure probability $2^{-l(|p|)}$.

We conclude this subsection with two examples which demonstrate the ease with which we can use *Uniform Reducer 4* to obtain probabilistic polynomial delay listing algorithms for interesting families of structures.

---

† If *S*-Sample halts without returning an output then *Uniform Reducer 4* halts immediately.

Example 1. A family of colorable graphs

We start by defining the family. Recall that the notation V_n is used to denote the vertex set $\{v_1, \ldots, v_n\}$. Suppose that n is a positive integer and that j is a positive integer that is less than or equal to n. A *j-coloring* of V_n is a partition $C = (C_1, \ldots, C_j)$ that divides the vertices of V_n between j disjoint subsets, $C_1, \ldots, C_j$, such that $1 \leq l < m \leq j$ implies that $|C_l| > |C_m|$ or that $|C_l| = |C_m|$ and $C_l \leq C_m$. Each set C_i is called a *color class* of C. (Note that the definition of a j-coloring does not forbid empty color classes.) Let G be a member of $\mathcal{G}(n)$ and let C be a j-coloring of V_n. C is a *j-coloring of G* if and only if it has the property that no two vertices that belong to the same color class are connected by an edge of G. A *j-colored graph* is a pair (C, G) such that C is a j-coloring of G.

We will say that a function k from $\mathbb{N}$ to $\mathbb{N}$ is a *sub-diagonal* function if and only if $k(n) \leq n$ for every $n \in \mathbb{N}$. For every sub-diagonal function k let P_k† be the family defined as follows. Every parameter value of P_k is a positive integer (encoded in unary). The value n is associated with the set $P_k(n)$ which contains all $k(n)$-colorings of V_n. Let $\mathcal{G}_k$ be the related family defined by the following equation:

$$\mathcal{G}_k(n) = \{(C, G) \,|\, (C \in P_k(n)) \wedge (G \in \mathcal{G}(n)) \wedge (C \text{ is a } k(n)\text{-coloring of } G)\}.$$

($\mathcal{G}_k(n)$ is the set of $k(n)$-colored n-vertex graphs.) Let $\sim$ be the equivalence relation on colored graphs that ignores the coloring. (i.e. $(C_1, G_1) \sim (C_2, G_2)$ if and only if $G_1 = G_2$.) Let $\widetilde{\mathcal{G}_k}$ be the family with the following definition. Every parameter value of $\widetilde{\mathcal{G}_k}$ is a positive integer. The value n is associated with the set $\widetilde{\mathcal{G}_k}(n)$ which contains the equivalence classes under $\sim$ of $\mathcal{G}_k(n)$. Each equivalence class in $\widetilde{\mathcal{G}_k}(n)$ is associated with a particular $k(n)$-colorable graph $G \in \mathcal{G}(n)$.

We say that a sub-diagonal function k satisfies *Kučera's condition* if and only if there is a positive constant n_0 such that for every $n \geq n_0$ we have $k(n) \leq \sqrt{n/28 \log(n)}$. Suppose that k is *any* sub-diagonal function that satisfies Kučera's condition. In the remainder of this example we will design an efficient random sampling algorithm, $\widetilde{\mathcal{G}_k}$-*Sample*, for $\widetilde{\mathcal{G}_k}$.

---

† The notation defined here will be used in subsection 2.3.2 and in chapter 3. It will help the reader to realize that colorings are denoted by symbols such as "C". Families of colorings are denoted by symbols such as "P" and "Π" (since colorings are *partitions* of vertex sets). Graphs are denoted by symbols such as "G" and families of graphs and of colored graphs by symbols such as "$\mathcal{G}$" and "Γ".

$\widetilde{\mathcal{G}_k}$-*Sample* can be combined with *Uniform Reducer 4* to obtain a probabilistic polynomial delay listing algorithm for $\widetilde{\mathcal{G}_k}$ which has exponentially small failure probability.

We start by defining the equivalence class naming function $\mathcal{N}$, which will be associated with $\widetilde{\mathcal{G}_k}$-*Sample*. The function will be defined by the equation $\mathcal{N}(n, (C, G)) = G$. That is, for every colored graph $(C, G) \in \mathcal{G}_k(n)$ the name of the equivalence class of (C, G) in $\widetilde{\mathcal{G}_k}(n)$ is G.

In order to design an efficient random sampling algorithm for $\widetilde{\mathcal{G}_k}$ we first consider the problem of designing an efficient random sampling algorithm for the simple family $\mathcal{G}_k$. We make the following observation.

Observation 7. There is an efficient random sampling algorithm for $\mathcal{G}_k$.

Proof: We will not give the details of the algorithm here but we will give an informal description. In order to simplify the description we will first assume that the algorithm is to be implemented on a random access machine that has the ability to flip *biased* coins†. Then we will appeal to a result of Sinclair which shows that the algorithm can be efficiently simulated on an ordinary probabilistic random access machine.

Let $f(m, j, i)$ denote the number of j-colored graphs with vertex set V_m in which the largest color class has size i. The algorithm begins by doing dynamic programming to compute the value of $f(m, j, i)$ for $1 \le i \le m \le n$ and $1 \le j \le k(n)$.

Then the algorithm uses the values of $f(m, j, i)$ (and its biased coins) to select a coloring C. The probability with which any given coloring C is selected is proportional to the number of members of $\mathcal{G}_k(n)$ that have coloring C.

Finally, the algorithm selects a graph $G \in \mathcal{G}(n)$ such that C is a $k(n)$-coloring of G. The graph is selected by considering each pair of vertices from different color classes of C and making it an edge of G with probability $1/2$.

It is easy to see that there is a polynomial time implementation of this algorithm on a probabilistic random access machine that has biased coins. Furthermore, the implementation is an unbiased random sampling algorithm for $\mathcal{G}_k$.

Using the techniques from section 1.3 of [Sin 88] we can simulate this algorithm on an ordinary probabilistic random access machine. The simulation does not increase the expected running time or the bias factor of the algorithm by more than a factor of a polynomial in n so the resulting algorithm is an efficient random sampling algorithm for $\mathcal{G}_k$. □

---

† That is, we will assume that for every rational q in the range $[0, 1]$ the random access machine can flip a coin which has probability q of coming up "heads".

Let $\mathcal{G}_k$-*Sample* be an efficient random sampling algorithm for $\mathcal{G}_k$. Let b denote the bias factor of $\mathcal{G}_k$-*Sample*. Consider the following random sampling algorithm for $\widetilde{\mathcal{G}_k}$.

Algorithm $\widetilde{\mathcal{G}_k}$-*Sample*

Input n (in unary)

$(C, G) \longleftarrow \mathcal{G}_k$-*Sample*$(n)$

Output $((C, G), G)$

We will prove the following observation.

Observation 8. If k satisfies Kučera's condition then $\widetilde{\mathcal{G}_k}$-*Sample* is an efficient random sampling algorithm for $\widetilde{\mathcal{G}_k}$.

Proof: Since the expected running time of $\mathcal{G}_k$-*Sample* is bounded from above by a polynomial in n the expected running time of $\widetilde{\mathcal{G}_k}$-*Sample* is bounded from above by a polynomial in n. Furthermore, Kučera has shown that for every sub-diagonal function k that satisfies Kučera's condition it is the case that $|\widetilde{\mathcal{G}_k}(n)| = (1 - o(1))|\mathcal{G}_k(n)|$. Therefore the bias factor of $\widetilde{\mathcal{G}_k}$-*Sample* is $b(1+o(1))$. $\square$

Finally, we use observation 8 to obtain a corollary of theorem 6.

Corollary 1. If k satisfies Kučera's condition then there is a probabilistic polynomial delay listing algorithm for $\widetilde{\mathcal{G}_k}$ which has exponentially small failure probability.

Proof: The algorithm is obtained by combining $\widetilde{\mathcal{G}_k}$-*Sample* with *Uniform Reducer 4*. $\square$

Example 2. A family of unlabeled graphs

Let $\approx$ be the isomorphism relation on undirected graphs. Let $\widetilde{\widetilde{\mathcal{G}}}$ be the family of unlabeled graphs which we defined in the introduction of this thesis.

The problem of designing an efficient listing algorithm for $\widetilde{\widetilde{\mathcal{G}}}$ has been studied in the past [Rea 78, CR2 79, Rea 81, DW 83†]. However, previous notions of "efficient" are less

---

† Dixon and Wilf's paper contains the following observation. Suppose that samples are drawn from $\mathcal{G}(n)$ in such a way that each sample is equally likely to belong to any class in $\widetilde{\widetilde{\mathcal{G}}}(n)$. The coupon collector argument shows that the probability that a set of $|\widetilde{\widetilde{\mathcal{G}}}(n)| \times \log(|\widetilde{\widetilde{\mathcal{G}}}(n)|/\epsilon)$ such samples contains a representative of *every* class is at least $1 - \epsilon$. This observation led to my development of the methods in section 2.1.2 and to their application to the problem of listing unlabeled graphs.

demanding than the notion studied in this thesis. Furthermore, known listing algorithms for $\widetilde{\widetilde{\mathcal{G}}}$ are not efficient using our definition of the word. Later in this section we will present a deterministic listing algorithm for $\widetilde{\widetilde{\mathcal{G}}}$ which has polynomial delay and runs in polynomial space. In this subsection we show how to combine existing algorithms to obtain an efficient random sampling algorithm $\widetilde{\widetilde{\mathcal{G}}}$-*Sample* for $\widetilde{\widetilde{\mathcal{G}}}$. $\widetilde{\widetilde{\mathcal{G}}}$-*Sample* can be combined with *Uniform Reducer 4* to obtain a probabilistic polynomial delay listing algorithm for $\widetilde{\widetilde{\mathcal{G}}}$ which has exponentially small failure probability.

We start by defining the equivalence class naming function, $\mathcal{N}$, which will be associated with $\widetilde{\widetilde{\mathcal{G}}}$-*Sample*. This function is based on Babai and Kučera's canonical labeling algorithm from [BK 79], which we refer to as *BK-Label*. *BK-Label* takes as input a graph $G \in \mathcal{G}(n)$ and returns a permutation ρ of V_n which is called a *canonical labeling* of G. If the vertices of G are permuted by ρ and the edges are permuted accordingly then the result, denoted $\rho(G)$, is the *canonical representative* of G's isomorphism class. We define $\mathcal{N}(n, G)$ to be equal to $\rho(G)$ for every graph $G \in \mathcal{G}(n)$.

The random sampling algorithm $\widetilde{\widetilde{\mathcal{G}}}$-*Sample* is based on an algorithm of Wormald [Wor 87] which we call *W-Sample*. *W-Sample* takes as input a unary integer n and outputs a member of $\mathcal{G}(n)$. On any given run of *W-Sample* with any input n, the output is equally likely to be a member of any isomorphism class in $\widetilde{\widetilde{\mathcal{G}}}(n)$. Furthermore, the expected running time of *W-Sample* is bounded from above by a polynomial in n. The algorithm $\widetilde{\widetilde{\mathcal{G}}}$-*Sample* is as follows:

Algorithm $\widetilde{\widetilde{\mathcal{G}}}$-*Sample*

Input n (in unary)

$G \longleftarrow$ *W-Sample*(n)

$\rho \longleftarrow$ *BK-Label*(G)

Output $(G, \rho(G))$

We will devote the rest of this subsection to the proof of the following lemma about $\widetilde{\widetilde{\mathcal{G}}}$-*Sample*. At the end of the subsection we will use the lemma to argue that $\widetilde{\widetilde{\mathcal{G}}}$-*Sample* can be combined with *Uniform Reducer 4* to obtain a probabilistic polynomial delay listing algorithm for $\widetilde{\widetilde{\mathcal{G}}}$ which has exponentially small failure probability.

Lemma 3. $\widetilde{\widetilde{\mathcal{G}}}$-*Sample* is an efficient random sampling algorithm for $\widetilde{\widetilde{\mathcal{G}}}$.

In order to prove lemma 3 we must show that the expected running time and the bias factor of $\widetilde{\widetilde{\mathcal{G}}}$-*Sample* are bounded from above by a polynomial in n. The claims that we have already made about *W-Sample* demonstrate that $\widetilde{\widetilde{\mathcal{G}}}$-*Sample* is unbiased. In order to show that its expected running time is bounded from above by a polynomial in n we must show that when inputs to *BK-Label* are drawn from the output distribution of *W-Sample*(n), the expected running time of *BK-Label* is bounded from above by a polynomial in n. The proof of this fact is straightforward but it requires some basic definitions and facts. In the remainder of this subsection we provide the definitions and facts that we need. Then we prove the result.

Here and elsewhere in the thesis, we will use *Oberschelp's formula* (See [HP 73] p. 196). This formula says that $|\widetilde{\mathcal{G}}(n)| = [n!]^{-1}2^{\binom{n}{2}}[1 + O(n^2/2^n)]$. We will also need the following definitions. We say that a probability distribution on $\mathcal{G}(n)$ is a *uniform distribution of unlabeled graphs* if a given sample is equally likely to belong to any class in $\widetilde{\widetilde{\mathcal{G}}}(n)$. (The output distribution of *W-Sample*(n) is a uniform distribution of unlabeled graphs.) Suppose that f is a function whose domain is the set of undirected graphs. We say that f is *isomorphism-invariant* if it is the case that for any two isomorphic graphs G_1 and G_2, $f(G_1) = f(G_2)$.

The size of the automorphism group of a graph is isomorphism-invariant. Therefore, for every isomorphism class $C \in \widetilde{\widetilde{\mathcal{G}}}(n)$ we can use the notation $|\mathrm{Aut}(C)|$ to denote the size of the automorphism group of every member of C. Given a uniform distribution of unlabeled graphs, the expected size of the automorphism group of a randomly chosen n-vertex graph is $1 + o(1)$. This fact does not seem to be proved in the literature, so we provide a short proof here:†

Lemma 4. $\displaystyle\sum_{C \in \widetilde{\widetilde{\mathcal{G}}}(n)} |\mathrm{Aut}(C)| = (1 + o(1))|\widetilde{\widetilde{\mathcal{G}}}(n)|.$

Proof: We know from a simple application of Burnside's lemma that each isomorphism class in $\widetilde{\widetilde{\mathcal{G}}}(n)$ is represented $n!$ times in $\{\langle G, \pi\rangle|\ G \in \mathcal{G}(n) \wedge \pi \in \mathrm{Aut}(G)\ \}$. Therefore

$$\sum_{C \in \widetilde{\widetilde{\mathcal{G}}}(n)} |\mathrm{Aut}(C)| = \frac{1}{n!} \sum_{G \in \mathcal{G}(n)} \sum_{\pi \in \mathrm{Aut}(G)} |\mathrm{Aut}(G)| = \frac{1}{n!} \sum_{G \in \mathcal{G}(n)} |\mathrm{Aut}(G)|^2.$$

---

† L. Babai pointed out that this result follows from [BK 79].

[BK 79] shows that for any t in the range $2 \le t < n^{\frac{1}{4}}$ the probability that a random member of $\mathcal{G}(n)$ has more than $(t-1)!$ automorphisms is at most $\exp(-ctn)$ for a positive constant c. Therefore

$$\sum_{C \in \widetilde{\widetilde{\mathcal{G}}}(n)} |\mathrm{Aut}(C)| \le \frac{1}{n!} 2^{\binom{n}{2}} \left[1 + \sum_{t=2}^{n^{\frac{1}{4}}-1} \exp(-ctn)[t!]^2 + \exp(-cn^{\frac{5}{4}})[n!]^2 \right]$$

$$\le \frac{1}{n!} 2^{\binom{n}{2}} (1 + o(1)).$$

The result now follows from Oberschelp's formula. □

In order to prove lemma 3 we must show that when inputs to *BK-Label* are drawn from the output distribution of *W-Sample*(n), the expected running time of *BK-Label* is bounded from above by a polynomial in n. We now proceed with this proof.

Let $T(G)$ denote the number of machine instructions that are executed in a call to *BK-Label*(G). Suppose that inputs to *BK-Label* are chosen uniformly at random from $\mathcal{G}(n)$. Babai and Kučera showed that for fixed j the expected value of $T(G)^j$ is $O(n^{2j})$. Since $T(G)$ is isomorphism-invariant, we can compute the expected value of $T(G)^j$ for a uniform distribution of unlabeled graphs. Given an isomorphism class $C \in \widetilde{\widetilde{\mathcal{G}}}(n)$, let $T(C)$ denote the running time of Babai and Kučera's algorithm when it is given as input a member of C. We can now prove the following lemma.

Lemma 5. If j is a constant greater than or equal to 1 and G is selected randomly from a uniform distribution of unlabeled n-vertex graphs then $\mathrm{E}(T(G)^j) = O(n^{2j})$.

Proof: If G is selected randomly from a uniform distribution of unlabeled n-vertex graphs then

$$\mathrm{E}(T(G)^j) = \frac{1}{|\widetilde{\widetilde{\mathcal{G}}}(n)|} \sum_{C \in \widetilde{\widetilde{\mathcal{G}}}(n)} T(C)^j.$$

Applying Burnside's lemma (as in the proof of lemma 4) we obtain

$$\mathrm{E}(T(G)^j) = \frac{1}{|\widetilde{\widetilde{\mathcal{G}}}(n)|} \sum_{C \in \widetilde{\widetilde{\mathcal{G}}}(n)} T(C)^j = \frac{1}{|\widetilde{\widetilde{\mathcal{G}}}(n)|} \frac{1}{n!} \sum_{G \in \mathcal{G}(n)} |\mathrm{Aut}(G)| \, T(G)^j.$$

Using Oberschelp's formula to approximate the size of $\widetilde{\widetilde{\mathcal{G}}}(n)$, the right hand side becomes

$$E(T(G)^j) = \frac{1}{(1 + o(1))\, 2^{\binom{n}{2}}} \sum_{G \in \mathcal{G}(n)} |\mathrm{Aut}(G)|\, T(G)^j.$$

For any real numbers x and y it is the case that $xy \leq (x^2 + y^2)/2$. Setting $x = n^j |\mathrm{Aut}(G)|$ and $y = n^{-j}\, T(G)^j$ we obtain

$$E(T(G)^j) \leq \frac{1}{2\,(1 + o(1))\, 2^{\binom{n}{2}}} \left(\sum_{G \in \mathcal{G}(n)} \left[n^{2j}\, |\mathrm{Aut}(G)|^2 \right] + \sum_{G \in \mathcal{G}(n)} \left[n^{-2j}\, T(G)^{2j} \right] \right).$$

We showed in the proof of lemma 4 that $\displaystyle\sum_{G \in \mathcal{G}(n)} |\mathrm{Aut}(G)|^2 \leq 2^{\binom{n}{2}}(1 + o(1))$

so the left hand summation is at most $2^{\binom{n}{2}}O(n^{2j})$.

Babai and Kučera showed that $\displaystyle\sum_{G \in \mathcal{G}(n)} T(G)^{2j} = 2^{\binom{n}{2}}O(n^{4j})$

so the right hand term is $2^{\binom{n}{2}}O(n^{2j})$, which proves the lemma. □

Since the output distribution of *W-Sample* is a uniform distribution of unlabeled graphs, we conclude that the expected running time of *BK-Label* is bounded from above by a polynomial in n when inputs to *BK-Label* are drawn from the output distribution of *W-Sample*(n). Therefore we have proved lemma 3.

We conclude the subsection by using lemma 3 to obtain a corollary of theorem 6.

Corollary 2. There is a probabilistic polynomial delay listing algorithm for $\widetilde{\widetilde{\mathcal{G}}}$ which has exponentially small failure probability.

Proof: The algorithm is obtained by combining $\widetilde{\widetilde{\mathcal{G}}}$-*Sample* with *Uniform Reducer 4*. □

2.3.2. Deterministic Algorithms

In this subsection we discuss the problem of designing deterministic listing algorithms for families of structures that are not simple. The framework that we consider is the following. Suppose that S is a simple family of combinatorial structures and that $\sim$ is an equivalence relation on the structures of S that divides each set $S(p)$ into disjoint equivalence classes. Let $\widetilde{S}$ be the family in which $\widetilde{S}(p)$ denotes the set of equivalence classes in $S(p)$. The problem that we address in this subsection is "How do we design an efficient listing algorithm for $\widetilde{S}$?" In many cases we will be able to use the methods described in sections 2.1 and 2.2 to design an efficient listing algorithm for the simple family S. In some cases we will be able to modify the listing algorithm for S to obtain an efficient listing algorithm for $\widetilde{S}$. In other cases, the listing algorithm for S will be used indirectly in the design of the listing algorithm for $\widetilde{S}$.

Before considering the general problem of designing an efficient listing algorithm for $\widetilde{S}$, we consider an example. Consider the family $\mathcal{G}$, which was discussed in the introduction to this thesis. We have used the notation $\approx$ to denote the isomorphism relation on graphs and the notation $\widetilde{\widetilde{\mathcal{G}}}$ to denote the family in which $\widetilde{\widetilde{\mathcal{G}}}(n)$ is the set of isomorphism classes in $\mathcal{G}(n)$. We described an efficient listing algorithm for $\mathcal{G}$ in section 2.1. We would like to modify this algorithm to obtain an efficient listing algorithm for $\widetilde{\widetilde{\mathcal{G}}}$. We start by writing down the recursive listing algorithm for $\mathcal{G}$ which we described in subsection 2.1.1.

Algorithm *List_$\mathcal{G}$*
Input n (in unary)
If $(n = 1)$ Then Output $(V_1, \varnothing)$
Else For Each $(n-1)$-vertex graph (V_{n-1}, E)
    For Each set $W \subseteq V_{n-1}$
        $G' \longleftarrow (V_n, E \cup \{(v_n, w) \mid w \in W\})$
        Output(G')

Our goal will be to modify algorithm *List_$\mathcal{G}$* to obtain an efficient listing algorithm for $\widetilde{\widetilde{\mathcal{G}}}$. The crucial problem will be to prevent the modified algorithm from listing more than one representative of any given isomorphism class.

Most known solutions to this problem are based on a method which Read and Colbourn call the "classical method" [Rea 78, CR2 79]. The basic idea is to check each augmentation G' against the list of graphs that have already been output, outputting G' if and only if it is the first representative of its isomorphism class. It is easy to see that solutions which are based on this method require quite a lot of space to store the list of graphs. Furthermore, they require quite a lot of time to do the checking so they have large delay.

In [Rea 78] Read describes his "orderly method" which is substantially more efficient than the classical method. In order to obtain an "orderly" listing algorithm for $\widetilde{\widetilde{\mathcal{G}}}$, Read and Colbourn devised a scheme for identifying a particular canonical representative of each equivalence class in $\widetilde{\widetilde{\mathcal{G}}}(n)$. They chose the canonical representatives in such a way that each n-vertex canonical representative is an augmentation of exactly one $(n-1)$-vertex canonical representative. Then they obtained the following polynomial space listing algorithm for $\widetilde{\widetilde{\mathcal{G}}}$ [CR2 79].

Algorithm *Orderly*

Input n (in unary)

If $(n = 1)$ Then Output $(V_1, \varnothing)$

Else For Each $(n-1)$-vertex canonical representative (V_{n-1}, E)

    For Each set $W \subseteq V_{n-1}$

        $G' \longleftarrow (V_n, E \cup \{(v_n, w) \,|\, w \in W\})$

        If G' is canonical Then Output(G')

In terms of space efficiency†, Read and Colbourn's algorithm is vastly superior to the algorithms which are based on the classical method and to the probabilistic algorithm that we described in subsection 2.3.1. Furthermore, Read and Colbourn save time by eliminating much of the search space that is examined by the algorithms which use the classical method. However, if our goal is to design a polynomial delay algorithm, then there are two problems with their approach.

1. The number of n-vertex augmentations that are constructed by algorithm *Orderly* is approximately n times the number of augmentations that get output. The algorithm contains no mechanism to ensure that there is no "gap" in which exponentially many augmentations are considered, each augmentation being found to be non-canonical.

2. The question "Is G' canonical?", which is answered before each output, is unlikely to be answerable in polynomial time.

Later in this subsection we will see how to get around these problems and we will present a deterministic polynomial space polynomial delay listing algorithm for $\widetilde{\widetilde{\mathcal{G}}}$. First, however, we observe that the problems that we have identified come up in the context of the general framework that we described at the beginning of this subsection. Suppose

---

† In [Rea 78], Read presents a convincing argument that space complexity is more important than time complexity in real applications, which necessarily involve small values of n.

that S is a simple family of combinatorial structures, that $\sim$ is an equivalence relation as defined previously, and that we attempt to modify an efficient listing algorithm for S to obtain an efficient listing algorithm for $\widetilde{S}$. We will encounter the following problems:

1. Since $|S(p)|$ can be much bigger than $|\widetilde{S}(p)|$, the new algorithm may contain "gaps" in which an exponential number of members of $S(p)$ are considered, none of which are output.

2. Once a member of $S(p)$ has been constructed, it may take an exponential number of computational steps to determine whether or not it should be output.

In this thesis we will take two approaches to solving the problems.

1. If S and $\widetilde{S}$ are polynomially related then we may be able to use the filter method to obtain an efficient listing algorithm for $\widetilde{S}$. Let S_p be the list of structures that are output when we run the listing algorithm for S with input p. Let $S'(p)$ be the set of structures $s \in S(p)$ that satisfy "s is the first member of its equivalence class in $\widetilde{S}(p)$ on the list S_p". If we can use the filter method to design a cumulative polynomial delay listing algorithm for S' then we can simply use the listing algorithm for S' as a listing algorithm for $\widetilde{S}$. Informally, this approach works when the list S_p is guaranteed to have two properties: First, there must be plenty of structures near the front of the list that are members of $S'(p)$ (that is, there must not be large "gaps" near the front of the list). Second, there must not be too many structures s near the front of the list for which the question "Is s a member of $S'(p)$?" is computationally difficult.

2. We may be able to use the interleaving method to obtain an efficient listing algorithm for $\widetilde{S}$. Our strategy would be to try to define a sub-family $\widetilde{E}$ of $\widetilde{S}$ such that $\widetilde{E}$ is polynomially related to $\widetilde{S}$ and $\widetilde{E}$ has a polynomial delay listing algorithm. We would then need to find a polynomial ℓ such that we could implement a listing algorithm for $\widetilde{S}-\widetilde{E}$ which executes at most $\ell(|p|) \times (|\widetilde{S}(p)| + 1)$ machine instructions when it is run with input p. If S and $\widetilde{S}$ are polynomially related then the listing algorithm for $\widetilde{S}-\widetilde{E}$ could be based on filtering the listing algorithm for S. Otherwise the listing algorithm for S can be used indirectly in the design of the listing algorithms for $\widetilde{E}$ and $\widetilde{S}-\widetilde{E}$.

In the remainder of this subsection we consider two examples of non-simple combinatorial families. We use the examples to illustrate the approaches that we have described in this subsection. First, we use the filter method to design an efficient listing algorithm for a certain family of colorable graphs. Second, we use the interleaving method to design an efficient listing algorithm for $\widetilde{\widetilde{G}}$.

Example 1.   A family of colorable graphs.

Consider the families P_k and $\mathcal{G}_k$, which were defined in subsection 2.3.1. It will be helpful to define two additional families, Π_k and Γ_k. Every parameter value of Π_k is an undirected graph. The value $G \in \mathcal{G}(n)$ is associated with the set $\Pi_k(G)$ which contains all $k(n)$-colorings of G. Every parameter value of Γ_k is a $k(n)$-coloring of some vertex set V_n. The value $C \in P_k(n)$ is associated with the set $\Gamma_k(C)$ which is defined to be $\{G \in \mathcal{G}(n) \mid C \in \Pi_k(G)\}$. Using the new definitions, we can see that

$$\mathcal{G}_k(n) = \{(C, G) \mid (G \in \mathcal{G}(n)) \wedge (C \in \Pi_k(G))\}$$
$$= \{(C, G) \mid (C \in P_k(n)) \wedge (G \in \Gamma_k(C))\}.$$

In chapter 3 we will use the families P_k, $\mathcal{G}_k$, Π_k, and Γ_k to develop an efficient listing algorithm for $\widetilde{\mathcal{G}_k}$ (provided that k satisfies certain conditions). At present, we will illustrate the filter method by using it to design an efficient listing algorithm for a sub-family of $\widetilde{\mathcal{G}_k}$ (again, provided that k satisfies certain conditions).

We start by defining the sub-family. We say that a coloring $C \in P_k(n)$ is *balanced* if and only if it is the case that $3n/2k(n) \geq |C_i| \geq n/2k(n)$ for each color class C_i of C. Let Pb_k be the sub-family of P_k defined by the relation $Pb_k(n) = \{C \in P_k(n) \mid C \text{ is balanced}\}$. Furthermore, let Πb_k be the sub-family of Π_k defined by the relation $\Pi b_k(G) = \{C \in \Pi_k(G) \mid C \text{ is balanced}\}$. Let $\mathcal{G}b_k$ be the sub-family of $\mathcal{G}_k$ defined by

$$\mathcal{G}b_k(n) = \{(C, G) \mid (G \in \mathcal{G}(n)) \wedge (C \in \Pi b_k(G))\}$$
$$= \{(C, G) \mid (C \in Pb_k(n)) \wedge (G \in \Gamma_k(C))\}.$$

Finally, let $\widetilde{\mathcal{G}b_k}(n)$ be the set of equivalence classes under $\sim$ of $\mathcal{G}b_k(n)$.

Lemma 1 of [Kuč 89] shows that $\mathcal{G}b_k$ and $\widetilde{\mathcal{G}b_k}$ are polynomially related when k satisfies Kučera's condition. We will show that in this case we can use the filter method and an efficient listing algorithm for $\mathcal{G}b_k$ to obtain a cumulative polynomial delay listing algorithm for $\widetilde{\mathcal{G}b_k}$. By the end of the example we will have proved the following theorem.

Theorem 7.   If k satisfies Kučera's condition then there is a cumulative polynomial delay listing algorithm for $\widetilde{\mathcal{G}b_k}$.

We start by presenting a polynomial space cumulative polynomial delay listing algorithm for $\mathcal{G}b_k$. The general framework for the algorithm is the following:

```
Algorithm List_Gbₖ
Input n (in unary)
For Each C ∈ Pbₖ(n)
    For Each G ∈ Γₖ(C)
        Output(C, G)
```

In order to fill in the details of algorithm $List\_\mathcal{G}b_k$, we will need to show how to implement polynomial space cumulative polynomial delay listing algorithms for the families Pb_k and Γ_k. We start by considering Pb_k. We will describe a polynomial space cumulative polynomial delay listing algorithm for Pb_k in the proof of the following lemma. The algorithm will be called $List\_Pb_k$. We will use the notation $Pb_{k,n}$ to denote the list of colorings of V_n that are produced when $List\_Pb_k$ is run with input n. The following lemma describes some properties of $Pb_{k,n}$.

Lemma 6. There is a polynomial space cumulative polynomial delay listing algorithm for Pb_k which takes input n (in unary) and outputs the list $Pb_{k,n}$. $Pb_{k,n}$ has the following properties.

1. $(i < j) \Rightarrow (\, |\Gamma_k(Pb_{k,n}[i])| \geq |\Gamma_k(Pb_{k,n}[j])| \,)$.

2. There is a polynomial space polynomial time algorithm that takes as input two members C and C' of the list $Pb_{k,n}$ and determines which of C and C' comes first on $Pb_{k,n}$.

Proof: For every $C = (C_1, \ldots, C_{k(n)}) \in Pb_k(n)$ let $S_i(C)$ denote $|C_i|$ and let $M(C)$ denote $\sum_{i=1}^{k(n)} [S_i(C)]^2$. It is easy to see that

$$|\Gamma_k(C)| = 2^{\sum_{i<j} S_i(C)S_j(C)} = 2^{(n^2 - M(C))/2}.$$

Therefore, condition 1 can be re-stated as

$$(i < j) \Rightarrow (M(Pb_{k,n}[i]) \leq M(Pb_{k,n}[j])).$$

For any positive integer j and any sequence $(s_1, \ldots, s_j)$ of positive integers let $\mu(s_1, \ldots, s_j) = \sum_{i=1}^{j} s_i^2$. Let I be the simple family with the following description. Each parameter value of I is a tuple (j, n, m, u, l) of positive integers (each integer is encoded in unary). $I(j, n, m, u, l)$ is the set of sequences $(s_1, \ldots, s_j)$ of positive integers such that $\sum_{i=1}^{j} s_i = n$ and $\mu(s_1, \ldots, s_j) = m$ and $u \geq s_1 \geq \cdots \geq s_j \geq l$. Let $\Psi(j, n, m, u, l)$ be the boolean predicate whose value is "true" if and only if the set $I(j, n, m, u, l)$ is non-empty.

Suppose that n is a positive integer. Then the values of $\Psi(j, n, m, u, l)$ for $1 \leq j \leq k(n)$, $1 \leq m \leq n^2$, and $1 \leq l \leq u \leq n$ can be computed in polynomial time using dynamic programming. (If $j > 1$ then $\Psi(j, n, m, u, l)$ is "true" if and only if $\Psi(j-1, n-s_1, m-s_1^2, \text{Min}(s_1, n-s_1), l)$ is "true" for some s_1 such that $u \geq s_1 \geq l$.)

It is fairly easy to see that there is a polynomial space polynomial delay listing algorithm for I which uses the values of $\Psi(j, n, m, u, l)$. Given such an algorithm we can implement a polynomial space polynomial delay listing algorithm for Pb_k.

```
Algorithm List_Pbₖ
Input n (in unary)
κ ⟵ k(n)
For m ⟵ 1 To n²
For Each (s₁,…,sₖ) ∈ I( κ , n , m , 3n/2κ , n/2κ )
    For Each C ∈ Pₖ(n) such that Sᵢ(C) = sᵢ for 1 ≤ i ≤ κ
        Output C
```

The fact that this algorithm satisfies condition 1 is immediate. It is not difficult to fill in the details in such a way that condition 2 is satisfied. □

Now that we have shown that there is a polynomial space cumulative polynomial delay listing algorithm for Pb_k, we turn to the problem of showing that there is a polynomial space cumulative polynomial delay listing algorithm for Γ_k. It is easy to use the definition of Γ_k to design such an algorithm since $\Gamma_k(C)$ is simply the set of all spanning subgraphs of a certain complete k-partite graph. Alternatively, we can observe that Γ_k is recursively listable and we can use the techniques from subsection 2.1.1 to design a polynomial space polynomial delay listing algorithm for Γ_k.

Now that we have shown that Pb_k and Γ_k have polynomial space cumulative polynomial delay listing algorithms we can conclude that algorithm $List\_Gb_k$ is a polynomial space cumulative polynomial delay listing algorithm for Gb_k. We wish to prove theorem 7 by showing how to use the filter method and algorithm $List\_Gb_k$ to obtain a cumulative polynomial delay listing algorithm for $\widetilde{Gb_k}$, assuming that k satisfies Kučera's condition.

We start by defining some notation. Let $\Gamma_{k,C}$ denote the list of graphs output by the listing algorithm for Γ_k when it is run with input C. Suppose that the lth coloring on $Pb_{k,n}$ is C and that $\Gamma_{k,C}$ is $G_1, G_2, \ldots$ Then the lth "chunk" of the list output by algorithm $List\_Gb_k$ is $(C, G_1), (C, G_2), \ldots$ We refer to this chunk as $Gb_{k,n,l}$. We use the notation $Gb_{k,n}$ to denote the concatenation of the lists $Gb_{k,n,1}, Gb_{k,n,2}, \ldots$ Clearly, $Gb_{k,n}$ is the list of colored graphs that is output when algorithm $List\_Gb_k$ is run with input n.

Let $Gb'_k(n)$ be the set of colored graphs $(C, G) \in Gb_k(n)$ that satisfy "(C, G) is the first member of its equivalence class in $\widetilde{Gb_k}(n)$ on the list $Gb_{k,n}$." We will show that when k satisfies Kučera's condition we can use the filter method and algorithm $List\_Gb_k$ to obtain a cumulative polynomial delay listing algorithm for Gb'_k. Then we will have proved theorem 7.

In order to use the filter method we will need to invent a subroutine $Filter_k$, which takes as input an integer n and a colored graph $(C, G) \in Gb_k(n)$ and returns "yes" if and only if the colored graph is a member of $Gb'_k(n)$. Then we can use the following listing algorithm for Gb'_k:

```
Algorithm List_Gb'_k
Input n
For j ⟵ 1 To |Gb_k(n)|
      continue simulating List_Gb_k(n) to obtain Gb_{k,n}[j]
      If Filter_k (n, Gb_{k,n}[j]) = "yes"
          Output Gb_{k,n}[j]
```

Suppose that we invent a subroutine $Filter_k$ with time complexity T_k. The following observation follows directly from observation 5 and remark 1 of subsection 2.2.2 and from the fact that every member of $Gb_{k,n,1}$ is a member of $Gb'_k(n)$.

Observation 9. Algorithm $List\_Gb'_k$ will run in polynomial space if and only if algorithm $Filter_k$ runs in polynomial space. Furthermore, algorithm $List\_Gb'_k$ will have cumulative polynomial delay if k satisfies Kučera's condition and there exists a polynomial r such that the following conditions are satisfied:

Condition 1.   For every integer i in the range $1 \leq i \leq |Gb_{k,n,1}|$ we have

$$T_k(n, Gb_{k,n}[i]) \leq r(n).$$

Condition 2.   For every integer l in the range range $1 \leq l < |Pb_k(n)|$ we have

$$\sum_{j=1}^{|Gb_{k,n,l+1}|} T_k(n, Gb_{k,n,l+1}[j]) \leq r(n) \times |Gb_{k,n,l} / Gb'_k(n)|.$$

In the remainder of this example we will prove theorem 7 by designing an algorithm $Filter_k$ whose time complexity, T_k, satisfies the conditions in observation 9. First, we make our task easier by simplifying condition 2. Lemma 1 of [Kuč 89] shows that if k satisfies Kučera's condition then

$$|Gb_{k,n,l} / Gb'_k(n)| \geq (1 - o(1))|Gb_{k,n,l}|$$

for every l in the appropriate range . Furthermore, condition 1 of lemma 6 guarantees that $|Gb_{k,n,l}| \geq |Gb_{k,n,l+1}|$ for every l in the appropriate range. Combining these two observations, we can replace condition 2 with the following (possibly stronger) condition:

Condition 2'.   For every integer l in the range $2 \leq l \leq |Pb_k(n)|$ we have

$$\sum_{j=1}^{|Gb_{k,n,l}|} T_k(n, Gb_{k,n,l}[j]) \leq r(n) \times |Gb_{k,n,l}|.$$

Observation 10 incorporates the simplification that we have discussed, rewriting condition 2' in an equivalent form. The notation G_C is used to denote a member of $\Gamma_k(C)$, chosen uniformly at random.

Observation 10. Algorithm $List\_Gb'_k$ will run in polynomial space if and only if algorithm $Filter_k$ runs in polynomial space. Furthermore, algorithm $List\_Gb'_k$ will have cumulative polynomial delay if k satisfies Kučera's condition and there exists a polynomial r such that the following conditions are satisfied:

Condition 1.   For every integer i in the range $1 \le i \le |Gb_{k,n,1}|$ we have

$$T_k(n, Gb_{k,n}[i]) \le r(n).$$

Condition 2.   For every $C \in Pb_k(n)$ (except possibly $C = Pb_{k,n}[1]$) we have

$$E(T_k(n, (C, G_C))) \le r(n).$$

In the remainder of our treatment of this example, we assume that k satisfies Kučera's condition. We consider the problem of designing an algorithm $Filter_k$ whose time complexity, T_k, satisfies the conditions in observation 10. First, we consider a simple dictionary-based implementation of $Filter_k$. We argue that its time complexity satisfies the conditions. Therefore, it can be combined with algorithm $List\_Gb'_k$ to obtain a cumulative polynomial delay listing algorithm for $\widetilde{Gb_k}$. At this point we will have finished the proof of theorem 7, which merely says that if k satisfies Kučera's condition then there is a cumulative polynomial delay listing algorithm for $\widetilde{Gb_k}$. We next consider the problem of designing a *polynomial space* algorithm $Filter_k$ whose time complexity, T_k, satisfies the conditions in observation 10. We are unable to solve this problem in the general case (this problem is discussed further in chapter 3) but we succeed in doing so when $k(n) = O(1)$. Thus, we prove the following theorem.

Theorem 8. If $k(n) = O(1)$ then there is a polynomial space cumulative polynomial delay listing algorithm for $\widetilde{Gb_k}$.

We start, then, by presenting the simple dictionary-based implementation of $Filter_k$. Recall that $Filter_k$ takes as input an integer n and a colored graph $(C, G) \in Gb_k(n)$. The output of $Filter_k(n, (C, G))$ should be "yes" if and only if (C, G) is the first member of $Gb_{k,n}$ which contains the graph G. By the time that algorithm $List\_Gb'_k$ makes the call $Filter_k(n, (C, G))$ it will already have called $Filter_k(n, (C', G'))$ for every colored graph (C', G') which precedes (C, G) on $Gb_{k,n}$. Therefore, the implementation of $Filter_k$ could be based on a dictionary of n-vertex graphs. The dictionary should be made empty at the beginning of algorithm $List\_Gb'_k$. $Filter_k$ would have the following form:

Algorithm $Filter_k(n, (C, G))$
If G is in the dictionary
    Return "no"
Else
    put G in the dictionary
    Return "yes"

Suppose that k satisfies Kučera's condition and that we use algorithm $Filter_k$ as a subroutine in algorithm $List\_Gb'_k$, implementing the dictionary as a 2–3 tree (see [AHU 74]). Then the time complexity of $Filter_k$, T_k, will be bounded from above by a polynomial in the size of its input. Therefore (by observation 10) algorithm $List\_Gb'_k$ will be a cumulative polynomial delay listing algorithm for $\widetilde{Gb_k}$. We have now proved theorem 7.

In the remainder of our treatment of this example we will assume that $k = O(1)$ and we will present a polynomial space implementation of $Filter_k$. We will demonstrate (using observation 10) that the resulting algorithm $List\_Gb'_k$ is a polynomial space cumulative polynomial delay listing algorithm for $\widetilde{Gb_k}$. Thus, we will prove theorem 8.

Recall that every member of $Gb_{k,n,1}$ is a member of $Gb'_k(n)$. Therefore, $Filter_k(n, (C, G))$ should always output "yes" if $C = Pb_k[1]$. Furthermore, recall from lemma 6 that there is a polynomial space polynomial time algorithm that takes as input two members C and C' of $Pb_k(n)$ and determines which of C and C' comes first on the list $Pb_{k,n}$. The general form of the algorithm $Filter_k$ is as follows:

```
Algorithm Filter_k(n, (C, G))
If  C = Pb_k[1]
    Return "yes"
Else
    old  ⟵  false
    For Each  C' ∈ Π_k(G)
        If  C'  is balanced
            If  C'  precedes  C  on  Pb_{k,n}
                old  ⟵  true
    If ( old = true)
        Return "no"
    Else
        Return "yes"
```

Before we can make any claims about the time complexity, T_k, of $Filter_k$, we must specify the listing algorithm that we will use for Π_k. Later in this subsection we will present a polynomial space algorithm $List\_\Pi_k$ which takes as input a graph $G \in \mathcal{G}(n)$ and lists the members of $\Pi_k(G)$. Let t_k denote the overall time complexity of $List\_\Pi_k$. We will show that there is a polynomial r such that for every $C \in Pb_k(n)$ we have $\mathrm{E}(t_k(G_C)) \leq r(n)$. Suppose that we implement algorithm $Filter_k$ using $List\_\Pi_k$ as a sub-routine. It is easy to see that algorithm $Filter_k$ runs in polynomial space and that its time complexity satisfies the conditions in observation 10. Therefore if we use algorithm $Filter_k$ as a sub-routine in algorithm $List\_\mathcal{G}b'_k$ we will find that algorithm $List\_\mathcal{G}b'_k$ is a polynomial space cumulative polynomial delay listing algorithm for $\widetilde{\mathcal{G}b_k}$. Thus, we will have proved theorem 8.

We will conclude our treatment of this example, then, by presenting a polynomial space algorithm $List\_\Pi_k$ which takes as input a graph $G \in \mathcal{G}(n)$ and lists the members of $\Pi_k(G)$. We will show that there is a polynomial r such that for every $C \in Pb_k(n)$ we have $\mathrm{E}(t_k(G_C)) \leq r(n)$ where t_k is the time complexity of $List\_\Pi_k$.

In order to describe algorithm $List\_\Pi_k$ we require some notation. Suppose that $C = (C_1, \ldots, C_k)$ is a k-coloring of V_n and that $C' = (C'_1, \ldots, C'_k)$ is a k-coloring of a subset of V_n. We will use the notation $\{C'\}$ to stand for the vertex set $C'_1 \cup \cdots \cup C'_k$. We say that C' is a *sub-coloring* of C if and only if $C'_j \subseteq C_j$ for $1 \le j \le k$. (We say that C is a *super-coloring* of C' in this case.) If C' is a sub-coloring of C and $|C'_1| = \cdots = |C'_k| = i$ then we say that C' is an *i-sub-coloring* of C.

Suppose that G is a member of $\mathcal{G}(n)$ and that V' is a subset of V_n. We use the notation $G[V']$ to represent the subgraph of G induced by the vertices in V'. Suppose that C' is a k-coloring of $G[V']$. An *extension* of C' to G is a super-coloring C of C' which is a k-coloring of G. We say that C' *directly forces* a vertex v_i of G if there is at most one extension of C' to $G[V' \cup \{v_i\}]$. We use the notation $DF(C', G)$ to stand for the set of vertices of G that are directly forced by C'. If C' is extendible to $G[DF(C', G)]$ then the unique extension of C' to $G[DF(C', G)]$ is called the *direct forced extension* of C' to G. Otherwise, C' is said to *directly clash* with G. Suppose that C' does not directly clash with G. We say that C' *indirectly forces* a vertex v_i of G if the direct forced extension of C' to G directly forces v_i. We use the notation $IF(C', G)$ to stand for the set of vertices of G that are indirectly forced by C'. If C' is extendible to $G[IF(C', G)]$ then the unique extension of C' to $G[IF(C', G)]$ is called the *indirect forced extension* of C' to G. Otherwise, C' is said to *indirectly clash* with G. (We say that C' *clashes* with G if it directly clashes with G or indirectly clashes with G.) We can now describe algorithm *List_Π_k*.

```
Algorithm List_Π_k
Input G
let n be the number of vertices of G
b ⟵ k! × ⌈log(n)⌉
list all k-cliques in G
use the greedy heuristic to construct a list of
    vertex-disjoint k-cliques in G
If fewer than b vertex-disjoint k-cliques are found
    BruteForce(G)
Else
    let G′ be a subgraph of G consisting of b vertex-disjoint k-cliques
    flag ⟵ false
    For Each C′ ∈ Π_k(G′)
        If C′ does not clash with G
            If |IF(C′, G)| < n − k⌈log(n)⌉
                flag ⟵ true
    If (flag = true)
        BruteForce(G)
    Else
        For Each C′ ∈ Π_k(G′)
            If C′ does not clash with G
                let C_f be the indirect forced extension of C′ to G
                For Each extension C″ of C_f to G
                    Output C″
```

Procedure *BruteForce*(G)

let n be the number of vertices of G

For Each $C \in P_k(n)$

    If C is a k-coloring of G

        Output(C)

It is easy to see that algorithm *List_Π_k* runs in polynomial space and that it produces the correct output. If procedure *BruteForce* is run with an input $G \in \mathcal{G}(n)$ then it will execute at most $q_1(n)\,k^n$ machine instructions for some polynomial q_1. The number of machine instructions executed by algorithm *List_Π_k* when it is given an input $G \in \mathcal{G}(n)$, exclusive of calls to procedure *BruteForce*, is at most $q_2(n)$ for some polynomial q_2. We wish to show that there is a polynomial r such that for every $C \in Pb_k(n)$ we have $E(t_k(G_C)) \leq r(n)$. This fact follows from the following lemma.

Lemma 7. Let $C = (C_1, \ldots, C_k)$ be a member of $Pb_k(n)$ and let G_C be a member of $\Gamma_k(C)$, chosen uniformly at random. If n is sufficiently large then the probability that procedure *BruteForce* will be called in a run of algorithm *List_Π_k* with input G_C is at most k^{-n}.

Proof: Let $c_1, c_2, \ldots$ stand for constants whose values are greater than 1. We will prove the lemma by proving the following two facts:

Fact 1.   The probability that *List_Π_k* calls *BruteForce* at the first opportunity is $c_1^{-n^2}$.

Fact 2.   The probability that *List_Π_k* calls *BruteForce* at the second opportunity is $c_2^{-n\log(n)}$.

We start by proving fact 1. We wish to show that with probability $1 - c_1^{-n^2}$ the greedy heuristic yields at least b vertex-disjoint k-cliques in G_C. Let m denote $n/2k - b$ and let ϵ be a constant in the range $0 < \epsilon < 1$. Let m_k denote m and for $0 \leq j < k$ let m_j denote $\lceil m_{j+1}(1 - \epsilon)/2 \rceil$. Suppose that the greedy heuristic yields fewer than b vertex-disjoint k-cliques in G_C. Then since the size of each color class C_i of C is at least $n/2k$ there is an m-sub-coloring C' of C such that $G_C[\{C'\}]$ contains no k-clique. Fact 1 now follows from fact 3:

Fact 3. Suppose that j is an integer in the range $1 \le j \le k$ and that $C' = (C'_1, \ldots, C'_j)$ is an m_j-sub-coloring of $(C_1, \ldots, C_j)$. The probability that $G_C[\{C'\}]$ contains a j-clique is at least $(1 - c_3{}^{-m^2})^j$.

We will prove fact 3 by induction on j. The base case $(j = 1)$ is trivial (provided that n is sufficiently large). So suppose that $j > 1$. Fix any vertex $v \in C'_j$ and any integer l in the range $1 \le l < j$. Let $C'_l[v]$ stand for the set of vertices in C'_l that are adjacent to v in G_C. Using Chernoff's bound [HR 90], we find that the probability that $|C'_l[v]| \ge m_{j-1}$ is at least $1 - c_4{}^{-m}$. So the probability that $|C'_l[v]| \ge m_{j-1}$ for every l in the range $1 \le l < j$ is at least $(1 - c_4{}^{-m})^{j-1}$ which is at least $1 - c_5{}^{-m}$ since $j \le k$. Finally, we see that the probability that there exists a vertex $v \in C'_j$ such that $|C'_l[v]| \ge m_{j-1}$ for every l in the range $1 \le l < j$ is at least $(1 - [c_5{}^{-m}]^{m_j}) = 1 - c_3{}^{-m^2}$. If there is such a vertex v then let $C'[v] = (C'_1[v], \ldots, C'_{j-1}[v])$. We can use the inductive hypothesis to show that the probability that $G_C[\{C'[v]\}]$ contains a $(j-1)$-clique is at least $(1 - c_3{}^{-m^2})^{j-1}$.

We have now finished the proof of fact 1 and we proceed to the proof of fact 2. We start by defining some notation. Suppose that $C' = (C'_1, \ldots, C'_k)$ is a sub-coloring of C. We say that C' is *i-close* to C if $|C_l - C'_l| \le i$ for $1 \le l \le k$. We say that C' is *i-forcing* for G_C if there is a sub-coloring $C'' = (C''_1, \ldots, C''_k)$ of C which is i-close to C and has the property that each vertex in $\{C''\}$ is directly forced by C'. Our proof of fact 2 will use the following fact:

Fact 4. Suppose that i and i' are positive integers in the range $k \le i, i' \le n$. The probability that every i-sub-coloring of C is i'-forcing is at least $1 - c_6{}^{n-ii'}$.

Before proving fact 4, we will use it to prove fact 2. Suppose that $List\_II_k$ is run with input G_C and that it constructs a subgraph G'_C consisting of b vertex-disjoint k-cliques from G_C. We wish to show that with probability $1 - c_2{}^{-n\log(n)}$ every k-coloring C' of G'_C that does not clash with G_C satisfies $|IF(C', G_C)| \ge n - k\lceil\log(n)\rceil$.

Let δ denote $\lfloor n/4k\rfloor$ and let δ' denote $\lceil n/2k\rceil - \delta$. Fact 4 shows that the probability that there exists a $\lceil\log(n)\rceil$-sub-coloring of C which is not δ-forcing is at most $c_6{}^{n-\lceil\log(n)\rceil\times\delta}$. Similarly, fact 4 shows that the probability that there exists a δ'-sub-coloring of C which is not $\lceil\log(n)\rceil$-forcing is at most $c_6{}^{n-\lceil\log(n)\rceil\times\delta'}$. Suppose that every $\lceil\log(n)\rceil$-sub-coloring of C is δ-forcing and that every δ'-sub-coloring of C is $\lceil\log(n)\rceil$-forcing (we now know that this occurs with probability at least $1 - c_6{}^{n-\lceil\log(n)\rceil\times\delta} - c_6{}^{n-\lceil\log(n)\rceil\times\delta'}$ which is at least $1 - c_2{}^{-n\log(n)}$ for some positive constant c_2).

Let $C' = (C'_1, \ldots, C'_k)$ be any k-coloring of G'_C that does not clash with G_C. We will show that $|IF(C', G_C)| \geq n - k\lceil\log(n)\rceil$ which proves fact 2. If C' is a sub-coloring of C then the proof is easy: C' is a super-coloring of a $\lceil\log(n)\rceil$-sub-coloring of C so it is δ-forcing. Furthermore, the direct forced extension of C' is a super-coloring of a δ'-sub-coloring of C so it is $\lceil\log(n)\rceil$-forcing. By the definition of $IF(C', G_C)$ we find that $|IF(C', G_C)| \geq n - k\lceil\log(n)\rceil$. If C' is not a sub-coloring of C then we cannot conclude that C' is a super-coloring of a $\lceil\log(n)\rceil$-sub-coloring of C. However, a simple counting argument shows that there is a permutation ρ of $[1, \ldots, k]$ such that $|C'_{\rho(l)} \cap C_l| \geq \lceil\log(n)\rceil$ for $1 \leq l \leq k$. Let C''_l denote $C'_{\rho(l)} \cap C_l$ and let $C'' = (C''_1, \ldots, C''_k)$. Then we can use the arguments that we used above to prove $|IF(C'', G_C)| \geq n - k\lceil\log(n)\rceil$ which implies $|IF(C', G_C)| \geq n - k\lceil\log(n)\rceil$ and therefore proves fact 2.

Having proved fact 2, we return to the proof of fact 4. Suppose that i and i' are positive integers in the range $k \leq i, i' \leq n$. Let $C' = (C'_1, \ldots, C'_k)$ be any i-sub-coloring of C. Let C''_l be $\{v \in C_l \mid v$ is directly forced by $C'\}$. Let $M_l = |C_l| - i$. The probability that $|C_l - C''_l| > i'$ is at most

$$\sum_{j=0}^{M_l - i'} \binom{M_l}{j} \times \left[\left(1 - 2^{-i}\right)^{k-1}\right]^j \times \left[1 - \left(1 - 2^{-i}\right)^{k-1}\right]^{M_l - j}$$

which is at most

$$\sum_{j=0}^{M_l - i'} 2^{M_l} \times 1 \times \left[(k-1)2^{-i}\right]^{M_l - j} \leq M_l\, 2^{M_l}\left[(k-1)2^{-i}\right]^{i'} \leq c_7{}^{n - ii'}.$$

We conclude that the probability that any particular i-sub-coloring of C is not i'-forcing is at most $k\, c_7{}^{n - ii'}$. Therefore, the probability that there exists an i-sub-coloring of C that is not i'-forcing is at most $k^n\, k\, c_7{}^{n - ii'}$. $\square$

Now that we have proved lemma 7 we can conclude that there is a polynomial r such that for every $C \in Pb_k(n)$ the expected value of $t_k(G_C)$ is bounded from above by $r(n)$. Therefore the time complexity of algorithm $Filter_k$ satisfies the conditions in observation 10. We conclude that algorithm $List\_Gb'_k$ is a polynomial space cumulative polynomial delay listing algorithm for $\widetilde{Gb_k}$ and we have therefore proved theorem 8.

Example 2.   A family of unlabeled graphs†.

Recall the framework that we described at the beginning of this subsection. We postulated the existence of a simple family S and an equivalence relation $\sim$ on the structures of S that divides each set $S(p)$ into disjoint equivalence classes. We let $\widetilde{S}$ be the family in which $\widetilde{S}(p)$ denotes the set of equivalence classes in $S(p)$. The problem that we posed was "How do we design an efficient listing algorithm for $\widetilde{S}$?" We noted that in many cases we could use the methods described in sections 2.1 and 2.2 to design an efficient listing algorithm for the simple family S and that in some cases we could modify the listing algorithm for S to obtain an efficient listing algorithm for $\widetilde{S}$. We identified two sources of difficulty which could hinder our attempts to come up with an efficient modified algorithm. First, since $|S(p)|$ could be much bigger than $|\widetilde{S}(p)|$, a modified listing algorithm for S could contain "gaps" in which an exponential number of members of $S(p)$ are considered, none of which are output. Second, once a member of $S(p)$ has been constructed, it could take an exponential number of computational steps to determine whether or not it should be output. We suggested two approaches to overcoming these difficulties. The first approach uses the filter method. It was illustrated in example 1. The second approach uses the interleaving method. The general idea is to try to define a sub-family $\widetilde{E}$ of $\widetilde{S}$ such that $\widetilde{E}$ is polynomially related to $\widetilde{S}$ and $\widetilde{E}$ has a polynomial delay listing algorithm. Having defined $\widetilde{E}$, we would then have to find a polynomial ℓ such that we could implement a listing algorithm for $\widetilde{S} - \widetilde{E}$ which executes at most $\ell(|p|) \times (|\widetilde{S}(p)| + 1)$ machine instructions when it is run with input p. We observed that the listing algorithm for S can be used indirectly in the design of the listing algorithms for $\widetilde{E}$ and $\widetilde{S} - \widetilde{E}$. We will conclude this subsection by illustrating the second approach. We will use the interleaving method to design a polynomial space polynomial delay listing algorithm for $\widetilde{\widetilde{G}}$.

We begin by describing the background material that we will need. We say that a graph is *rigid* if its automorphism group is the trivial group ID which contains only one element. Let $\mathcal{G}_{nr}(n)$ denote the set of non-rigid graphs in $\mathcal{G}(n)$ and let $\widetilde{\widetilde{\mathcal{G}}}_{nr}(n)$ denote the set of equivalence classes in $\widetilde{\widetilde{\mathcal{G}}}(n)$ whose members are not rigid. We will use the following lemma.

---

† The author is grateful to Brendan McKay for a helpful discussion concerning the problem of listing unlabeled graphs.

Lemma 8. For any polynomial q it is the case that

$$\sum_{C \in \widetilde{\widetilde{\mathcal{G}}}_{nr}(n)} |\mathrm{Aut}(C)| \;=\; o(q(n)^{-1})\,|\widetilde{\widetilde{\mathcal{G}}}(n)|.$$

Proof: Applying Burnside's lemma (as in the proof of lemma 4) we obtain

$$\sum_{C \in \widetilde{\widetilde{\mathcal{G}}}_{nr}(n)} |\mathrm{Aut}(C)| \;=\; \frac{1}{n!} \sum_{G \in \mathcal{G}_{nr}(n)} |\mathrm{Aut}(G)|^2.$$

The result now follows from the proof of lemma 4 and from Oberschelp's formula. □

Our listing algorithm will use a modified version of subroutine *BK-Label*. The modified version takes as input an n-vertex graph G and returns both a canonical labeling of G and the automorphism group of G.

Before we can describe the appropriate modifications to *BK-Label*, we must designate the method that we will use to computationally represent permutation groups. The method that we will use is due to Sims, Furst, Hopcroft, and Luks. It is described thoroughly in [Hof 82]. For completeness, we provide a brief description here.

Suppose that Γ is a group of permutations of $\{1, \ldots, n\}$. Let Γ_i denote the pointwise stabilizer of $\{i, \ldots, n\}$ in Γ for $1 \leq i \leq n$. Let Γ_{n+1} denote Γ. For each integer i in the range $1 \leq i \leq n$ we can establish an equivalence relation on the elements in Γ_{i+1} (see [Hof 82], pp. 14–15) in which π_1 is related to π_2 if and only if $\pi_2^{-1}\pi_1 \in \Gamma_i$. (Note that composition is written from right to left.) The equivalence classes of Γ_{i+1} are called the *right cosets* of Γ_i in Γ_{i+1}. A *complete right transversal* for Γ_i in Γ_{i+1} is a set which contains exactly one member of each right coset of Γ_i in Γ_{i+1}. If U_i is a complete right transversal for Γ_i in Γ_{i+1} for every integer i in the range $1 \leq i \leq n$ then every permutation $\pi \in \Gamma$ can be written as $\pi_n \pi_{n-1} \cdots \pi_1$ where $\pi_i \in U_i$ (See [Hof 82], p. 28). Therefore, we can recover any information about Γ if we store the members of a complete right transversal for Γ_i in Γ_{i+1} for every i in the range $1 \leq i \leq n$.

It is easily shown (see [Hof 82], theorem 3) that each right coset of Γ_i in Γ_{i+1} can be associated with a particular integer $j \leq i$ such that the members of the coset are precisely the members of Γ_{i+1} that map i to j. Therefore, a complete right transversal for Γ_i in Γ_{i+1} is simply a set which contains, for each integer j in the range $1 \leq j \leq i$, either a member of Γ which pointwise stabilizes $\{i+1, \ldots, n\}$ and maps i to j or nothing if no such member exists.

We will represent the automorphism group of an n-vertex graph as an $n \times n$ table in which the $\{i,j\}^{th}$ entry is any automorphism which pointwise stabilizes $v_{i+1}, \ldots, v_n$ and maps v_i to v_j. (The $\{i,j\}^{th}$ entry will be empty if no such automorphism exists.) Given a list of the automorphisms of an n-vertex graph G we can construct such a table in $O(n^2 + n |\text{Aut}(G)|)$ time steps. Once we have a table representing the automorphism group of an n-vertex graph G, we can list the automorphisms of G with $O(n^2)$ delay and we can determine in $O(1)$ time steps whether G has an automorphism which maps v_n to any specified vertex.

At certain times during the execution of our listing algorithm we will wish to combine the automorphisms of a given graph with $O(n)$ new generators to obtain a larger group. In order to save time we will simply store a list of the new generators until we actually need to know the elements of the new group. When we do need to know the elements of the new group we will use Furst, Hopcroft, and Luks' algorithm from [FHL 80] to construct a new table in $O(n^6)$ time steps.

We are now ready to describe the modified version of *BK-Label*. We start by defining some notation. Suppose that s is a sequence of vertices from a graph G. Then the *trace* of a vertex v_j relative to s (denoted $tr(v_j, s)$) is simply a list $b_1, \ldots, b_{|s|}$ of binary digits in which $b_i = 1$ if v_j is adjacent to the ith element of the sequence and $b_i = 0$ otherwise. We say that a sequence s is *trace-distinguishing* if all of the vertices outside of s have different traces relative to s. *BK-Label* works in the following manner: after receiving as input a graph $G \in \mathcal{G}(n)$, it divides the vertices of G into equivalence classes according to their degrees. The equivalence classes, $C_1, C_2, \ldots$ are indexed by integers so that for any $u \in C_i$, $v \in C_{i+1}$ it is the case that $\deg(u) < \deg(v)$. Having divided the vertices into equivalence classes, *BK-Label* attempts to refine the equivalence relation by considering the number of neighbors that each vertex has in each equivalence class. After two refinement steps, it calculates the size of the equivalence classes. If every equivalence class has size one, the canonical labeling of G is simply the permutation which maps the vertex in equivalence class j to v_j for $1 \le j \le n$. In this case, the automorphism group of G is simply the trivial group. If there is an equivalence class which contains more than one vertex then *BK-Label* searches for a small trace-distinguishing sequence s. If the smallest trace-distinguishing sequence which it finds has size z, then it uses $O(n^3 n^z)$ time steps to find a canonical labeling of G. We can arrange for the canonical labeling to map a vertex of maximum degree to v_n. Once it has chosen s, the modified version of *BK-Label* uses the following method to find a list of the automorphisms of G in $O(q(n)n^z)$ time steps (for some polynomial q).

Procedure *List_Automorphisms*(G, s)

/* G is a member of $\mathcal{G}(n)$ */

/* s is a trace-distinguishing sequence of vertices from G */

/* $bad(\lambda)$ becomes true as soon as it is discovered */

/* that no extension of λ is an automorphism of G. */

For each function $\lambda : s \to V_n$

    $bad(\lambda) \longleftarrow$ **false**

    $W \longleftarrow$ the image of s under λ

    For each $v \in V_n - W$

        If there exists a vertex $u \in V_n - s$ such that $tr(u, s) = tr(v, W)$

            $\lambda(u) \longleftarrow v$

        Else $bad(\lambda) \longleftarrow$ **true**

    If $(bad(\lambda) = $ **false**$)$

        If λ is a permutation of V_n

            If $(\lambda(G) = G)$

                put λ in the table representing the automorphism group of G

In subsection 2.3.1 we used the notation $T(G)$ to stand for the number of machine instructions that are executed when *BK-Label* is run with input G. We showed that when inputs to *BK-Label* are drawn from a uniform distribution of unlabeled graphs and j is a constant which is at least 1 we have $E(T(G)^j) = O(n^{2j})$. Since the time complexity of the modified version of *BK-Label* is not much greater than the time complexity of the unmodified version this result remains true when we use the notation $T(G)$ to stand for the number of machine instructions that are executed when the modified version of *BK-Label* is run with input G.

We are now ready to use the interleaving method to obtain an efficient listing algorithm for $\widetilde{\widetilde{\mathcal{G}}}$. Our strategy will be to define a sub-family $\widetilde{\widetilde{E}}$ of $\widetilde{\widetilde{\mathcal{G}}}$ such that $\widetilde{\widetilde{E}}$ is polynomially related to $\widetilde{\widetilde{\mathcal{G}}}$ and $\widetilde{\widetilde{E}}$ has a polynomial delay listing algorithm. We start by reconsidering algorithm *Orderly*. This algorithm determines whether or not to output a given augmentation by deciding whether or not the augmentation is the canonical representative of its isomorphism class. Since there is no known polynomial-time algorithm for determining whether a given graph is the canonical representative of its isomorphism class, our listing algorithm for $\tilde{\tilde{E}}$ will have to replace the canonicity test in algorithm *Orderly* with another test†. In order to efficiently implement the new test, we maintain the automorphism groups of the graphs that are constructed. That is, instead of simply listing n-vertex graphs, our algorithm will list a series of pairs $\langle G, \text{Aut}(G) \rangle$ in which G is an n-vertex graph and $\text{Aut}(G)$ is the automorphism group of G, represented in the manner that we described. We will say that a pair $\langle G, \text{Aut}(G) \rangle$ is the *algorithmic* representative of its class in $\tilde{\tilde{\mathcal{G}}}(n)$ if $\langle G, \text{Aut}(G) \rangle$ is output by our algorithm. (Sometimes we refer to G as the algorithmic representative of its class.)

We can now define the sub-family $\tilde{\tilde{E}}$. We will say that an n-vertex graph G is easy to process if and only if it satisfies at least one of the following conditions:

(i) G has a vertex with degree $n - 1$.

(ii) G has a unique vertex v of maximum degree and $G - v$ is rigid.

The property of being easy to process is isomorphism-invariant. We can therefore define $\tilde{\tilde{E}}(n)$ to be the set of all classes in $\tilde{\tilde{\mathcal{G}}}(n)$ whose members are easy to process. We will use the symbol $\tilde{\tilde{H}}$ to stand for the family $\tilde{\tilde{\mathcal{G}}} - \tilde{\tilde{E}}$.

Let c_e and c_h be positive constants (which will be defined implicitly later in this subsection). We give an inductive definition for the polynomials d and e:

$d(0) = 0.$

$d(n) = 2c_s c_h n^4 + e(n) + c_s$ for $n > 0.$

$e(n) = c_e n + d(n - 1).$

Observation 1 shows that the interleaving method gives a polynomial space listing algorithm for $\tilde{\tilde{\mathcal{G}}}$ with delay d provided that the following three conditions are satisfied:

(i) $|\tilde{\tilde{\mathcal{G}}}(n)| \le 2|\tilde{\tilde{E}}(n)|.$

(ii) There is a polynomial space listing algorithm for $\tilde{\tilde{E}}$ which has delay e.

(iii) There is a polynomial space listing algorithm for $\tilde{\tilde{H}}$ which executes at most $c_h n^4 (|\tilde{\tilde{\mathcal{G}}}(n)| + 1)$ machine instructions when it is run with input n.

In the remainder of this subsection we give an inductive proof that these conditions can be satisfied. We therefore prove the following theorem

Theorem 9. There is a polynomial space polynomial delay listing algorithm for $\tilde{\tilde{\mathcal{G}}}$.

The proof consists of three lemmas.

---

† The idea of avoiding canonical labeling when alternative tests are more efficient was used in [MR 86].

Lemma 9. $|\widetilde{\widetilde{\mathcal{G}}}(n)| \le 2|\widetilde{\widetilde{E}}(n)|$.

Proof: [Bol 85 p. 64] shows that at most o(1) of the $2^{\binom{n}{2}}$ graphs in $\mathcal{G}(n)$ fail to have a unique vertex of maximum degree. The number of n-vertex graphs G which have a unique vertex v of maximum degree such that $G-v$ is not rigid is at most a factor of $n2^{n-1}$ larger than the number of non-rigid $(n-1)$-vertex graphs. By [BK 79] the number of non-rigid $(n-1)$-vertex graphs is at most $c^{-(n-1)}2^{\binom{n-1}{2}}$ for some fixed $c > 1$. Thus $[1 - o(1)]2^{\binom{n}{2}}$ graphs in $\mathcal{G}(n)$ are easy to process. We conclude that at least $[1 - o(1)]2^{\binom{n}{2}}[n!]^{-1}$ classes in $\widetilde{\widetilde{\mathcal{G}}}(n)$ must be members of $\widetilde{\widetilde{E}}(n)$. Using Oberschelp's formula, we find that more than half of the classes in $\widetilde{\widetilde{\mathcal{G}}}(n)$ are members of $\widetilde{\widetilde{E}}(n)$.

Lemma 10.   There is a polynomial space listing algorithm for $\widetilde{\widetilde{E}}$ which has delay e.

Proof: The following algorithm suffices:

Algorithm $\mathcal{E}$

Input n

For each algorithmic representative $\langle G, \mathrm{Aut}(G)\rangle$ of a class in $\widetilde{\widetilde{\mathcal{G}}}(n - 1)$

    $G' \longleftarrow G \cup \{(v_i, v_n) \mid i < n\}$

    $\mathrm{Aut}(G') \longleftarrow$ the group generated by the generators of $\mathrm{Aut}(G)$

                and $\{(v_i, v_n) \mid v_i$ has degree $n-2$ in $G\}$

    Output $\langle G', \mathrm{Aut}(G')\rangle$

    If G is rigid

        For all subsets $W \subset V_{n-1}$ such that

        v_n is the unique vertex of maximum degree in $G \cup \{(w, v_n) \mid w \in W\}$

        Output $\langle G \cup \{(w, v_n) \mid w \in W\}, \mathrm{ID}\rangle$

If we maintain an array which allows the degree of each vertex to be obtained in a constant number of steps, we can implement this algorithm with at most $d(n - 1) + \mathrm{O}(n)$ delay.

Lemma 11.   There is a polynomial space listing algorithm for $\widetilde{\widetilde{H}}$ which executes at most $c_h n^4 |\widetilde{\widetilde{\mathcal{G}}}(n)|$ machine instructions when it is run with input n.

Proof: The basic outline of the algorithm is the following:

Algorithm $\mathcal{H}$

Input n

For each algorithmic representative $\langle G, \mathrm{Aut}(G) \rangle$ **of a class in** $\widetilde{\widetilde{\mathcal{G}}}(n-1)$

    If G **is rigid**

        For all subsets $W \subset V_{n-1}$ **such that**

        v_n **is a** *non-unique* **vertex of maximum degree in** $G \cup \{(w, v_n) \mid w \in W\}$

            Test_Augmentation$(G \cup \{(w, v_n) \mid w \in W\})$

    Else For all subsets $W \subset V_{n-1}$ **such that**

        v_n **is a vertex of maximum degree in** $G \cup \{(w, v_n) \mid w \in W\}$

        If *Is_Smallest*$(W, \mathrm{Aut}(G))$

            Test_Augmentation$(G \cup \{(w, v_n) \mid w \in W\})$

The algorithm uses two subroutines, *Test_Augmentation* and *Is_Smallest*:

Procedure *Test_Augmentation*(G')

/* G' is a graph with vertex set $\{v_1, \ldots, v_n\}$ */

$(\rho, \mathrm{Aut}(G')) \longleftarrow$ *BK-Label*(G')

If $\exists \pi \in \mathrm{Aut}(G')$ **such that** $\pi(v_n) = \rho^{-1}(v_n)$ **Then Output** $\langle G', \mathrm{Aut}(G') \rangle$

Function *Is_Smallest(W, Group)*
/* W is a subset of $\{v_1, \ldots, v_n\}$ */
/* *Group* is a group of permutations of $\{v_1, \ldots, v_n\}$ */
W_Is_Smallest ⟵ **true**
For all $\pi \in$ *Group*
    If the image of W under π is lexicographically smaller than W
        W_Is_Smallest ⟵ **false**
Return(*W_Is_Smallest*)

Before considering the running time of algorithm $\mathcal{H}$ we prove that it is correct by establishing the following facts:

(i) Algorithm $\mathcal{H}$ never outputs a graph whose isomorphism class is in $\overset{\approx}{E}(n)$.

The proof of this fact is straightforward. □

(ii) Algorithm $\mathcal{H}$ outputs *at least* one representative of each class $C \in \overset{\approx}{H}(n)$.

Let CR be the canonical representative of a class in $\overset{\approx}{H}(n)$. Let G be the algorithmic representative of the class of $CR - v_n$ and let π_1 be an isomorphism mapping $CR - v_n$ to G. Let W be the image in G under π_1 of the neighbors of v_n in CR. Let π_2 be an automorphism of G mapping W to a set W' such that W' is lexicographically as small as possible over all automorphisms of G. Finally, extend π_1 and π_2 to the domain $\{v_1, \ldots, v_n\}$ by setting $\pi_1(v_n) = \pi_2(v_n) = v_n$:

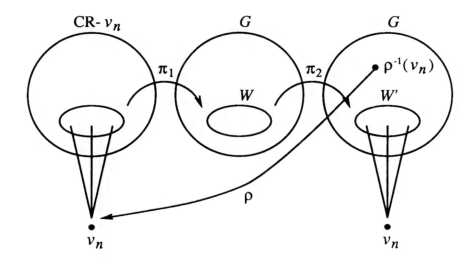

As mentioned earlier, we can arrange to make v_n a vertex of maximum degree in CR. Therefore, $\mathcal{H}$ will construct the augmentation $G' = (G \cup \{(w, v_n) \mid w \in W'\})$ when it examines G. *Test_Augmentation*(G') will compute a canonical labeling ρ of G'. It is easy to see that the automorphism $\rho^{-1}\pi_1{}^{-1}\pi_2{}^{-1}$ maps v_n to $\rho^{-1}(v_n)$, so G' will be output. $\square$

(iii) Algorithm $\mathcal{H}$ outputs *at most* one representative of each class $C \in \overset{\approx}{\tilde{H}}(n)$.

Suppose G_1 and G_2 are two isomorphic graphs and that the test in *Test_Augmentation* succeeds for both of them. The test in *Test_Augmentation* guarantees that there is an isomorphism from G_1 to its canonical representative which fixes v_n and that there is an isomorphism from G_2 to the same canonical representative which fixes v_n, so there must be an isomorphism from G_1 to G_2 which fixes v_n. Let G be the algorithmic representative of $G_1 - v_n$ and $G_2 - v_n$. Let π_1 be an isomorphism mapping $G_1 - v_n$ to G and let W_1 be the image in G under π_1 of the neighbors of v_n in G_1. Let π_2 be an isomorphism mapping $G_2 - v_n$ to G and let W_2 be the image in G under π_2 of the neighbors of v_n in G_2:

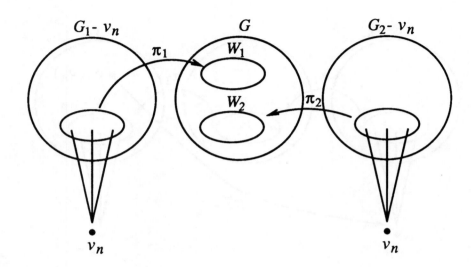

Clearly G has an automorphism mapping W_1 to W_2. Therefore calls to *Is_Smallest* will prevent $\mathcal{H}$ from calling both of *Test_Augmentation*(G_1) and *Test_Augmentation*(G_2). □

At this point we have shown that $\mathcal{H}$ lists exactly one representative from each isomorphism class in $\widetilde{\widetilde{H}}(n)$. It remains to show that the algorithm runs in $c_h n^4 |\widetilde{\widetilde{\mathcal{G}}}(n)|$ time steps.

We know from the inductive hypothesis that the delay of the outer **for** loop is bounded by $d(n-1)$. We will charge the selection of W to the appropriate call to *Test_Augmentation* if G is rigid and to the appropriate call to *Is_Smallest* otherwise. Therefore we need only show that the number of time steps which are spent in calling *Is_Smallest* and *Test_Augmentation* is bounded by $c_h n^4 |\widetilde{\widetilde{\mathcal{G}}}(n)|$.

For each non-rigid algorithmic representative G of a class in $\widetilde{\widetilde{\mathcal{G}}}(n-1)$ we will make at most 2^{n-1} calls to *Is_Smallest*. The time complexity of a single call is at most $O(n^6) + O(n^2)|\text{Aut}(G)|$. (The $O(n^6)$ time steps are used to construct a table of generators for $\text{Aut}(G)$ in the case that we have a list of new generators which need to be added to the existing table.) Therefore the number of time steps which $\mathcal{H}$ spends calling *Is_Smallest* is bounded by $O(n^6)2^{n-1} \sum_{C \in \widetilde{\widetilde{\mathcal{G}}}_{nr}(n-1)} |\text{Aut}(C)|$. Lemma 8 shows that this expression is bounded from above by $o(1)|\widetilde{\widetilde{\mathcal{G}}}(n)|$.

If we consider a uniform distribution of unlabeled graphs, the expected time of *Test_Augmentation* is $O(n^2)$. We will show that $\mathcal{H}$ calls *Test_Augmentation* for at most n^2 members of each class in $\widetilde{\widetilde{\mathcal{G}}}(n)$, which establishes the result:

The only way that $\mathcal{H}$ can produce a graph whose canonical representative is CR is to augment the algorithmic representative G_i of the isomorphism class of $CR - v_i$ for some v_i in $\{v_1, \ldots, v_n\}$. Suppose that the algorithmic representative G_i of the class $CR - v_i$ contains two sets of vertices, W_1 and W_2, such that $(G_i \cup \{(w, v_n) \mid w \in W_1\})$ and $(G_i \cup \{(w, v_n) \mid w \in W_2\})$ are both members of CR's isomorphism class. Suppose further that there are canonical labelings π_1 of $(G_i \cup \{(w, v_n) \mid w \in W_1\})$ and π_2 of $(G_i \cup \{(w, v_n) \mid w \in W_2\})$ such that $\pi_1(v_n) = \pi_2(v_n)$:

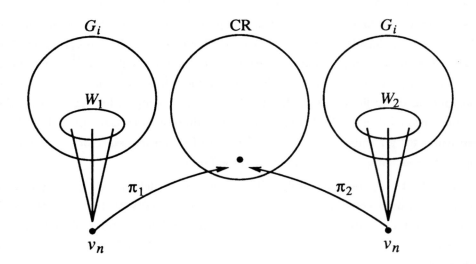

Then it is easy to see that G_i has an automorphism mapping W_1 to W_2. Therefore calls to *Is_Smallest* will prevent $\mathcal{H}$ from calling both *Test_Augmentation*$(G_i \cup \{(w, v_n) \mid w \in W_1\})$ and
Test_Augmentation$(G_i \cup \{(w, v_n) \mid w \in W_2\})$. We conclude that at most n augmentations of G_i will be tested. □

We have now shown that algorithm $\mathcal{E}$ can be interleaved with algorithm $\mathcal{H}$ to obtain a polynomial space polynomial delay listing algorithm for $\widetilde{\widetilde{\mathcal{G}}}$. We have therefore proved theorem 9.

3. Applications to Particular Families of Structures

Chapter 2 described several general methods for listing combinatorial structures. In order to illustrate the methods we applied them to a few specific families of structures. In addition, we made some observations concerning the application of the methods to various classes of combinatorial families including graph properties and recursively listable families.

While the examples in chapter 2 involved particular combinatorial families, the focus of our attention was on the general listing methods. In this chapter we will shift the focus of our attention to applications. We will be interested in looking at the particular algorithms that we have developed in the course of this work and in finding out what we have learned about particular combinatorial families in the course of the work.

We start by considering a few results from chapter 2 which we will not pursue farther in this chapter. First, consider *Uniform Reducer 2* which we described in subsection 2.1.2. In theorem 2 we proved that whenever *Uniform Reducer 2* is combined with any efficient random sampling algorithm *S-Sample* for any simple family S it becomes a probabilistic polynomial delay listing algorithm for S. The listing algorithm has exponentially small failure probability. This theorem leads immediately to efficient probabilistic listing algorithms for a number of interesting families of structures since other people have developed random sampling algorithms for these families.

For example, let Sp be the family with the following definition. Every parameter value of Sp is an undirected graph. The value G is associated with the set $Sp(G)$ which contains all spanning trees of G. There is an efficient random sampling algorithm for Sp (see [CDN 89]). Therefore, we can use *Uniform Reducer 2* to obtain an efficient listing algorithm for Sp†.

As another example, let $\mathcal{G}_{\text{deg}}$ be the family with the following definition. Every parameter value of $\mathcal{G}_{\text{deg}}$ is a finite sequence of non-negative numbers. The sequence must satisfy a condition described in [JS 90]. The value $(d_1, \ldots, d_n)$ is associated with the set $\mathcal{G}_{\text{deg}}(d_1, \ldots, d_n)$ which contains all undirected graphs with degree sequence $(d_1, \ldots, d_n)$. [JS 90] contains an efficient random sampling algorithm for $\mathcal{G}_{\text{deg}}$. Therefore, we can use

---

† We mention this example only to illustrate the use of theorem 2. The algorithm that we obtain by applying the theorem is not the first (or even the best) listing algorithm for Sp. A deterministic polynomial space polynomial delay algorithm is described in [RT 75].

Uniform Reducer 2 to obtain an efficient listing algorithm for $\mathcal{G}_{\mathrm{deg}}$. [JMS 89] shows that the condition in [JS 90] is sufficiently general that this result is interesting. For example, all regular sequences satisfy the condition.

Next, consider observation 6 of subsection 2.2.2. This observation says that if S is a graph property such that $S(n)$ is large enough and there is a polynomial expected time algorithm that takes as input a graph $G \in \mathcal{G}(n)$ and determines whether or not G is a member of $S(n)$ then there is a probabilistic polynomial delay listing algorithm for S that has exponentially small failure probability. This observation seems to be fairly general and is likely to be useful for practical applications.

Finally, consider the polynomial space polynomial delay listing algorithm for $\widetilde{\widetilde{\mathcal{G}}}$ which is described in subsection 2.3.2. It has been known for some time that algorithms for listing unlabeled graphs can be used to solve a variety of practical problems (see, for example, [Rea 81]). Our algorithm is particularly useful since it is the most efficient known algorithm for listing unlabeled graphs. (Our algorithm is the only known deterministic listing algorithm for $\widetilde{\widetilde{\mathcal{G}}}$ which can be proven to have polynomial delay. Since Read and Colbourn's algorithm is unlikely to have a polynomial delay implementation (see chapter 2) our algorithm is likely to be the only known deterministic polynomial delay listing algorithm for $\widetilde{\widetilde{\mathcal{G}}}$.) Moreover, our algorithm would be fairly easy to implement. It does not depend upon any of the group-theoretic concepts which are currently being used for moderately exponential graph isomorphism algorithms. (The only group-theoretic result which is used is the application in [FHL 80] of the "tower of groups" idea.)

In this chapter we consider various other applications of our listing methods. First, in section 3.1, we apply our methods to the problem of designing efficient listing algorithms for first order graph properties. In section 3.2 we apply the methods to the problem of designing efficient listing algorithms for Hamiltonian graphs. In section 3.3 we apply the methods to the problem of designing efficient listing algorithms for graphs with cliques of specified size. Finally, in section 3.4 we apply the methods to the problem of designing efficient listing algorithms for graphs which can be colored with a specified number of colors.

3.1. First Order Graph Properties

The first order language of graphs consists of the following symbols:

1. Variables $x_1, x_2, \ldots$, ranging over vertices

2. The binary predicate "=", representing equality of vertices

3. The binary predicate "A", representing adjacency of vertices

4. The propositional connectives "$\neg$", "$\wedge$", "$\vee$", and "$\Rightarrow$"

5. The quantifiers "$\exists$" and "$\forall$"

6. The constants "**true**" and "**false**"

7. parentheses

Formulas and sentences in this language are constructed in the same manner as sentences in any other first order language (see [BH 79]). Given a sentence θ in the first order language of graphs and a graph $G = (V_n, E)$ in $\mathcal{G}(n)$ we say that $\theta(G) = $ **true** if and only if the sentence θ evaluates to **true** when the variables in θ are allowed to range over the vertices in V_n and the adjacency predicate A is defined by $A(v_i, v_j) = $ **true** $\iff (v_i, v_j) \in E$. The graph property corresponding to θ is denoted F_θ and is defined as follows: $F_\theta(n) = \{G \in \mathcal{G}(n) \mid \theta(G) = $ **true**$\}$. Many graph properties can be described by first order sentences. For example, consider the formula $\psi = \exists x_1 \forall x_2 \neg A(x_1, x_2)$. $F_\psi(n)$ is the set of n-vertex graphs that have one or more isolated vertices.

It is fairly easy to design a polynomial space polynomial delay listing algorithm for F_ψ. Furthermore, given any particular graph property F_θ, it seems to be easy to design a polynomial space polynomial delay listing algorithm for F_θ. It would be interesting to know whether it is the case that all first order graph properties are easy to list. That is, it would be interesting to know whether there exists a first order graph property which has no efficient listing algorithm. If there is no such graph property then it would be interesting to know whether there is a general method that can be used to obtain a polynomial space polynomial delay listing algorithm for any first order graph property F_θ.

We do not provide complete answers to these questions in this thesis. The answers that we do provide depend upon a result of Fagin. Fagin showed in [Fag 76] that for every sentence θ in the first order language of graphs either $|F_\theta(n)| = (1-o(1))|\mathcal{G}(n)|$ or $|F_\theta(n)| = o(1)|\mathcal{G}(n)|$. In the former case, we say that F_θ is a *first order one property*. Otherwise, we say that it is a *first order zero property*. In this thesis we do not study first order zero properties. However, we are able to give complete answers to the questions concerning the difficulty of listing first order one properties. That is, we show that every first order one property has an efficient listing algorithm and we describe a general method that can be used to obtain a polynomial space polynomial delay listing algorithm for any first order one property F_θ. The method is based upon a modification of Spencer and Raghavan's *method of pessimistic estimators*† [Spe 87,Rag 88].

We will begin this section by showing that if a graph property $\mathcal{P}$ satisfies certain conditions then the method of pessimistic estimators can be used to obtain an efficient construction algorithm for $\mathcal{P}$. Next, we will show that if $\mathcal{P}$ satisfies certain (stronger) conditions then a modified method of pessimistic estimators can be used to obtain an efficient listing algorithm for $\mathcal{P}$. Finally, we will show that every first order one property satisfies the stronger conditions.

We start with some definitions. For every positive integer n let $U(n)$ be $\{(v_i, v_j) \mid 1 \leq i < j \leq n\}$. Let $\mathcal{G}'$ be the family with the following description. Every parameter value of $\mathcal{G}'$ is a triple (n, E, N) in which n is a positive integer (encoded in unary) and E and N are disjoint subsets of $U(n)$. $\mathcal{G}'(n, E, N) = \{G \in \mathcal{G}(n) \mid$ the edge set of G contains every member of E and no member of $N\}$. The *measure* of a parameter value (n, E, N) is the size of the set $U(n) - E - N$. We will use the fact that $|\mathcal{G}'(p)|$ is equal to 2 raised to the power of the measure of p. Suppose that $p = (n, E, N)$ is a parameter value of $\mathcal{G}'$ whose measure is positive and that (v_i, v_j) is the lexicographically smallest pair in $U(n) - E - N$. We use the notation $p[1]$ to stand for the parameter value $(n, E \cup \{(v_i, v_j)\}, N)$ and the notation $p[0]$ to stand for the parameter value $(n, E, N \cup \{(v_i, v_j)\})$.

Suppose that $\mathcal{P}$ is a graph property. Let $\mathcal{P}'$ be the sub-family of $\mathcal{G}'$ defined by the relation $\mathcal{P}'(n, E, N) = \mathcal{P}(n) \cap \mathcal{G}'(n, E, N)$. It is easy to see that $\mathcal{P}'(n, \varnothing, \varnothing) = \mathcal{P}(n)$ for every positive integer n. Suppose that there is a polynomial-time computable function e that maps each parameter value p of $\mathcal{P}'$ to a positive real number $e(p)$ which satisfies $e(p) \geq |\mathcal{G}'(p) - \mathcal{P}'(p)|$. e is called a *pessimistic estimator function* for $\mathcal{P}$. e is a *good* pessimistic estimator function if and only if $e(p) \geq 2 \min(e(p[0]), e(p[1]))$ for every parameter value p of $\mathcal{P}'$ whose measure is positive.

Suppose that e is a pessimistic estimator function for $\mathcal{P}$ and that p is a parameter value of $\mathcal{G}'$ such that $e(p) < |\mathcal{G}'(p)|$. Then $\mathcal{G}'(p)$ contains a member of $\mathcal{P}'(p)$. If e is a

---

† Although Raghavan distinguishes between "the method of conditional probabilities" and the refinement of it which he calls "the method of pessimistic estimators", the two methods are often referred to together as the "method of conditional probabilities".

good pessimistic estimator function then we can find a member of $\mathcal{P}'(p)$ by running the following binary search algorithm.

Procedure $Search(p)$
/* $Search(p)$ uses the method of pessimistic estimators */
/* to find a member of $\mathcal{P}'(p)$ in $\mathcal{G}'(p)$ */
If $e(p) \geq |\mathcal{G}'(p)|$ Then Return
If the measure of p is 0
    Output the only member of $\mathcal{G}'(p)$
Else
    choose $b \in \{0,1\}$ such that $e(p[b]) \leq e(p[1-b])$
    $Search(p[b])$

Lemma 12. Procedure $Search$ runs in polynomial time. If $e(p) \geq |\mathcal{G}'(p)|$ then $Search(p)$ returns without output. If e is a good pessimistic estimator function for $\mathcal{P}$ and $e(p) < |\mathcal{G}'(p)|$ then $Search(p)$ outputs some $G \in \mathcal{P}'(p)$.

Proof: It is easy to see that procedure $Search$ runs in polynomial time and that $Search(p)$ returns without output if $e(p) \geq |\mathcal{G}'(p)|$. Suppose that e is a good pessimistic estimator function for $\mathcal{P}$ and that $e(p) < |\mathcal{G}'(p)|$. The fact that $Search(p)$ outputs some $G \in \mathcal{P}'(p)$ can be proved by induction on the measure of p. (In the proof of the inductive step we use the fact that $e(p) < |\mathcal{G}'(p)|$ and the fact that e is good to show that $e(p[b]) < |\mathcal{G}'(p[b])|$.)

Corollary 3. Suppose that $\mathcal{P}$ is a graph property and that e is a good pessimistic estimator function for $\mathcal{P}$ which satisfies $e(n, \varnothing, \varnothing) < |\mathcal{G}(n)|$ for every positive integer n. Then there is a polynomial time algorithm that takes input n (in unary) and outputs a member of $\mathcal{P}(n)$.

We have now shown that if a graph property $\mathcal{P}$ satisfies certain conditions then the method of pessimistic estimators can be used to obtain an efficient construction algorithm for $\mathcal{P}$. Next, we will show that if $\mathcal{P}$ satisfies certain (stronger) conditions then a modified method of pessimistic estimators can be used to obtain an efficient listing algorithm for $\mathcal{P}$. The modified method combines the method of pessimistic estimators with the interleaving method from chapter 2. We start by strengthening the notion of a *good* pessimistic estimator function. Suppose that e is a pessimistic estimator function for a graph property $\mathcal{P}$. We say that e is a *recursive* pessimistic estimator function if $e(p) \geq e(p[0]) + e(p[1])$ for every parameter value p of $\mathcal{P}'$ whose measure is positive. Suppose that e is a recursive pessimistic estimator function for $\mathcal{P}$ and consider the following listing algorithm.

```
Procedure List(p)
If e(p) ≥ |G'(p)| Then Return
If the measure of p is 0
    Output the only member of G'(p)
Else
    List(p[0])
    List(p[1])
```

Let $\mathcal{L}'(p)$ be the set of graphs that are output by this algorithm when it is run with input p. We will use the following facts, each of which can be proved by induction on the measure of p.

Fact 1. $\mathcal{L}'(p) \subseteq \mathcal{P}'(p)$.

Fact 2. $|\mathcal{L}'(p)| \geq |\mathcal{G}'(p)| - e(p)$.

We will also use the following fact.

Fact 3. Procedure $List$ runs in polynomial space with polynomial delay.

Proof: It is easy to see that $List$ runs in polynomial space. To see that it has polynomial delay, note that at every level of recursion it is the case that if $e(p) \geq |\mathcal{G}'(p)|$ then $List(p)$ returns without recursing further. If $e(p) < |\mathcal{G}'(p)|$ then we know from fact 2 that $List(p)$ will produce an output. □

Suppose that $\mathcal{P}$ is a graph property. Let $\mathcal{L}$ be the sub-family of $\mathcal{P}$ defined by the relation $\mathcal{L}(n) = \mathcal{L}'(n, \varnothing, \varnothing)$. (We can use fact 1 to show that $\mathcal{L}$ is indeed a sub-family of $\mathcal{P}$.) Procedure $List$ can be used as a polynomial delay listing algorithm for $\mathcal{L}$. If the sets in $\mathcal{L}$ are sufficiently large and there is a standard graph listing algorithm for $\mathcal{P} - \mathcal{L}$ which is sufficiently fast then we can interleave procedure $List$ with the standard graph listing algorithm to obtain a polynomial delay listing algorithm for $\mathcal{P}$. We refer to this particular application of the interleaving method as "the modified method of pessimistic estimators". The following lemma establishes certain conditions whose satisfaction guarantees that the modified method of pessimistic estimators yields an efficient listing algorithm.

Lemma 13. Suppose that $\mathcal{P}$ is a graph property and that e is a recursive pessimistic estimator function for $\mathcal{P}$. Suppose that there is a polynomial q such that $e(n, \varnothing, \varnothing) \leq (1 - q(n)^{-1}) |\mathcal{G}(n)|$ for every large enough integer n. Suppose further that there is a polynomial space polynomial expected time algorithm that takes as input a graph $G \in \mathcal{G}(n)$ and determines whether or not $G \in \mathcal{P}(n)$. Then procedure *List* and a standard graph listing algorithm for $\mathcal{P} - \mathcal{L}$ can be interleaved to obtain a polynomial space polynomial delay listing algorithm for $\mathcal{P}$.

Proof: We can use fact 2 and the condition on e to show that for every large enough integer n it is the case that $q(n) |\mathcal{L}(n)| \geq |\mathcal{G}(n)|$. Fact 3 shows that procedure *List* can be used as a polynomial space polynomial delay listing algorithm for $\mathcal{L}$. It is easy to see that there is a polynomial time algorithm that takes as input a graph $G \in \mathcal{G}(n)$ and determines whether or not $G \in \mathcal{L}(n)$. The result now follows from observation 2. $\square$

In order to make it easier to apply lemma 13 to the problem of listing first order one properties we will now consider a particular class of graph properties which Blass and Harary used in their combinatorial proof of Fagin's result [BH 79]. Suppose that V and W are disjoint subsets of V_n and that G is a member of $\mathcal{G}(n)$. We say that a vertex $u \in V_n$ is *good* for (V, W) in G if u is a member of $V_n - W$ which is adjacent in G to every vertex in V but to no vertex in W. Otherwise, we say that it is *bad* for (V, W) in G. We say that a pair $((V, W), G)$ is *bad* if V and W are subsets of the vertex set of G and every vertex in G is bad for (V, W) in G. Suppose that k is a positive integer. For every graph G let $B_k(G) = \{(V, W) \mid ((V, W), G) \text{ is bad and } |V| = |W| = k\}$ and let Ψ_k be the graph property defined by the relation $\Psi_k(n) = \{G \in \mathcal{G}(n) \mid B_k(G) = \varnothing\}$.

Let e be the function whose domain is the set of parameter values of $\mathcal{G}'$ and which satisfies $e(p) = \sum_{G \in \mathcal{G}'(p)} |B_k(G)|$. The following fact is easily established:

Fact 4. $e(p) \geq |\mathcal{G}'(p) - \Psi_k'(p)|$.

Since $\mathcal{G}'(p) = \mathcal{G}'(p[0]) \uplus \mathcal{G}'(p[1])$ for every parameter value p whose measure is positive we also have:

Fact 5. $e(p) = e(p[0]) + e(p[1])$ for every parameter value p whose measure is positive.

To compute the value of $e(n, E, N)$ we can simply consider each of the $\binom{n}{k}\binom{n-k}{k}$ pairs (V, W) such that V and W are subsets of V_n and $|V| = |W| = k$. Given a particular pair (V, W), we need only count the graphs $G \in \mathcal{G}'(n, E, N)$ such that $((V, W), G)$ is bad. It is easy to see that this can be accomplished in polynomial time. Therefore, we have:

Fact 6. There is a polynomial time algorithm that takes input p and computes $e(p)$.

Furthermore, the value of $e(n, \varnothing, \varnothing)$ is

$$\binom{n}{k}\binom{n-k}{k}(2^{2k} - 1)^{n-2k} 2^{\binom{n-2k}{2}} 2^{\binom{2k}{2}} = \binom{n}{k}\binom{n-k}{k}(1 - 2^{-2k})^{n-2k}|\mathcal{G}(n)|$$

$$= o(1)|\mathcal{G}(n)|.$$

(See [HP 73] for a justification of this calculation.) Therefore, we have established:

Fact 7. There is a polynomial q such that $e(n, \varnothing, \varnothing) \leq (1 - q(n)^{-1})|\mathcal{G}(n)|$ for every large enough integer n.

Using facts 4–7 we get the following corollary of lemma 13:

Corollary 4. Suppose that $\mathcal{P}$ is a graph property and that there is a positive integer k such that $\mathcal{P}$ is a super-family of Ψ_k. Suppose further that there is a polynomial space polynomial expected time algorithm that takes as input a graph $G \in \mathcal{G}(n)$ and determines whether or not $G \in \mathcal{P}(n)$. Then the modified method of pessimistic estimators can be used to obtain a polynomial space polynomial delay listing algorithm for $\mathcal{P}$.

Proof: The fact that $\mathcal{P}$ is a super-family of Ψ_k implies that $|\mathcal{G}'(p) - \mathcal{P}'(p)|$ is at most $|\mathcal{G}'(p) - \Psi_k'(p)|$. Using facts 4 and 5 we see that e is a recursive pessimistic estimator function for $\mathcal{P}$. The result now follows from lemma 13 and from fact 7.

The main result of this section follows immediately from corollary 4.

Theorem 10. Suppose that F_θ is a first order one property. The modified method of pessimistic estimators can be used to obtain a polynomial space polynomial delay listing algorithm for F_θ.

Proof: Blass and Harary show that there is a positive constant k (which depends on θ) such that F_θ is a super-family of Ψ_k. It is easy to see that there is a polynomial time algorithm that takes as input a graph $G \in \mathcal{G}(n)$ and determines whether or not $G \in F_\theta(n)$. The result now follows from corollary 4.

We will further illustrate the strength of corollary 4 by describing some particular graph properties that meet the conditions in the corollary. These graph properties are described more fully in section 2 of [BH 79] which lists a number of interesting graph properties and shows that each is a super-family of Ψ_k for some positive integer k. For many graph properties $\mathcal{P}$ on Blass and Harary's list it is the case that there is a well known polynomial space polynomial expected time algorithm that takes as input a graph $G \in \mathcal{G}(n)$ and determines whether or not $G \in \mathcal{P}(n)$. The following corollaries follow directly from corollary 4 and from [BH 79].

Corollary 5. Let H_1 be an induced subgraph of H_2. Let $\mathcal{G}_{H_1,H_2}$ be the graph property with the following definition. A graph $G \in \mathcal{G}(n)$ is a member of $\mathcal{G}_{H_1,H_2}(n)$ if and only if it is the case that every isomorphism from H_1 onto an induced subgraph of G can be extended to an isomorphism from H_2 onto a induced subgraph of G. The modified method of pessimistic estimators can be used to obtain a polynomial space polynomial delay listing algorithm for $\mathcal{G}_{H_1,H_2}$.

Corollary 6. Let H be any graph. Let $\mathcal{G}_H$ be the graph property with the following definition. A graph $G \in \mathcal{G}(n)$ is a member of $\mathcal{G}_H(n)$ if and only if G has an induced subgraph which is isomorphic to H. The modified method of pessimistic estimators can be used to obtain a polynomial space polynomial delay listing algorithm for $\mathcal{G}_H$.

Corollary 7. Let $\overline{P}$ be the graph property with the following definition. A graph $G \in \mathcal{G}(n)$ is a member of $\overline{P}(n)$ if and only if G is non-planar. The modified method of pessimistic estimators can be used to obtain a polynomial space polynomial delay listing algorithm for $\overline{P}$.

Corollary 8. Let j be a positive integer and let C_j be the graph property with the following definition. A graph $G \in \mathcal{G}(n)$ is a member of $C_j(n)$ if and only if G is j-connected. The modified method of pessimistic estimators can be used to obtain polynomial space polynomial delay listing algorithms for C_j.

Corollary 9. Let j be a positive integer. Let N_j be the graph property with the following definition. A graph $G \in \mathcal{G}(n)$ is a member of $N_j(n)$ if and only if G has no j-coloring. The modified method of pessimistic estimators can be used to obtain a polynomial space polynomial delay listing algorithm for N_j.

(The proof of corollary 9 depends upon the existence of a polynomial space polynomial expected time algorithm that takes as input a graph $G \in \mathcal{G}(n)$ and determines whether or not $G \in N_j(n)$. It is easy to see that such an algorithm exists since the probability that a random graph $G \in \mathcal{G}(n)$ has a clique of size $j+1$ is at least $1-j^{-n}$ (See [Bol 85]).

We conclude this section by making a remark about the modified method of pessimistic estimators. We have presented this method as a technique for designing listing algorithms for graph properties. However, it is easy to see that the method could be generalized and used to design listing algorithms for other combinatorial families. For example, suppose that $m: \mathsf{N} \to \mathsf{N}$ is a function which is bounded from above by a polynomial and that I_m is a family in which each parameter value is a positive integer encoded in unary and $I_m(n)$ is the set of binary words of length $m(n)$. It is easy to see that we could revise our description of the modified method so that it can be used to design listing algorithms for sub-families of I_m.

3.2. Hamiltonian Graphs

Let $\mathcal{H}$ be the graph property defined by the formula

$$\mathcal{H}(n) = \{G \in \mathcal{G}(n) \,|\, G \text{ contains a Hamiltonian cycle}\}.$$

In this section we prove the following theorem.

Theorem 11. There is a deterministic polynomial delay listing algorithm for $\mathcal{H}$.

We start by observing that the results that we obtained in section 3.1 do not tell us how to design an efficient listing algorithm for $\mathcal{H}$. In fact, corollary 2 of section 3.1 is provably inapplicable to this problem since Blass and Harary showed in [BH 79] that there is no positive integer k such that $\mathcal{H}$ is a super-family of Ψ_k. Nevertheless, we show in this section that the interleaving method can be used to design a polynomial delay listing algorithm for $\mathcal{H}$. The algorithm that we describe requires exponential space so we conclude the section by discussing the prospects for designing a *polynomial space* polynomial delay listing algorithm for $\mathcal{H}$.

Let $\mathcal{E}$ be the graph property with the following definition. A graph $G \in \mathcal{G}(n)$ is a member of $\mathcal{E}(n)$ if and only if $n > 2$ and G is 2-connected and every pair of vertices $(u, v) \in V_n \times V_n$ satisfies $|\Gamma_G(u) \cup \Gamma_G(v)| \geq [2n-1]/3$. [FGJS 89] shows that $\mathcal{E}$ is a sub-family of $\mathcal{H}$. In the remainder of this section we will prove three lemmas about $\mathcal{E}$ and $\mathcal{H}$. The lemmas state that $\mathcal{E}$ and $\mathcal{H}$ satisfy the conditions in observation 2. Therefore, we can conclude that the interleaving method can be used to obtain a polynomial delay listing algorithm for $\mathcal{H}$. The algorithm itself consists of interleaving a polynomial delay listing algorithm for $\mathcal{E}$ (which is described in the proof of lemma 15) with a standard graph listing algorithm for $\mathcal{H} - \mathcal{E}$.

Lemma 14. $|\mathcal{E}(n)| = (1 - o(1)) |\mathcal{G}(n)|$.

Proof: For every integer $n > 2$ let G_n denote a randomly chosen member of $\mathcal{G}(n)$. It is well known (see, for example, [HP 73]) that the probability that G_n is 2-connected is $1 - o(1)$. Let u and v be two (arbitrarily chosen) members of V_n. The probability that a vertex $w \in V_n - \{u, v\}$ is in $\Gamma_{G_n}(u) \cup \Gamma_{G_n}(v)$ is $3/4$. Using Chernoff's bound [HR 90], we see that the probability that $|\Gamma_{G_n}(u) \cup \Gamma_{G_n}(v)| < [2n - 1]/3$ is at most c^{-n} for some fixed $c > 1$. Therefore the probability that V_n contains two vertices u and v such that $|\Gamma_{G_n}(u) \cup \Gamma_{G_n}(v)| < [2n - 1]/3$ is at most $\binom{n}{2} c^{-n} = o(1)$ □

Lemma 15.   There is a polynomial delay listing algorithm for $\mathcal{E}$.

Proof: It is easy to design a polynomial delay listing algorithm for $\mathcal{E}$ because the following conditions are satisfied.

1. There is a polynomial time algorithm for determining whether or not a given member of $\mathcal{G}(n)$ is in $\mathcal{E}(n)$.

2. $\mathcal{E}$ is a *monotonic* graph property. (That is, if $G \in \mathcal{E}(n)$ then every n-vertex super-graph of G is a member of $\mathcal{E}(n)$.)

We will use some notation from section 3.1. For every positive integer n let $U(n)$ be $\{(v_i, v_j) \mid 1 \leq i < j \leq n\}$. Let m denote $\binom{n}{2}$ and let the (lexicographically ordered) members of $U(n)$ be written as $u_1, \ldots, u_m$. For every pair (E, N) of disjoint subsets of $U(n)$ let $\mathcal{G}'(n, E, N) = \{G \in \mathcal{G}(n) \mid$ the edge set of G contains every member of E and no member of Since $\mathcal{E}$ is monotonic we know that $\mathcal{G}'(n, E, N)$ contains a member of $\mathcal{E}(n)$ if and only if the graph $(V_n, U(n) - N)$ is a member of $\mathcal{E}(n)$. Using this observation we see that the following listing algorithm for $\mathcal{E}$ has polynomial delay. $\square$

```
Algorithm List_E
Input n
Special_List(n, 0, ∅, ∅)

Procedure Special_List(n, j, E, N)
/* 0 ≤ j ≤ (n choose 2) */
/* (E, N) is a partition of {u₁, ..., u_j} for j ≥ 1 */
If (j = (n choose 2))
     If ((V_n, E) ∈ E(n))
         Output (V_n, E)
Else
     If (G'(n, E, N) contains a member of E(n))
         Special_List(n, j+1, E ∪ {u_{j+1}}, N)
         Special_List(n, j+1, E, N ∪ {u_{j+1}})
```

Lemma 16.   There is a polynomial expected time algorithm that takes as input a graph $G \in \mathcal{G}(n)$ and determines whether or not G is a member of $\mathcal{H}(n) - \mathcal{E}(n)$.

Proof: It is easy to see that there is a polynomial time algorithm that takes as input a graph $G \in \mathcal{G}(n)$ and determines whether or not G is a member of $\mathcal{E}(n)$. It is proved in [BFF 85] that there is also a polynomial expected time algorithm that takes as input a graph $G \in \mathcal{G}(n)$ and determines whether or not G is a member of $\mathcal{H}(n)$. □

Remark. It would be useful to have a *polynomial space* polynomial delay listing algorithm for $\mathcal{H}$. The algorithm described in this section does not run in polynomial space because the polynomial expected time algorithm for determining whether a graph is Hamiltonian [BFF 85] requires exponential space. The probability that Bollobás, Fenner, and Frieze's algorithm fails to run in polynomial space is $o(2^{-n})$. Therefore, it would suffice to find a polynomial space algorithm which finds a Hamiltonian cycle in an n-vertex graph (or determines that none exists) in $O(q(n)\,2^n)$ time steps for some polynomial q. Determining whether or not such an algorithm exists may be an interesting problem in its own right.

3.3. Graphs with Cliques of Specified Sizes

Let G be an undirected graph. A *clique*† of G is a subgraph of G in which every pair of vertices is connected by an edge. The size of a clique is the number of vertices that it contains. Suppose that j is a sub-diagonal function and let Cl_j be the graph property defined by the relation $Cl_j(n) = \{G \in \mathcal{G}(n)\,|\,G$ contains a clique of size $j(n)\}$.

If $j(n) = O(1)$ then the methods from section 3.1 can be used to design a polynomial space polynomial delay listing algorithm for Cl_j. (See corollary 6 of section 3.1.) If $j(n) = \omega(1)$, however, the methods from section 3.1 are inapplicable. In this section we study the general problem of designing an efficient listing algorithm for Cl_j. The results that we obtain depend upon the function j. We consider several cases, depending on whether or not j satisfies one of the following conditions.

Condition 1. There are positive constants ϵ and n_0 such that $j(n) \leq (1-\epsilon)\log(n)$ for every $n \geq n_0$.

Condition 2. There are positive constants ϵ and n_0 such that $j(n) \geq (2+\epsilon)\log(n)$ for every $n \geq n_0$.

The remainder of this section has the following structure. In subsection 3.3.1 we show that if j satisfies condition 1 then we can use the interleaving method to obtain a

---

† Note that some texts such as [Bol 85] use the word *clique* to mean a *maximal* complete subgraph.

polynomial space polynomial delay listing algorithm for Cl_j. In subsection 3.3.2 we show that if j satisfies condition 2 then we can use the filter method to obtain a polynomial delay listing algorithm for Cl_j. (This algorithm uses exponential space.) Finally, in subsection 3.3.3 we discuss the problem of designing an efficient listing algorithm for Cl_j when j fails to satisfy either of conditions 1 and 2.

3.3.1. Graphs with Small Cliques

In this subsection we prove the following theorem.

Theorem 12. If j satisfies condition 1 then there is a polynomial space polynomial delay listing algorithm for Cl_j.

We will use the interleaving method to prove the theorem. We start with some definitions. Given a graph $G \in \mathcal{G}(n)$ and two cliques C_1 and C_2 of G we say that C_1 is lexicographically smaller than C_2 if and only if the vertex set of C_1 is lexicographically smaller than the vertex set of C_2. Let $\mathcal{W}_j$ be the simple family with the following definition. Every parameter value of $\mathcal{W}_j$ is a positive integer. The value n is associated with the set $\mathcal{W}_j(n) = \{W \subseteq V_n \mid |W| = j(n)\}$. Let $\mathcal{W}'_j$ be the sub-family of $\mathcal{W}_j$ defined by the relation $\mathcal{W}'_j(n) = \{W \in \mathcal{W}_j(n) \mid v_1 \in W\}$. Let L_j be the simple family with the following definition. Every parameter value of L_j is a pair (n, W) such that $W \in \mathcal{W}'_j(n)$. $L_j(n, W)$ is the set $\{G \in Cl_j(n) \mid G[W] \text{ contains the lexicographically smallest } k\text{-clique in } G \text{ for every } k \leq j(n)\}$. Finally, let E_j be the graph property defined by the relation $E_j(n) = \bigcup_{W \in \mathcal{W}'_j(n)} L_j(n, W)$. In the remainder of this subsection we will prove three lemmas about E_j and Cl_j. The lemmas state that E_j and Cl_j satisfy the conditions in observation 2. Therefore, we can conclude that the interleaving method can be used to obtain a polynomial space polynomial delay listing algorithm for Cl_j. The algorithm itself consists of interleaving a polynomial space polynomial delay listing algorithm for E_j (which is described in the proof of lemma 18) with a standard graph listing algorithm for $Cl_j - E_j$.

Lemma 17. If j satisfies condition 1 then $|E_j(n)| \geq (1 - \binom{n}{j(n)}^{-1}) |\mathcal{G}(n)|$.

Proof: Let G_n be a member of $\mathcal{G}(n)$, chosen uniformly at random. The probability that G_n is not in $E_j(n)$ is less than or equal to the probability that for some $r < j(n)$ there exists an r-clique of G_n which cannot be extended to an $(r+1)$-clique. Following Turner [Tur 88] and letting j denote $j(n)$, we see that this probability is at most:

$$\sum_{r=1}^{j-1} \binom{n}{r} (1 - 2^{-r})^{(n-r)} \quad \leq \quad j \binom{n}{j} (1 - 2^{-j})^{(n-j)} \quad \leq \quad j \, n^j \, 2^{-[(n-j)/2^j]}.$$

If j satisfies condition 1 then this probability is easily shown to be less than $\binom{n}{j(n)}^{-1}$. □

Lemma 18. There is a polynomial space polynomial delay listing algorithm for E_j.

Proof: the general form of the algorithm is the following:

```
Algorithm List_Ej
Input n
For Each W ∈ W'j(n)
    For Each G ∈ Lj(n, W)
        Output G
```

The fact that algorithm $List\_E_j$ lists the members of $E_j(n)$ (without duplicates) follows from the fact that if W_1 and W_2 are distinct members of $W'_j(n)$ then $L_j(n, W_1)$ and $L_j(n, W_2)$ are disjoint. It is easy to see that there is a polynomial space polynomial delay listing algorithm for W'_j and that every set $L_j(n, W)$ is non-empty. Therefore algorithm $List\_E_j$ can be made to run in polynomial space with polynomial delay so long as there is a polynomial space polynomial delay listing algorithm for L_j. To see that there is a polynomial space polynomial delay listing algorithm for L_j observe that $L_j(n, W)$ is simply the set of graphs $G \in \mathcal{G}(n)$ satisfying:

1. W is a clique of G.

2. For every vertex $v \in V_n - W$ either

    a. v is larger than every vertex in W,

or b. there is a vertex $w \in W$ such that $w < v$ and (v, w) is not an edge of G. □

Lemma 19. If j satisfies condition 1 then there is a polynomial space polynomial expected time algorithm that takes as input a graph $G \in \mathcal{G}(n)$ and determines whether or not G is a member of $Cl_j(n) - E_j(n)$.

Proof: The algorithm is straightforward: Take input $G \in \mathcal{G}(n)$. Using the "greedy heuristic" (see section 4 of [GM 75]), attempt to construct a set $W \in W'_j(n)$ such that $G \in L_j(n, W)$. If a suitable W is constructed then $G \in E_j(n)$. Otherwise, consider each of the $\binom{n}{j(n)}$ subsets $W \in W_j(n)$. If $G[W]$ is a clique for some $W \in W_j(n)$ then G is in $Cl_j(n) - E_j(n)$. Otherwise it is not. To see that the algorithm runs in polynomial expected time note that the greedy heuristic runs in polynomial time and that (see lemma 17) the probability that $G \notin E_j(n)$ is at most $\binom{n}{j(n)}^{-1}$. It is easy to see that the space requirement of the algorithm is bounded from above by a polynomial.

3.3.2. Graphs with Large Cliques

In this subsection we prove the following theorem.

Theorem 13. If j satisfies condition 2 then there is a polynomial delay listing algorithm for Cl_j.

We will use the filter method to prove the theorem. We start with some definitions. Let W_j denote the family that was defined in subsection 3.3.1. Let Cl denote the family with the following definition. Every parameter value of Cl is a pair (n, W) such that $W \subseteq V_n$. The set $Cl(n, W)$ is defined by the equation

$$Cl(n, W) = \{G \in \mathcal{G}(n) \mid G[W] \text{ is a clique of } G\}.$$

Let Cl' be the sub-family of Cl which is defined by the following equation.

$$Cl'(n, W) = \left\{ G \in Cl(n, W) \; \middle| \; \begin{array}{l} G[W] \text{ is the lexicographically smallest} \\ \text{clique of its size in } G \end{array} \right\}.$$

Let C_j be the family defined by the relation

$$C_j(n) = \bigcup_{W \in \mathcal{W}_j(n)} \{(G, W) \mid G \in Cl(n, W)\}$$

and let C'_j be the sub-family defined by the relation

$$C'_j(n) = \bigcup_{W \in \mathcal{W}_j(n)} \{(G, W) \mid G \in Cl'(n, W)\}.$$

Using the notation that we have defined, we can see that

$$Cl_j(n) = \{G \in \mathcal{G}(n) \mid (G, W) \in C'_j(n) \text{ for some } W \in \mathcal{W}_j(n)\}.$$

Furthermore, for every pair $W, W' \in \mathcal{W}_j(n)$ it is the case that at most one of (G, W) and (G, W') is a member of $C'_j(n)$. Therefore, we can use a listing algorithm for C'_j as a listing algorithm for Cl_j. In the remainder of this subsection we will show that when j satisfies condition 2 we can use the filter method and an efficient listing algorithm for C_j

to obtain a cumulative polynomial delay listing algorithm for C'_j†. We start by observing that when j satisfies condition 2, C_j and C'_j are polynomially related. This fact can be deduced from the following lemma:

Lemma 20. Suppose that j satisfies condition 2. Then there is a positive integer n_1 such that for every $n \geq n_1$ and for every $W \in \mathcal{W}_j(n)$ we have $|Cl'(n, W)| \geq |Cl(n, W)|/2$.

Proof: Suppose that n is a positive integer. Let W be a member of $\mathcal{W}_j(n)$ and let $G_{n,W}$ be a member of $Cl(n, W)$, chosen uniformly at random. Let j denote $j(n)$. By definition, $G_{n,W}[W]$ is a clique of $G_{n,W}$. The expected number of additional cliques of size j in $G_{n,W}$ is

$$\sum_{r=1}^{j} \binom{n-j}{r} \binom{j}{j-r} 2^{-\binom{r}{2}} 2^{-r(j-r)} \leq \sum_{r=1}^{j} \frac{[(n-j)j]^r}{2^{(j-(r+1)/2)r}} \leq \sum_{r=1}^{j} \frac{[(n-j)j]^r}{2^{((j-1)/2)r}}.$$

Using the fact that j satisfies condition 2 and the fact that n can be assumed to be suitably large, we can do some elementary calculations which show that the expected number of additional cliques is at most $1/2$. We conclude that at least half of the members of $Cl(n, W)$ are members of $Cl'(n, W)$ □

As we stated before, we wish to show how to use the filter method and an efficient listing algorithm for C_j to obtain a cumulative polynomial delay listing algorithm for C'_j. We start by developing a polynomial space polynomial delay listing algorithm for C_j.

It is easy to see that there are polynomial space polynomial delay listing algorithms for the families $\mathcal{W}_j$ and Cl, which were defined earlier. In particular, there is a polynomial space polynomial delay listing algorithm for $\mathcal{W}_j$ which takes input n and lists the members of $\mathcal{W}_j(n)$ in lexicographical order. Suppose that we choose this listing algorithm for $\mathcal{W}_j$ and some polynomial space polynomial delay listing algorithm for Cl and that we use them as subroutines in the following polynomial space polynomial delay listing algorithm for C_j:

---

† The cumulative polynomial delay listing algorithm can be converted to a polynomial delay listing algorithm using the method described in the introduction to this thesis.

```
Algorithm List_C_j
Input n
For Each W ∈ W_j(n)
    For Each G ∈ Cl(n, W)
        Output (G, W)
```

We now wish to show how to use the filter method and algorithm $List\_C_j$ to obtain a cumulative polynomial delay listing algorithm for C_j'. We start by defining some notation. Let $C_{j,n,l}$ be the list of members of $C_j(n)$ that are output during the lth iteration of the loop "For Each $W \in W_j(n)$" when algorithm $List\_C_j$ is run with input n. Let $C_{j,n}$ be the concatenation of the lists $C_{j,n,1}, C_{j,n,2}, \ldots$

In order to use the filter method we will need to invent a subroutine $Filter_j$, which takes as input an integer n and a pair $(G, W) \in C_j(n)$ and returns "yes" if and only if (G, W) is a member of $C_j'(n)$. Then we can use the following listing algorithm for C_j':

```
Algorithm List_C_j'
Input n
For l ⟵ 1 To |C_j(n)|
    continue simulating List_C_j(n) to obtain C_{j,n}[l]
    If Filter_j(n, C_{j,n}[l]) = "yes"
        Output C_{j,n}[l]
```

Suppose that we invent a subroutine $Filter_j$ with time complexity T_j. The following observation follows directly from observation 5 and remark 1 of subsection 2.2.2 and from the fact that (since the members of $W_j(n)$ are listed in lexicographical order) every member of $C_{j,n,1}$ is a member of $C_j'(n)$.

Observation 11. Algorithm *List_$\mathcal{C}'_j$* will run in polynomial space if and only if algorithm *Filter_j* runs in polynomial space. Furthermore, algorithm *List_$\mathcal{C}'_j$* will have cumulative polynomial delay if j satisfies condition 2 and there exists a polynomial r such that the following conditions are satisfied:

Condition A. For every integer i in the range $1 \leq i \leq |\mathcal{C}_{j,n,1}|$ we have $T_j(n, \mathcal{C}_{j,n}[i]) \leq r(n)$.

Condition B. For every integer l in the range range $1 \leq l < |\mathcal{W}_j(n)|$ we have

$$\sum_{k=1}^{|\mathcal{C}_{j,n,l+1}|} T_j(n, \mathcal{C}_{j,n,l+1}[k]) \leq r(n) \times |\mathcal{C}_{j,n,l} / C'_j(n)|.$$

In the remainder of this subsection we will show how to make *List_$\mathcal{C}'_j$* a cumulative polynomial delay listing algorithm by designing an algorithm *Filter_j* whose time complexity, T_j, satisfies the conditions in observation 11. First, we make our task easier by using lemma 20 to simplify condition B. We start by observing that $|\mathcal{C}_{j,n,l} / C'_j(n)|$ is greater than or equal to $|\mathcal{C}_{j,n,l}|/2$ for every l in the appropriate range. Furthermore, $|\mathcal{C}_{j,n,l}| = |\mathcal{C}_{j,n,l+1}|$ for every appropriate value of l. Combining these two observations, we can replace condition B with the following (possibly stronger) condition:

Condition B'. For every integer l in the range $2 \leq l \leq |\mathcal{W}_j(n)|$ we have

$$\sum_{k=1}^{|\mathcal{C}_{j,n,l}|} T_j(n, \mathcal{C}_{j,n,l}[k]) \leq r(n) \times |\mathcal{C}_{j,n,l}|.$$

Observation 12 incorporates the simplification that we have discussed, rewriting condition B' in an equivalent form. Once again, the notation $G_{n,W}$ is used to denote a member of $Cl(n, W)$, chosen uniformly at random.

Observation 12. Algorithm *List_$\mathcal{C}'_j$* will run in polynomial space if and only if algorithm *Filter_j* runs in polynomial space. Furthermore, algorithm *List_$\mathcal{C}'_j$* will have cumulative polynomial delay if j satisfies condition 2 and there exists a polynomial r such that the following conditions are satisfied:

Condition A. For every integer i in the range $1 \leq i \leq |\mathcal{C}_{j,n,1}|$ we have $T_j(n, \mathcal{C}_{j,n}[i]) \leq r(n)$.

Condition B. For every $W \in \mathcal{W}_j(n)$ we have $\mathrm{E}(T_j(n, (G_{n,W}, W))) \leq r(n)$.

As in section 2.3.2, we could use a dictionary-based approach to the problem of designing algorithm $Filter_j$. Recall that $Filter_j$ takes as input an integer n and a pair $(G, W) \in C_j(n)$. The output of $Filter_j(n, (G, W))$ should be "yes" if and only if $G[W]$ is the lexicographically smallest clique in G. Since the listing algorithm for W_j lists the members of $W_j(n)$ in lexicographical order, $G[W]$ will be the lexicographically smallest clique in G if and only if (G, W) is the first member of $C_{j,n}$ which contains the graph G. By the time that algorithm $List\_C'_j$ makes the call $Filter_j(n, (G, W))$ it will already have called $Filter_j(n, (G', W'))$ for every pair (G', W') which precedes (G, W) on $C_{j,n}$. Therefore, the implementation of $Filter_j$ could be based on a dictionary of n-vertex graphs. The dictionary should be made empty at the beginning of algorithm $List\_C'_j$. $Filter_j$ would then have the following form:

```
Algorithm Filter_j(n,(G,W))
If G is in the dictionary
     Return "no"
Else
     put G in the dictionary
     Return "yes"
```

Suppose that j satisfies condition 2 and that we use algorithm $Filter_j$ as a subroutine in algorithm $List\_C'_j$, implementing the dictionary as a 2–3 tree (see [AHU 74]). Then the time complexity of $Filter_j$ will be bounded from above by a polynomial in the size of its input. Therefore (by observation 12) algorithm $List\_C'_j$ will have cumulative polynomial delay. We conclude that algorithm $List\_C'_j$ is a cumulative polynomial delay listing algorithm for Cl_j and that it can be converted to a polynomial delay listing algorithm using the method described in the introduction to this thesis. Therefore, we have proved theorem 13.

The space requirement of algorithm $List\_C'_j$ will be at least as large as the space requirement of $Filter_j$. In particular, it will be super-polynomial. It would be interesting to know whether there is a polynomial space cumulative polynomial delay listing algorithm for Cl_j. This question is not answered in this thesis.

3.3.3. Graphs with Cliques whose Sizes are Between $\log(n)$ and $2\log(n)$

Suppose that j is a sub-diagonal function. In subsection 2.3.1 we showed that if there are positive constants ϵ and n_0 such that $j(n) \le (1-\epsilon)\log(n)$ for every $n \ge n_0$ then the interleaving method can be used to obtain a polynomial delay listing algorithm for Cl_j. In subsection 2.3.2 we showed that if there are positive constants ϵ and n_0 such that $j(n) \ge (2+\epsilon)\log(n)$ for every $n \ge n_0$ then the filter method can be used to obtain a polynomial delay listing algorithm for Cl_j. Of course we can combine these results to get the following theorem:

Theorem 14. Suppose that j is a sub-diagonal function. If there are positive constants ϵ and n_0 such that for every $n \ge n_0$ either $j(n) \le (1-\epsilon)\log(n)$ or $j(n) \ge (2+\epsilon)\log(n)$ then there is a polynomial delay listing algorithm for Cl_j.

Let $\mathcal{H}$ be the set of sub-diagonal functions which fail to satisfy the conditions of theorem 14. That is, let

$$\mathcal{H} = \left\{ j : \mathsf{N} \to \mathsf{N} \,\middle|\, \begin{array}{l} \text{for every positive constant } \epsilon \\ j(n) \le n \quad \text{and} \quad (1-\epsilon)\log(n) \le j(n) \le (2+\epsilon)\log(n) \\ \text{infinitely often} \end{array} \right\}$$

It is clear that there are functions $j \in \mathcal{H}$ such that Cl_j has a polynomial delay listing algorithm. For example, it is fairly easy to see that the proofs in subsection 2.3.2 would still work if we replaced condition 2 with the following weaker but more cumbersome condition:

Condition 2'. There is a positive constant n_0 such that

$$j(n) \ge 2\log(n) + 4\log(j(n)) + 3$$

for every $n \ge n_0$.

Furthermore, it is easy to see that there are members of $\mathcal{H}$ which satisfy condition 2'.

The methods that we have described in this section are likely to fail for many functions $j \in \mathcal{H}$, however. Let

$$\mathcal{H}' = \left\{ j \in \mathcal{H} \,\middle|\, \begin{array}{l} \text{There exists a positive constant } \epsilon \text{ such that} \\ (1+\epsilon)\log(n) \le j(n) \le (2-\epsilon)\log(n) \\ \text{infinitely often} \end{array} \right\}$$

Suppose that j is a member of $\mathcal{H}'$ and consider the listing algorithms for Cl_j which were described in subsections 2.3.1 and 2.3.2. These algorithms do not have polynomial delay when $j \in \mathcal{H}'$. Furthermore, it is unlikely that they can be modified so that they do have polynomial delay in this case.

First consider the (interleaving) listing algorithm from subsection 2.3.1. This algorithm contains a subroutine (which is described in the proof of lemma 19) that takes as input a graph $G \in \mathcal{G}(n)$ and finds a $j(n)$-clique in G or determines that none exists. The argument that the listing algorithm has polynomial delay depends upon the fact that the subroutine runs in polynomial expected time. However, the expected running time of the subroutine is super-polynomial (see [GM 75], theorem 7) if there exists a positive constant ϵ such that $j(n) \geq (1+\epsilon) \log(n)$ infinitely often. Furthermore, there is evidence [Jer 90] supporting the conjecture that there is no polynomial expected time algorithm that performs the task of the subroutine in this case.

Next, consider the (filter) listing algorithm from subsection 2.3.2. This algorithm combines an efficient listing algorithm for $\mathcal{C}_j$ with an efficient filtering subroutine to obtain a cumulative polynomial delay listing algorithm for $\mathcal{C}_j'$. However, if there is a positive constant ϵ such that $j(n) \leq (2-\epsilon) \log(n)$ infinitely often (and $j(n) = \omega(1)$) then the expected number of cliques of size $j(n)$ in a random n-vertex graph is super-polynomial in n. Therefore, $\mathcal{C}_j$ and $\mathcal{C}_j'$ are not polynomially related so we cannot use the filter method and an efficient listing algorithm for $\mathcal{C}_j$ to obtain a cumulative polynomial delay listing algorithm for $\mathcal{C}_j'$.

It would be interesting to determine for which of the functions $j \in \mathcal{H}$ there is a polynomial delay listing algorithm for Cl_j. We leave this question as an open problem.

3.4. Graphs which can be Colored with a Specified Number of Colors

Suppose that k is a sub-diagonal function. Consider the families $\mathcal{G}_k$ and $\widetilde{\mathcal{G}_k}$ which were defined in chapter 2. ($\mathcal{G}_k(n)$ is the set of $k(n)$-*colored* n-vertex graphs and each equivalence class in $\widetilde{\mathcal{G}_k}(n)$ is associated with a particular $k(n)$-*colorable* graph $G \in \mathcal{G}(n)$.) In this section we consider the problem of designing efficient listing algorithms for $\widetilde{\mathcal{G}_k}$. This turns out to be a much more difficult problem than the other problems that we have considered so far in this chapter. Therefore, the results that we obtain are less complete.

In order to state the results that are described in this section we require the following definition. We say that a sub-diagonal function k satisfies the *greedy condition* if and only if there are positive constants ϵ and n_0 such that for every $n \geq n_0$ we have $k(n) \geq (1+\epsilon) n / \log(n)$.

The results that we obtain are the following:

Theorem 15. If k satisfies Kučera's condition then there is a deterministic cumulative polynomial delay† listing algorithm for $\widetilde{\mathcal{G}_k}$. (The algorithm requires exponential space.)

Theorem 16. If $k(n) = O(1)$ then there is a deterministic polynomial space cumulative polynomial delay listing algorithm for $\widetilde{\mathcal{G}_k}$.

Theorem 17. If k satisfies the greedy condition then there is a probabilistic polynomial delay listing algorithm for $\widetilde{\mathcal{G}_k}$. (The algorithm requires exponential space.)

It is easy to see that there are many sub-diagonal functions that fail to satisfy either Kučera's condition or the greedy condition. If k is one of these functions then the problem of designing an efficient listing algorithm for $\widetilde{\mathcal{G}_k}$ remains open. In the final portion of this section we address this problem. There we discuss the prospects of strengthening theorems 15 and 17 by weakening the relevant conditions.

There are many interesting questions that are suggested by the results presented in this section. For example, is there a deterministic *polynomial space* cumulative polynomial delay listing algorithm for $\widetilde{\mathcal{G}_k}$ for any $k(n) = \omega(1)$? Is there a deterministic polynomial space *polynomial delay* listing algorithm for $\widetilde{\mathcal{G}_k}$ when $k(n) = O(1)$? Is there a *deterministic* polynomial delay listing algorithm for $\widetilde{\mathcal{G}_k}$ when k satisfies the greedy condition? These questions remain open. I hope to resolve them in the future.

We begin this section by defining a sub-family $\widetilde{\mathcal{G}_k}'$ of $\widetilde{\mathcal{G}_k}$. The definition of $\widetilde{\mathcal{G}_k}'$ is based on the definition of the family $\widetilde{\mathcal{G}b_k}$, which was given in chapter 2.

Recall that

$$\mathcal{G}_k(n) \;=\; \{(C,G) \mid G \in \mathcal{G}(n) \text{ and } C \text{ is a } k(n)\text{-coloring of } G\}$$

and that $\sim$ is the equivalence relation on colored graphs that ignores the coloring. $\widetilde{\mathcal{G}_k}(n)$ is the set of equivalence classes under $\sim$ of $\mathcal{G}_k(n)$. Furthermore,

$$\mathcal{G}b_k(n) \;=\; \{(C,G) \mid G \in \mathcal{G}(n) \text{ and } C \text{ is a } \textit{balanced } k(n)\text{-coloring of } G\}$$

and $\widetilde{\mathcal{G}b_k}(n)$ is the set of equivalence classes under $\sim$ of $\mathcal{G}b_k(n)$.

Let $\widetilde{\mathcal{G}_k}'$ be the sub-family of $\widetilde{\mathcal{G}_k}$ defined as follows:

$$\widetilde{\mathcal{G}_k}'(n) \;=\; \{E \in \widetilde{\mathcal{G}_k}(n) \mid \text{There exists a } (C,G) \in E \text{ such that } C \text{ is balanced}\}.$$

---

† Of course, we can convert this algorithm to a *polynomial delay* algorithm using the method described in the introduction to this thesis.

It is easy to see that there is a one-to-one correspondence between the equivalence classes in $\widetilde{\mathcal{G}_k}'(n)$ and $\widetilde{\mathcal{G}b_k}(n)$. In fact, there is a one-to-one correspondence which has the property that each equivalence class in $\widetilde{\mathcal{G}b_k}(n)$ is a subset of the corresponding class in $\widetilde{\mathcal{G}_k}'(n)$. Therefore, we can use a listing algorithm for $\widetilde{\mathcal{G}b_k}$ as a listing algorithm for $\widetilde{\mathcal{G}_k}'$.

Suppose that k satisfies Kučera's condition. In this case we will be able to show that $\widetilde{\mathcal{G}_k}$ and $\widetilde{\mathcal{G}_k}'$ are polynomially related. Furthermore, the listing algorithm for $\widetilde{\mathcal{G}b_k}$ which is described in subsection 2.3.2 has cumulative polynomial delay. Using this algorithm (as a listing algorithm for $\widetilde{\mathcal{G}_k}'$) and the interleaving method, we will obtain a cumulative polynomial delay listing algorithm for $\widetilde{\mathcal{G}_k}$.

Suppose further that $k(n) = O(1)$. In this case there is a *polynomial space* cumulative polynomial delay listing algorithm for $\widetilde{\mathcal{G}b_k}$ which is described in subsection 2.3.2. Using this algorithm (as a listing algorithm for $\widetilde{\mathcal{G}_k}'$) and the interleaving method, we will obtain a polynomial space cumulative polynomial delay listing algorithm for $\widetilde{\mathcal{G}_k}$.

We start, then, by assuming that k satisfies Kučera's condition and showing that $\widetilde{\mathcal{G}_k}$ and $\widetilde{\mathcal{G}_k}'$ are polynomially related. We mentioned in chapter 2 that when k satisfies Kučera's condition $\widetilde{\mathcal{G}_k}$ and $\mathcal{G}_k$ are polynomially related. Furthermore, we mentioned that under the same condition $\mathcal{G}b_k$ and $\widetilde{\mathcal{G}b_k}$ are polynomially related. Since $|\widetilde{\mathcal{G}b_k}(n)| = |\widetilde{\mathcal{G}_k}'(n)|$, it follows that $\mathcal{G}b_k$ and $\widetilde{\mathcal{G}_k}'$ are polynomially related. The property of being polynomially related is transitive so it suffices to show that when k satisfies Kučera's condition $\mathcal{G}_k$ and $\mathcal{G}b_k$ are polynomially related.

To show that $\mathcal{G}_k$ and $\mathcal{G}b_k$ are polynomially related when k satisfies Kučera's condition we must show that in this case there is a polynomial q such that $|\mathcal{G}_k(n)|/|\mathcal{G}b_k(n)| \leq q(n)$. The following technical lemma establishes a stronger result assuming a weaker condition. (We will use the results in the lemma later in the section.) The proof of the lemma is a modification of proofs found in [Wri 61] and [Wri 64]. We repeat details found in Wright's proofs for the sake of completeness.

Lemma 21. Let k be a sub-diagonal function. If there are positive constants ϵ and n_0 such that for every $n \geq n_0$ we have $k(n) \leq n^{2/3-\epsilon}$ then $|\mathcal{G}_k(n) - \mathcal{G}b_k(n)| = o(1)\,|\mathcal{G}_k(n)|$. Furthermore, if there are positive constants ϵ and n_0 such that for every $n \geq n_0$ we have $k(n) \leq n^{1/2-\epsilon}$ then $|\mathcal{G}_k(n) - \mathcal{G}b_k(n)| \times k(n)^n = o(1)\,|\mathcal{G}_k(n)|$.

Proof: We start by defining some notation. We say that sequence $s = (s_1, \ldots, s_{k(n)})$ of non-negative integers is a *k-of-n sequence* if $s_1 \geq \cdots \geq s_{k(n)}$ and $\sum_{i=1}^{k(n)} s_i = n$. Note that every $k(n)$-coloring $C = (C_1, \cdots, C_{k(n)})$ of V_n can be associated with a k-of-n sequence

$s = (s_1, \ldots, s_{k(n)})$ such that $|C_i| = s_i$ for every integer i in the range $1 \leq i \leq k(n)$. We use the notation $Col(s)$ to denote the set of colorings

$$\{C = (C_1, \cdots, C_{k(n)}) \in P_k(n) \mid |C_i| = s_i \text{ for every integer } i \text{ in the range } 1 \leq i \leq k(n)\}.$$

Suppose that $s = (s_1, \ldots, s_{k(n)})$ is a k-of-n sequence and that C is a coloring in $Col(s)$. We established in the proof of lemma 6 that $|\Gamma_k(C)| = 2^{(n^2 - \sum_i s_i^2)/2}$. Therefore,

$$|\mathcal{G}_k(n)| = \sum_s |Col(s)| \times 2^{(n^2 - \sum_i s_i^2)/2} \qquad (1)$$

where the sum is over k-of-n sequences s. Let k denote $k(n)$ and let K denote $(1 - k^{-1})/2$. In [Wri 61] Wright noted that

$$(n^2 - \sum_i s_i^2)/2 = Kn^2 - (1/2k^2) \sum_i (ks_i - n)^2.$$

He re-wrote (1) as

$$|\mathcal{G}_k(n)| = 2^{Kn^2} \sum_s |Col(s)| \times 2^{-(1/2k^2) \sum_i (ks_i - n)^2} \qquad (2)$$

Using the idea from the proof of theorem 1 of [Wri 61], we observe that $|\mathcal{G}_k(n) - \mathcal{G}b_k(n)|$ can be written

$$|\mathcal{G}_k(n) - \mathcal{G}b_k(n)| = 2^{Kn^2} {\sum_s}' |Col(s)| \times 2^{-(1/2k^2) \sum_i (ks_i - n)^2}$$

where ${\sum_s}'$ ranges over all k-of-n sequences $s = (s_1, \ldots, s_k)$ such that $|ks_i - n| > n/2$ for some i in the range $1 \leq i \leq k$. For these k-of-n sequences we have $\sum_i (ks_i - n)^2 \geq n^2/4$. Therefore, observing that ${\sum_s}' |Col(s)| \leq k^n$, we get

$$|\mathcal{G}_k(n) - \mathcal{G}b_k(n)| \leq 2^{Kn^2} k^n 2^{-n^2/8k^2} \qquad (3)$$

In order to derive a lower bound for the size of $\mathcal{G}_k(n)$ we need a lower bound for the size of $Col(s)$. This requires a bit more notation. Suppose that $s = (s_1, \ldots, s_k)$ is a k-of-n sequence. Let $|s|$ be the positive integer such that $s_l > 0$ for every $l \leq |s|$ and $s_l = 0$ for l in the range $|s| < l \leq k$. Finally, let $perm(s)$ be the number of permutations π of $(s_1, \ldots, s_{|s|})$ such that $(s_1, \ldots, s_{|s|}) = (\pi(s_1), \ldots, \pi(s_{|s|}))$. Now it is easy to see that

$$|Col(s)| = \frac{n!}{s_1! \cdots s_k!} \frac{1}{perm(s)} \qquad (4)$$

Let N denote $\lfloor n/k \rfloor$ and let $s' = (s_1', \ldots, s_k')$ be the k-of-n sequence in which $s_i' = N+1$ for $1 \le i \le n-kN$ and $s_i' = N$ for $n-kN < i \le k$. Wright shows in [Wri 64] that $n!/s_1'! \cdots s_k'! \ge k^{n-k}(n+k)^{-k}$. For completeness, we include his derivation of this fact:

$$\frac{n!}{s_1'! \cdots s_k'!} = \frac{n!}{((N+1)!)^{n-kN}(N!)^{k-(n-kN)}} = \frac{n!}{(N+1)^{n-kN}(N!)^k}$$

$$= \frac{(kN + (n-kN)) \cdots (kN+1)\,((kN)!)}{(N+1)^{n-kN}(N!)^k}$$

$$\ge \frac{(kN)!}{(N!)^k} = \frac{(kN+k-1)!}{(kN+k-1)\cdots(kN+1)\,(N!)^k} \tag{5}$$

Now

$$(kN+k-1)! = (k-1)! \prod_{l=0}^{k-1} \prod_{t=1}^{N}(kt+l) \ge \left\{ \prod_{t=1}^{N} tk \right\}^k = k^{kN}(N!)^k \tag{6}$$

Combining (5) and (6) we get

$$\frac{n!}{s_1'! \cdots s_k'!} \ge \frac{k^{kN}}{(kN+k-1)\cdots(kN+1)} \ge \frac{k^{n-k}}{(n+k)^k} \tag{7}$$

Returning to equation (2) note that

$$\frac{1}{2k^2} \sum_i (ks_i' - n)^2 = \frac{1}{2} \sum_i (s_i' - n/k)^2 \le k/2 \tag{8}$$

Furthermore in (4)

$$perm(s) \le k! \tag{9}$$

Finally, we combine (2), (4), (7), (8), and (9) to get

$$|\mathcal{G}_k(n)| \ge 2^{Kn^2} \frac{k^{n-k}}{(n+k)^k} \frac{1}{k!} 2^{-k/2} \tag{10}$$

Combining (3) and (10) and using the fact that $k(n) \le n$ we get

$$\frac{|\mathcal{G}_k(n) - \mathcal{G}b_k(n)|}{|\mathcal{G}_k(n)|} \le \frac{k^k (n+k)^k k! \, 2^{k/2}}{2^{n^2/8k^2}} \le 2^{-(n^2/8k^2 - ck\log(n))} \tag{11}$$

for a positive constant c. It is easy to see that the right hand side of (11) is $o(1)$ if there are positive constants ϵ and n_0 such that for every $n \ge n_0$ we have $k(n) \le n^{2/3-\epsilon}$.

Furthermore, the right hand side of (11) is $k^{-n}o(1)$ if there are positive constants ϵ and n_0 such that $k(n) \leq n^{1/2-\epsilon}$ for every $n \geq n_0$. □

So far, then, we have established the following facts:

1. If k satisfies Kučera's condition then $\widetilde{\mathcal{G}_k}$ and $\widetilde{\mathcal{G}_k}'$ are polynomially related.

2. If k satisfies Kučera's condition then there is a cumulative polynomial delay listing algorithm for $\widetilde{\mathcal{G}_k}'$. (This algorithm is described in subsection 2.3.2.)

3. If $k(n) = O(1)$ then there is a polynomial space cumulative polynomial delay listing algorithm for $\widetilde{\mathcal{G}_k}'$. (This algorithm is described in subsection 2.3.2.)

After reading the description of the interleaving method in subsection 2.2.1, we can make the following observations.

Observation 13. Suppose that k satisfies Kučera's condition and that l is a polynomial. Suppose further that there a listing algorithm for $\widetilde{\mathcal{G}_k} - \widetilde{\mathcal{G}_k}'$ which executes at most $l(n)|\widetilde{\mathcal{G}_k}(n)|$ machine instructions when it is run with input n. Then we can interleave the cumulative polynomial delay listing algorithm for $\widetilde{\mathcal{G}_k}'$ with the listing algorithm for $\widetilde{\mathcal{G}_k} - \widetilde{\mathcal{G}_k}'$ to obtain a cumulative polynomial delay listing algorithm for $\widetilde{\mathcal{G}_k}$.

Observation 14. Suppose that $k(n) = O(1)$ and that l is a polynomial. Suppose further that there is a *polynomial space* listing algorithm for $\widetilde{\mathcal{G}_k} - \widetilde{\mathcal{G}_k}'$ which executes at most $l(n)|\widetilde{\mathcal{G}_k}(n)|$ machine instructions when it is run with input n. Then we can interleave the polynomial space cumulative polynomial delay listing algorithm for $\widetilde{\mathcal{G}_k}'$ with the listing algorithm for $\widetilde{\mathcal{G}_k} - \widetilde{\mathcal{G}_k}'$ to obtain a polynomial space cumulative polynomial delay listing algorithm for $\widetilde{\mathcal{G}_k}$.

In order to prove theorems 15 and 16, then, we need only design listing algorithms for $\widetilde{\mathcal{G}_k} - \widetilde{\mathcal{G}_k}'$ which satisfy the conditions in observations 13 and 14. We start with some definitions. Let Pu_k denote the family $P_k - Pb_k$. ($Pu_k(n)$ is the set of *unbalanced* $k(n)$-colorings of V_n.) It is fairly easy to see that there is a polynomial space polynomial delay listing algorithm for Pu_k. (For example, we could design a dynamic programming listing algorithm for Pu_k which would be similar to the listing algorithm for Pb_k that we described in chapter 2.) Let $List\_Pu_k$ be a polynomial space polynomial delay listing algorithm for Pu_k and let $Pu_{k,n}$ be the list of unbalanced $k(n)$-colorings that are output by $List\_Pu_k$ when it is run with input n. Recall from chapter 2 that there are polynomial space polynomial delay listing algorithms for Γ_k and Pb_k. Once again, let the listing algorithm for Pb_k be called $List\_Pb_k$ and let $Pb_{k,n}$ be the list of balanced $k(n)$-colorings that are output by $List\_Pb_k$ when it is run with input n.

Suppose that k satisfies Kučera's condition and consider the following listing algorithm for $\widetilde{\mathcal{G}_k} - \widetilde{\mathcal{G}_k}'$.

```
Algorithm Listₖ
Input n
construct an empty dictionary (to contain n-vertex graphs)
For j ⟵ 1 To |Pbₖ(n)|
    simulate List_Pbₖ to obtain Pbₖ,ₙ[j]
    For Each G ∈ Γₖ(Pbₖ,ₙ[j])
        put G in the dictionary
For j ⟵ 1 To |Puₖ(n)|
    simulate List_Puₖ to obtain Puₖ,ₙ[j]
    For Each G ∈ Γₖ(Pbₖ,ₙ[j])
        If G is not in the dictionary
            Output (Puₖ,ₙ[j], G)
            put G in the dictionary
```

It is easy to see that algorithm $List_k$ outputs exactly one member of each equivalence class in $\widetilde{\mathcal{G}_k}(n) - \widetilde{\mathcal{G}_k}'(n)$ when it is run with input n. Furthermore, if the dictionary is implemented using an efficient data structure such as a 2–3 tree (see [AHU 74]) then the algorithm will execute at most $q(n)\,|\mathcal{G}_k(n)|$ machine instructions when it is run with input n, for some polynomial q. Since $\mathcal{G}_k$ and $\widetilde{\mathcal{G}_k}$ are polynomially related, there is a polynomial l such that $q(n)\,|\mathcal{G}_k(n)| \leq l(n)\,|\widetilde{\mathcal{G}_k}(n)|$. We conclude that algorithm $List_k$ satisfies the condition in observation 13. Therefore, it can be interleaved with a cumulative polynomial delay listing algorithm for $\widetilde{\mathcal{G}_k}'$ to obtain a cumulative polynomial delay listing algorithm for $\widetilde{\mathcal{G}_k}$. We have now proved theorem 15.

Now suppose that $k(n) = O(1)$ and consider the following listing algorithm for $\widetilde{\mathcal{G}_k} - \widetilde{\mathcal{G}_k}'$.

```
Algorithm List'_k
Input n
For i  ⟵  1 To |Pu_k(n)|
      simulate List_Pu_k to obtain Pu_{k,n}[i]
      For Each G ∈ Γ_k(Pu_{k,n}[i])
          bad  ⟵  false
          For j  ⟵  1 To |Pb_k(n)|
                simulate List_Pb_k to obtain Pb_{k,n}[j]
                If Pb_{k,n}[j] is a k(n)-coloring of G
                    bad  ⟵  true
          For j  ⟵  1 To i − 1
                simulate List_Pu_k to obtain Pu_{k,n}[j]
                If Pu_{k,n}[j] is a k(n)-coloring of G
                    bad  ⟵  true
          If bad = false
              Output (Pu_{k,n}[i], G)
```

It is easy to see that algorithm $List'_k$ lists exactly one member of each equivalence class in $\widetilde{\mathcal{G}_k}(n) - \widetilde{\mathcal{G}_k}'(n)$ when it is run with input n. Furthermore, the algorithm will execute at most $q(n) \times |\mathcal{G}_k(n) - \mathcal{G}b_k(n)| \times |P_k(n)|$ machine instructions when it is run with input n, for some polynomial q. Now, $|P_k(n)| \leq k^n$. Furthermore, by lemma 21 we have $|\mathcal{G}_k(n) - \mathcal{G}b_k(n)| \times k^n = o(1)|\mathcal{G}_k(n)|$. Since $\mathcal{G}_k$ and $\widetilde{\mathcal{G}_k}$ are polynomially related, we conclude that there is a polynomial l such that the algorithm executes at most $l(n)|\widetilde{\mathcal{G}_k}(n)|$ machine instructions when it is run with input n. Furthermore, algorithm $List'_k$ is a polynomial space algorithm. We conclude that algorithm $List'_k$ satisfies the conditions in observation 14. Therefore it can be interleaved with a polynomial space cumulative polynomial delay listing algorithm for $\widetilde{\mathcal{G}_k}'$ to obtain a polynomial space cumulative polynomial delay listing algorithm for $\widetilde{\mathcal{G}_k}$. We have now proved theorem 16.

Now that we have proved theorems 15 and 16, we will proceed to prove theorem 17 — if k satisfies the greedy condition then there is a probabilistic polynomial delay listing algorithm for $\widetilde{\mathcal{G}_k}$.

We will need to use two known graph coloring algorithms. The first (which we refer to as *Greedy_Color*) is a polynomial time algorithm that takes as input a graph G and uses the "greedy heuristic" to construct a coloring of G. It then outputs the coloring. Algorithm *Greedy_Color* is described in [McD 79] and in [Bol 85]. In [McD 79] McDiarmid proves† that the probability that algorithm *Greedy_Color* returns a coloring with more than $(1+\epsilon)n/\log(n)$ color classes when it is given as input a randomly chosen member of $\mathcal{G}(n)$ is at most 2.5^{-n}. The second coloring algorithm (which we refer to as *Lawler_Color* is described in [Law 76]. It takes as input a graph G and returns a coloring of G. The coloring that is returned is guaranteed to have as few color classes as possible. Lawler proves in [Law 76] that the time complexity of his algorithm is $O(2.5^n)$.

Suppose that k satisfies the greedy condition. We can combine algorithms *Greedy_Color* and *Lawler_Color* to obtain a deterministic polynomial expected time algorithm (which we refer to as *Color$_k$*) that takes as input an n-vertex graph G and returns a $k(n)$-coloring of G if G has a $k(n)$-coloring and "false" otherwise. Let $Color_k(G)$ denote the output of *Color$_k$* when it is run with input G.

Let $\mathcal{C}_k$ be the family of structures defined by the relation

$$\mathcal{C}_k(n) = \{(C, G) \mid G \in \mathcal{G}(n) \text{ and } C = Color_k(G)\}.$$

Let $\mathcal{C}'_k$ be the sub-family of $\mathcal{C}_k$ defined by the relation

$$\mathcal{C}'_k(n) = \mathcal{C}_k(n) \cap \mathcal{G}_k(n) = \{(C, G) \in \mathcal{C}_k(n) \mid C \neq \text{"false"}\}.$$

It is easy to see that $\mathcal{C}'_k(n)$ contains exactly one representative from each equivalence class in $\widetilde{\mathcal{G}_k}(n)$. We will show that if k satisfies the greedy condition then there is a probabilistic polynomial delay listing algorithm for $\mathcal{C}'_k$.

We start by observing that if k satisfies the greedy condition then $\mathcal{C}_k$ and $\mathcal{C}'_k$ are polynomially related. (This fact follows from McDiarmid's proof concerning algorithm *Greedy_Color*.) Furthermore, there is an efficient random sampling algorithm for $\mathcal{C}_k$. (The algorithm simply chooses a random n-vertex graph, G, and runs $Color_k(G)$.) Finally, there is a polynomial time algorithm that takes as input a pair $(C, G) \in \mathcal{C}_k(n)$ and determines whether or not $(C, G) \in \mathcal{C}'_k(n)$. Using the method discussed in remark 2 of subsection 2.2.2, we can construct an efficient random sampling algorithm for $\mathcal{C}'_k$. Then we can apply the methods from subsection 2.1.2 to obtain a probabilistic listing algorithm

---

† McDiarmid actually proves a stronger result. See [McD 79] and [Bol 85].

for C_k' that has polynomial delay and exponentially small failure probability. As we indicated previously, this algorithm can be used as a listing algorithm for $\widetilde{\mathcal{G}_k}$. So we have proved theorem 17.

Now that we have proved theorems 15 – 17 we discuss the prospects for strengthening the theorems. We begin by observing that we could combine theorems 15 and 17 to get the following theorem:

Theorem 18. Suppose that k is a sub-diagonal function. If there are positive constants ϵ and n_0 such that for every $n \geq n_0$ either $k(n) \leq \sqrt{n/28 \log(n)}$ or $k(n) \geq (1+\epsilon)n/\log(n)$ then there is a probabilistic polynomial delay listing algorithm for $\widetilde{\mathcal{G}_k}$.

It is clear that there are many sub-diagonal functions which fail to satisfy the conditions of the theorem. If k is such a function then it is unknown whether or not there is an efficient listing algorithm for $\widetilde{\mathcal{G}_k}$. One approach to resolving this open question is to attempt to strengthen theorem 15 and 17 by weakening the relevant conditions. We discuss this approach here.

First, consider theorem 15.

Theorem 15. If k satisfies Kučera's condition then there is a deterministic cumulative polynomial delay listing algorithm for $\widetilde{\mathcal{G}_k}$.

In order to prove this theorem we developed a deterministic listing algorithm for $\widetilde{\mathcal{G}_k}$. The algorithm is based on interleaving a cumulative polynomial delay listing algorithm for $\widetilde{\mathcal{G}_k}'$ (which is described in chapter 2) with a dictionary-based listing algorithm for $\widetilde{\mathcal{G}_k} - \widetilde{\mathcal{G}_k}'$. The proof that the final algorithm has cumulative polynomial delay uses the fact that when k satisfies Kučera's condition the following statements are true:

1. For every member C of $Pb_k(n)$ the probability that G_C is uniquely $k(n)$-colorable is $1 - o(1)$, where G_C stands for a member of $\Pi_k(C)$, chosen uniformly at random.

2. $\mathcal{G}_k$, $\widetilde{\mathcal{G}_k}$, $\widetilde{\mathcal{G}b_k}$, and $\mathcal{G}b_k$ are all polynomially related.

The proof does not use any other facts that depend upon the function k (except that k is assumed to be a sub-diagonal function). It would be interesting to see whether we could strengthen theorem 15 by assuming that k satisfies some condition which is weaker than Kučera's condition and proving statements 1 and 2. (It is clear that at least some of the relationships described in statement 2 hold under conditions which are weaker than Kučera's condition — see lemma 21 for details.)

Next, consider theorem 17.

Theorem 17. If k satisfies the greedy condition then there is a probabilistic polynomial delay listing algorithm for $\widetilde{\mathcal{G}_k}$.

Consider the probabilistic listing algorithm for $\widetilde{\mathcal{G}_k}$ which we designed in order to prove this theorem. The fact that the algorithm has polynomial delay when k satisfies the greedy condition depends upon the fact that C_k and C'_k are polynomially related in this case. Equivalently, it depends upon the fact that when k satisfies the greedy condition there is a polynomial q such that at least $q(n)^{-1}$ of the graphs in $\mathcal{G}(n)$ have chromatic number less than or equal to $k(n)$.

Suppose that k is a sub-diagonal function. We say that k satisfies *Bollobás's condition* if and only if there is a positive constant n_0 such that for every $n \geq n_0$ we have

$$k(n) \geq \left(1 + \frac{3 \log \log(n)}{\log(n)}\right) \frac{n}{\lceil 2 \log(n) - \log \log(n) + 2 \log(e/2) + 1 \rceil}.$$

In [Bol 88] Bollobás shows that if k satisfies Bollobás's condition then at least $1 - o(1)$ of the graphs in $\mathcal{G}(n)$ have chromatic number less than or equal to $k(n)$.

It is possible that we could strengthen theorem 17 by using Bollobás's condition instead of the greedy condition. However, to do so we would need to design a polynomial expected time algorithm that takes as input an n-vertex graph G and returns a $k(n)$-coloring of G if G has a $k(n)$-coloring and "false" otherwise.

If we could design such an algorithm for a sub-diagonal function k which fails to satisfy the greedy condition then we would be improving the best known clique-finding algorithm. (This observation follows from the fact that every $k(n)$-coloring of an n-vertex graph contains an independent set of size at least $n/k(n)$.) We conclude from the discussion in section 3.3 (see especially subsection 3.3.3) that designing such an algorithm is a difficult (if not impossible) task.

Now that we have discussed the prospects for strengthening theorems 15 and 17 by weakening the relevant conditions we discuss the possibility of strengthening theorem 16 in this manner. Recall the statement of theorem 16.

Theorem 16. If $k(n) = O(1)$ then there is a deterministic polynomial space cumulative polynomial delay listing algorithm for $\widetilde{\mathcal{G}_k}$.

In order to prove this theorem we designed a deterministic polynomial space cumulative polynomial delay listing algorithm for $\widetilde{\mathcal{G}_k}$. The algorithm is based on interleaving a polynomial space cumulative polynomial delay listing algorithm for $\widetilde{\mathcal{G}_k}'$ (which is described in chapter 2) with a polynomial space listing algorithm for $\widetilde{\mathcal{G}_k} - \widetilde{\mathcal{G}_k}'$. The question that we consider now is — can we modify the algorithm so that it has polynomial space and cumulative polynomial delay even when $k(n) = \omega(1)$?

We start by observing that the listing algorithm for $\widetilde{\mathcal{G}_k} - \widetilde{\mathcal{G}_k}'$ runs in polynomial space for any sub-diagonal function k. Furthermore, it is sufficiently fast as long as there are positive constants ϵ and n_0 such that for every $n \geq n_0$ we have $k(n) \leq n^{1/2-\epsilon}$. (In this case, lemma 21 shows that $|\mathcal{G}_k(n) - \mathcal{G}b_k(n)|$ is sufficiently small and Kučera's paper [Kuč 89] shows that $\mathcal{G}_k$ and $\widetilde{\mathcal{G}_k}$ are polynomially related.)

However the listing algorithm for $\widetilde{\mathcal{G}_k}'$ does not have cumulative polynomial delay unless $k(n) = O(1)$. In particular, algorithm $List\_\Pi_k$ does not run in polynomial expected time if $k(n) = \omega(1)$. It would be interesting to see whether a polynomial expected time algorithm could be designed which performs the task of algorithm $List\_\Pi_k$ for $k(n) = \omega(1)$. Such an algorithm would be interesting in its own right (see the note at the end of this section) and it would enable us to design a polynomial space cumulative polynomial delay listing algorithm for $\widetilde{\mathcal{G}_k}$ when $k(n) = \omega(1)$.

3.4.1. Digression — The Problem of Listing k-Colorings

Consider the family Π_k, which was defined in chapter 2. Every parameter of Π_k is an undirected graph. The value $G \in \mathcal{G}(n)$ is associated with the set $\Pi_k(G)$ which contains the $k(n)$-colorings of G. In chapter 2 we described a listing algorithm for Π_k. In this note we consider the performance of that algorithm and we compare the algorithm with other known graph coloring algorithms.

We start out by observing that the problem of coloring graphs is likely to be computationally difficult. In particular, suppose that k is a positive integer which is greater than or equal to 3. It is well known that the problem of determining whether or not an undirected graph is k-colorable is NP-complete (see [GJ 79]). Therefore, it is unlikely that there is a polynomial time algorithm that takes as input a parameter value G of Π_k and returns a coloring in $\Pi_k(G)$ if $\Pi_k(G)$ is non-empty.

Nevertheless, various researchers have developed graph-coloring algorithms which perform fairly well in a *probabilistic* sense. For example, Turner [Tur 88] designed a polynomial-time algorithm that takes as input a graph $G \in \mathcal{G}(n)$ and either returns a member of $\Pi_k(G)$ or halts without output. He showed that his algorithm constructs a k-coloring for all but o(1) of the k-colorable n-vertex graphs. In fact, Turner showed that his algorithm constructs a $k(n)$-coloring for almost every $k(n)$-colorable n-vertex graph, provided that k satisfies $k(n) \leq (1-\epsilon)\log(n)$.

Turner's result is improved by Kučera in [Kuč 89]. Kučera develops a new polynomial-time graph coloring algorithm and shows that his algorithm constructs a

$k(n)$-coloring for almost every $k(n)$-colorable n-vertex graph, provided that k satisfies $k(n) \leq \sqrt{n/196 \log(n)}$.

The fraction of n-vertex graphs which Kučera's algorithm fails to $k(n)$-color in polynomial time is $\omega(k^{-n})$. Similarly, the fraction of n-vertex graphs which Turner's algorithm fails to $k(n)$-color is $\omega(k^{-n})$. Therefore, neither of these two coloring algorithms could be combined with a brute force coloring algorithm to obtain a *polynomial expected time* algorithm for constructing $k(n)$-colorings.

Nevertheless, Dyer and Frieze have developed a probabilistic graph coloring algorithm which does run in polynomial expected time when $k(n) = O(1)$. In particular, suppose that k is a fixed positive integer. Dyer and Frieze's algorithm [DF 89] takes as input an undirected graph G and outputs a member of $\Pi_k(G)$ if $\Pi_k(G)$ is non-empty. If the input is chosen uniformly at random from the set of k-colorable n-vertex graphs then the expected running time of the algorithms is bounded from above by a polynomial in n.

Kučera has shown in [Kuč 89] that if $k(n) \leq \sqrt{n/28 \log(n)}$ then almost every $k(n)$-colorable n-vertex graph has only one $k(n)$-coloring. Nevertheless, it seems unlikely that Dyer and Frieze's algorithm could be modified to provide a polynomial expected time *listing* algorithm for Π_k.

We have provided such an algorithm in this thesis. In particular, algorithm $List\_\Pi_k$ from chapter 2 takes as input an undirected graph G and lists the members of $\Pi_k(G)$. We will prove the following theorem.

Theorem 19. If $k(n) = O(1)$ and the input to algorithm $List\_\Pi_k$ is chosen uniformly at random from the set of k-colorable n-vertex graphs then the expected running time of $List\_\Pi_k$ is bounded form above by a polynomial in n.

Proof: In order to prove this theorem we will need some notation. Let t_k denote the time complexity of $List\_\Pi_k$. Recall that $\mathcal{G}_k(n)$ is the set of $k(n)$-colored n-vertex graphs and that each equivalence class in $\widetilde{\mathcal{G}_k}(n)$ corresponds to a particular $k(n)$-colorable n-vertex graph. If E is an equivalence class in $\widetilde{\mathcal{G}_k}(n)$ then we will write $t_k(E)$ to denote the running time of $List\_\Pi_k$ when it is given as input the $k(n)$-colorable graph which corresponds to E. We will prove that if $k(n) = O(1)$ then there is a polynomial p such that

$$\frac{1}{|\widetilde{\mathcal{G}_k}(n)|} \sum_{E \in \widetilde{\mathcal{G}_k}(n)} t_k(E) \leq p(n).$$

In the proof we will use the notation $U_k(n)$ to refer to the set of $k(n)$-colored n-vertex graphs which belong to singleton equivalence classes in $\widetilde{\mathcal{G}_k}(n)$. The definitions that we have provided show that

$$\frac{1}{|\widetilde{\mathcal{G}_k}(n)|} \sum_{E \in \widetilde{\mathcal{G}_k}(n)} t_k(E) \le \frac{1}{|U_k(n)|} \sum_{E \in \widetilde{\mathcal{G}_k}(n)} t_k(E) \le \frac{1}{|U_k(n)|} \sum_{(C,G) \in \mathcal{G}_k(n)} t_k(G)$$

$$= \frac{|\mathcal{G}_k(n)|}{|U_k(n)|} \left(\frac{1}{|\mathcal{G}_k(n)|} \sum_{(C,G) \in \mathcal{G}_k(n)} t_k(G) \right)$$

Kučera shows in [Kuč 89] that $|\mathcal{G}_k(n)|/|U_k(n)| = 1 + o(1)$. Therefore we will complete the proof by showing that the parenthesized expression (which is the expected running time of *List_II$_k$* when it is run with a random k-*colored* n-vertex graph) is bounded from above by a polynomial in n. Recall that $\mathcal{G}b_k$ is a sub-family of $\mathcal{G}_k$. ($\mathcal{G}b_k$ was defined in chapter 2.) In addition, recall that there is a polynomial p such that $t_k(G) \le p(n) \times k^n$. (This observation was made in subsection 2.3.2.) Using these observations, we see that

$$\frac{1}{|\mathcal{G}_k(n)|} \sum_{(C,G) \in \mathcal{G}_k(n)} t_k(G) \le \frac{1}{|\mathcal{G}_k(n)|} \sum_{(C,G) \in \mathcal{G}b_k(n)} t_k(G)$$

$$+ \frac{1}{|\mathcal{G}_k(n)|} \sum_{(C,G) \in \mathcal{G}_k(n) - \mathcal{G}b_k(n)} p(n) \times k^n.$$

We know from lemma 21 that $|\mathcal{G}_k(n) - \mathcal{G}b_k(n)| \times k(n)^n = o(1) |\mathcal{G}_k(n)|$. Therefore, the right hand term is bounded from above by a polynomial in n. To show that the left hand term is bounded from above by a polynomial in n we use the definitions from chapter 2 . . .

$$\frac{1}{|\mathcal{G}_k(n)|} \sum_{(C,G) \in \mathcal{G}b_k(n)} t_k(G) = \frac{1}{|\mathcal{G}_k(n)|} \sum_{C \in Pb_k(n)} \sum_{G \in \Gamma_k(C)} t_k(G)$$

$$= \frac{1}{|\mathcal{G}_k(n)|} \sum_{C \in Pb_k(n)} |\Gamma_k(C)| \left(\frac{1}{|\Gamma_k(C)|} \sum_{G \in \Gamma_k(C)} t_k(G) \right).$$

We showed in chapter 2 (see the paragraph preceding lemma 7) that there is a polynomial r such that for every $C \in Pb_k(n)$ the value of the parenthesized expression is at most $r(n)$. Therefore, the right hand side is at most

$$\frac{r(n)}{|\mathcal{G}_k(n)|} \sum_{(C,G) \in Pb_k(n)} |\Gamma_k(C)| \le r(n).$$

We have now proved theorem 19. □

We complete this subsection by observing that we can use algorithm $List\_\Pi_k$ to remove the bias from algorithm $\widetilde{\mathcal{G}_k}\text{-}Sample$ from chapter 2. The revised algorithm is an *unbiased* random sampling algorithm for $\widetilde{\mathcal{G}_k}$. It has the following form:

Procedure $Unbiased\text{-}\widetilde{\mathcal{G}_k}\text{-}Sample$

Input n (in unary)

Do forever

   $(C, G) \longleftarrow \mathcal{G}_k\text{-}Sample(n)$

   use algorithm $List\_\Pi_k$ to compute $|\Pi_k(G)|$

   with probability $1/|\Pi_k(G)|$

      Output $((C, G), G)$

      Halt

The proof of theorem 19 shows that the expected running time of $List\_\Pi_k$ is bounded from above by a polynomial in n when it is run with a random k-colored n-vertex graph. The probability that procedure $Unbiased\text{-}\widetilde{\mathcal{G}_k}\text{-}Sample$ halts during any given iteration of the "Do **forever**" loop is at least $1/2$ since almost every k-colored graph is *uniquely k-colorable* [Kuč 89]. Therefore, the expected number of iterations of the loop is at most 2 (to understand why see the proof of lemma 2 in subsection 2.2.2). We conclude that the expected running time of $Unbiased\text{-}\widetilde{\mathcal{G}_k}\text{-}Sample$ is bounded from above by a polynomial in n and that we have therefore proved the following theorem.

Theorem 20. There is an efficient unbiased random sampling algorithm for $\widetilde{\mathcal{G}_k}$.

4. Directions for Future Work on Listing

In chapter 3 we described various applications of our listing methods. As we described each specific application we mentioned one or more related open problems. In this chapter we take a more comprehensive look at open problems in listing and we discuss directions for future work on listing combinatorial structures.

We start by observing that there are several aspects of computational listing which we have not considered in this thesis. It is likely that consideration of these aspects of listing could lead to interesting results. In particular, it would be interesting to study the problem of listing combinatorial structures *in a specified order* (see [JYP 88]). It would also be interesting to study the problem of designing efficient *parallel* algorithms for listing combinatorial structures.

While it would be interesting to study these new aspects of computational listing it would be equally interesting to consider the plethora of open problems which crop up within the context already studied in this thesis. We will discuss some of these problems here.

First, we observe that there are interesting families of combinatorial structures for which there are no known cumulative polynomial delay listing algorithms. Designing efficient listing algorithms for some of these families may require new methods. For example, it would be interesting to know whether or not there is a cumulative polynomial delay listing algorithm for $\mathcal{G} - \mathcal{C}l_j$ when j is a sub-diagonal function such that $j(n) = \omega(1)$. It is not clear how the methods from this thesis could be used to solve this problem.

Another interesting problem comes from example 2 of subsection 2.3.2. In that example we used the interleaving method to obtain a polynomial space polynomial delay listing algorithm for $\widetilde{\widetilde{\mathcal{G}}}$. In fact, the delay of the algorithm that we presented is $O(n^5)$. It would be interesting to see whether the algorithm could be modified to yield an *optimal* algorithm (i.e. one which has $O(n^2)$ delay.) It would also be interesting to see whether or not the techniques from this thesis could be used to design efficient listing algorithms for certain sub-families of $\widetilde{\widetilde{\mathcal{G}}}$. (Sub-families of $\widetilde{\widetilde{\mathcal{G}}}$ are called *unlabeled graph properties*.)

The orderly method has been used to design listing algorithms for various unlabeled graph properties including unlabeled Hamiltonian graphs [CR1 79], unlabeled graphs with a given clique [CR1 79], unlabeled k-colorable graphs [CR1 79], and unlabeled connected cubic graphs [MR 86]. As we explained in chapter 2, the orderly method does not yield polynomial delay listing algorithms. Therefore it would be interesting to determine whether or not the methods from this thesis could be used to design polynomial delay listing algorithms for unlabeled graph properties.

The unlabeled graph properties that we will consider will be described in the following manner. Suppose that S is a graph property which is isomorphism-invariant. That is, suppose that for any two isomorphic n-vertex graphs, G_1 and G_2, G_1 is a member of $S(n)$ if and only if G_2 is a member of $S(n)$. Then we can define an unlabeled graph property $\widetilde{\widetilde{S}}$ using the relation

$$\widetilde{\widetilde{S}}(n) = \{C \in \widetilde{\widetilde{\mathcal{G}}}(n) \mid \text{The graphs in isomorphism class } C \text{ are members of } S(n)\}.$$

It is clear that there are some cases in which the methods from this thesis can be used to design efficient listing algorithms for $\widetilde{\widetilde{S}}$. For example, suppose that $\widetilde{\widetilde{S}}$ is polynomially related to $\widetilde{\widetilde{\mathcal{G}}}$. Suppose further that there is a polynomial expected time algorithm that takes as input the canonical representative G of some isomorphism class in $\widetilde{\widetilde{\mathcal{G}}}(n)$ and returns "yes" if and only if G is a member of $S(n)$. Then we can use the algorithm $\widetilde{\widetilde{\mathcal{G}}}$-$Sample$ from subsection 2.3.1 and the method described in remark 2 of subsection 2.2.2 to obtain a probabilistic listing algorithm for $\widetilde{\widetilde{S}}$ which has polynomial delay and exponentially small failure probability.

We have not yet considered the possibilities for applying the deterministic methods from this thesis to the problem of designing efficient listing algorithms for interesting unlabeled graph properties. However we give some evidence that the methods may be applicable by using them to derive an efficient listing algorithm for a rather "easy" unlabeled graph property.

Recall that Cl_j is the graph property defined by the relation

$$Cl_j(n) = \{G \in \mathcal{G}(n) \mid G \text{ contains a clique of size } j(n)\}.$$

Suppose that $j(n) = O(1)$. It is not difficult to see that we can modify the algorithm from example 2 of subsection 2.3.2 to obtain a polynomial space polynomial delay listing algorithm for $\widetilde{\widetilde{Cl_j}}$.

In particular, we modify the definition of "easy to process" as follows. We say that an n-vertex graph G is easy to process if and only if it satisfies at least one of the following conditions:

(i) G has a vertex v with degree $n-1$ and $G-v$ has a j-clique.

(ii) G has a unique vertex v of maximum degree and $G-v$ is rigid and $G-v$ has a j-clique.

Following example 2, we define $\widetilde{\widetilde{E_j}}$ to be the set of all classes in $\widetilde{\widetilde{Cl}}_j(n)$ whose members are easy to process and we use the symbol $\widetilde{\widetilde{H_j}}$ to stand for the family $\widetilde{\widetilde{Cl}}_j - \widetilde{\widetilde{E_j}}$. Our algorithm interleaves a polynomial delay listing algorithm for $\widetilde{\widetilde{E_j}}$ with a listing algorithm for $\widetilde{\widetilde{H_j}}$.

The listing algorithm for $\widetilde{\widetilde{E_j}}$ is the same as the listing algorithm for $\widetilde{\widetilde{E}}$ which we described in example 2, except that it starts by constructing the representatives of classes in $\widetilde{\widetilde{Cl}}_j(n-1)$ rather than the representatives of classes in $\widetilde{\widetilde{\mathcal{G}}}(n-1)$.

For convenience, we provide an outline of the listing algorithm for $\widetilde{\widetilde{H_j}}$.

Algorithm $\mathcal{H}_j$

Input n

For each algorithmic representative $\langle G, \text{Aut}(G) \rangle$ of a class in $\widetilde{\widetilde{\mathcal{G}}}(n-1)$

    If G has a $(j-1)$-clique and no j-clique

        $G' \longleftarrow G \cup \{(v_i, v_n) \mid i < n\}$

        $\text{Aut}(G') \longleftarrow$ the group generated by the generators of $\text{Aut}(G)$

                and $\{(v_i, v_n) \mid v_i$ has degree $n-2$ in $G\}$

        Output $\langle G', \text{Aut}(G') \rangle$

    If G is rigid

        If G has a j-clique

            For all subsets $W \subset V_{n-1}$ such that

            v_n is a *non-unique* vertex of maximum degree in $G \cup \{(w, v_n) \mid w \in W\}$

                $Test\_Augmentation(G \cup \{(w, v_n) \mid w \in W\})$

        Else

            For all subsets $W \subset V_{n-1}$ such that

            v_n is a vertex of maximum degree in $G \cup \{(w, v_n) \mid w \in W\}$

                If $G \cup \{(w, v_n) \mid w \in W\}$ has a j-clique

                    $Test\_Augmentation(G \cup \{(w, v_n) \mid w \in W\})$

    Else For all subsets $W \subset V_{n-1}$ such that

        v_n is a vertex of maximum degree in $G \cup \{(w, v_n) \mid w \in W\}$

            If $Is\_Smallest(W, \text{Aut}(G))$

                If $(G \cup \{(w, v_n) \mid w \in W\})$ has a j-clique

                    $Test\_Augmentation(G \cup \{(w, v_n) \mid w \in W\})$

We conjecture that the algorithm from example 2 of section 2.3.2 can be modified to obtain an efficient listing algorithm for $\widetilde{\widetilde{Cl_j}}$ in some cases in which $j(n) = \omega(1)$. The necessary modifications would be more complicated than the ones described here, however.

We conclude our discussion of unlabeled graph properties by observing that it would be useful to have a polynomial delay algorithm which lists unlabeled graphs with specified numbers of edges.

Having considered the problem of designing efficient listing algorithms for unlabeled graph properties we now consider alternative directions for future work on listing. The remaining questions that we will consider are generalizations of questions that we have considered earlier in the thesis.

In section 3.1 we considered the problem of designing listing algorithms for graph properties which are defined by formulas in the first order language of graphs. It would be interesting to extend this research by considering the problem of designing listing algorithms for graph properties which are defined by formulas in other languages (see, for example, the languages described in [Imm 87]).

In section 3.3 we considered the problem of designing listing algorithms for graphs with cliques of specified sizes. It would be interesting to generalize this problem by considering the design of listing algorithms for graphs with *induced subgraphs* of specified sizes. The general framework that we have in mind is similar to one of the frameworks studied in [Ruc 87]. We give a brief description here.

Recall from subsection 2.1.1 that we *augment* a graph $G \in \mathcal{G}(n)$ by selecting a subset W of V_n and adding a new vertex v_{n+1} which is adjacent to the members of W. A sequence $H = H_1, H_2, \ldots$ of undirected graphs is called an *augmentation sequence* if $H_1 = (V_1, \varnothing)$ and H_i is an augmentation of H_{i-1} for every $i > 1$.

Suppose that H is an augmentation sequence and that j is a sub-diagonal function. Let $\mathcal{G}_{H,j}$ be the graph property defined by the relation

$$\mathcal{G}_{H,j}(n) = \{G \in \mathcal{G}(n) \mid G \text{ contains an induced subgraph which is isomorphic to } H_{j(n)}\}.$$

It is now clear that the family Cl_j which we studied in section 3.3 is identical to $\mathcal{G}_{K,j}$ where $K = K_1, K_2, \ldots$ is an augmentation sequence in which K_i is the complete graph on V_i. Therefore, it is possible that the techniques from section 3.3 could be generalized to yield efficient listing algorithms for $\mathcal{G}_{H,j}$†.

---

† We are assuming here that $j(n) = \omega(1)$. If $j(n) = O(1)$ then we can use corollary 6 of section 3.1 to obtain a polynomial space polynomial delay listing algorithm for $\mathcal{G}_{H,j}$.

The final problem that we discuss in this chapter is a generalization of the problem of designing an efficient algorithm for listing unlabeled graphs.

Before describing the general problem we discuss a particular encoding for graphs and unlabeled graphs. Suppose that p is a positive integer and that H is a member of $\mathcal{G}(p)$†. We can encode H as a function f from the set $\{1, \ldots, \binom{p}{2}\}$ to the set $\{1, 2\}$. The encoding that we use is straightforward. We order the $\binom{p}{2}$ 2-element subsets of V_p lexicographically. Then we define f as follows:

$$f(i) = \begin{cases} 1 & \text{if the } i^{\text{th}} \text{ 2-element subset of } V_p \text{ is an edge of } H \\ 2 & \text{otherwise} \end{cases}$$

For example, suppose that H_1 is defined as follows:

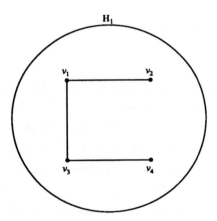

The 2-element subsets of V_4 are ordered $\{v_1, v_2\}$, $\{v_1, v_3\}$, $\{v_1, v_4\}$, $\{v_2, v_3\}$, $\{v_2, v_4\}$, $\{v_3, v_4\}$. Therefore, the encoding of H_1 is the function f_1:

---

† Our description of the generalized problem will use the notation in the literature, using the symbol "G" to stand for a permutation group and the symbol "n" to refer to the degree of G. To avoid confusion, we will use the symbol "H" to stand for a graph and the symbol "p" to stand for the number of vertices (or *points*) of H.

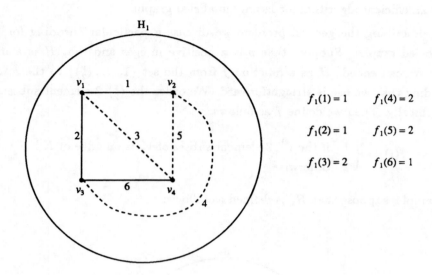

$$f_1(1) = 1 \qquad f_1(4) = 2$$

$$f_1(2) = 1 \qquad f_1(5) = 2$$

$$f_1(3) = 2 \qquad f_1(6) = 1$$

Let S_p denote the symmetric group acting on the set $\{1, \ldots, p\}$. The *pair group*† of S_p (denoted S_p^2) is the group of permutations of $\{1, \ldots, \binom{p}{2}\}$ defined as follows. For every permutation $\pi \in S_p$ there is a permutation $\pi' \in S_p^2$. If $\{a, b\}$ is the ith 2-element subset of $\{1, \ldots, p\}$ and $\{\pi(a), \pi(b)\}$ is the jth 2-element subset of $\{1, \ldots, p\}$ then $\pi'(i) = j$.

For example, suppose that π is the permutation $(1\,2)(3\,4)$. The permutation π' corresponding to π is defined by $\pi' = (2\,5)(3\,4)$.

We will use the permutation group S_p^2 to define an equivalence relation $\sim$ on encoded graphs. Suppose that f_1 and f_2 are two functions from $\{1, \ldots, \binom{p}{2}\}$ to $\{1, 2\}$. We will say that f_1 is related to f_2 by $\sim$ if and only if there is a permutation $\pi \in S_p^2$ such that $f_1\pi = f_2$‡. It is not too difficult to see that f_1 is related to f_2 by $\sim$ if and only if the graphs encoded by f_1 and f_2 are isomorphic. That is, $\sim$ is the usual graph isomorphism relation.

For example, let f_2 be the function with the following definition and let H_2 denote the graph encoded by f_2:

---

† For a more detailed description of pair groups see [HP 73].
‡ Note that composition of functions is written from right to left.

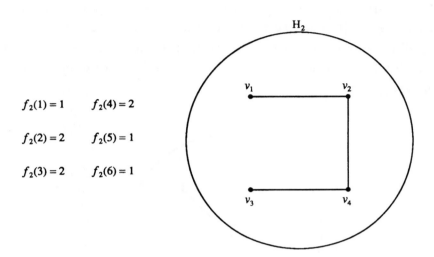

$f_2(1) = 1 \qquad f_2(4) = 2$

$f_2(2) = 2 \qquad f_2(5) = 1$

$f_2(3) = 2 \qquad f_2(6) = 1$

H_2 is isomorphic to the graph H_1 which we described earlier. Furthermore, the permutation π' satisfies $f_1 \pi' = f_2$.

To generalize the framework that we have just described suppose that n and m are positive integers and that G is a group of permutations of $\{1, \ldots, n\}$. We will use the permutation group G to define an equivalence relation $\sim_{G,m}$ on the set of functions from $\{1, \ldots, n\}$ to $\{1, \ldots, m\}$. Suppose that f_1 and f_2 are two functions from $\{1, \ldots, n\}$ to $\{1, \ldots, m\}$. We will say that f_1 is related to f_2 by $\sim_{G,m}$ if and only if there is a permutation $\pi \in G$ such that $f_1 \pi = f_2$.

For every positive integer m we can use the equivalence relations that we have defined to define an interesting family of combinatorial structures, which we will call $\widetilde{\mathcal{F}_m}$. Every parameter value of $\widetilde{\mathcal{F}_m}$ is a group of permutations. Suppose that n is a positive integer and that G is a group of permutations of $\{1, \ldots, n\}$. We will define $\widetilde{\mathcal{F}_m}(G)$ to be the set of equivalence classes in the set of functions from $\{1, \ldots, n\}$ to $\{1, \ldots, m\}$ under the equivalence relation $\sim_{G,m}$.

Given these definitions it is easy to verify that each equivalence class in $\widetilde{\mathcal{F}_2}(S_p^2)$ contains the (encoded) members of an isomorphism class in $\widetilde{\widetilde{\mathcal{G}}}(p)$. Therefore, the problem of designing an efficient listing algorithm for $\widetilde{\widetilde{\mathcal{G}}}$ can be viewed as a special case of the problem of designing an efficient listing algorithm for $\widetilde{\mathcal{F}_2}$.

In the following paragraphs we will further generalize the framework that we have described. We start by reconsidering our encoded unlabeled graphs. A graph is said to be *self-complementary* [Rea 63, Pal 70] if it is isomorphic to the graph that is obtained by turning all of its edges into non-edges and its non-edges into edges. For example, the graph H_2 is self-complementary because it is isomorphic to its complement, which is depicted below:

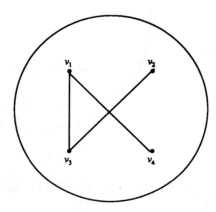

Suppose that f is an encoded p-vertex graph (i.e. f is a function from $\{1, \ldots, \binom{p}{2}\}$ to $\{1, 2\}$). Using the definition of "self-complementary" we see that f is self-complementary if and only if it is related by $\sim$ to to the function $(1\,2)f$ where composition of functions is written from right to left and $\sim$ is the isomorphism relation that we defined earlier.

It is easy to see that the property of being self-complementary is isomorphism-invariant. That is, every isomorphism class $C \in \widetilde{\mathcal{F}_2}(S_p^2)$ has the property that either every graph in C is self-complementary or none of the graphs in C are self-complementary. We will say that an isomorphism class is self-complementary if and only if its members are.

We can generalize the notion of a self-complementary graph by returning to our general framework. Suppose that n and m are positive integers and that G is a group of permutations of $\{1, \ldots, n\}$. Suppose further that h is a permutation of $\{1, \ldots, m\}$. We will say that a function f from $\{1, \ldots, n\}$ to $\{1, \ldots, m\}$ is *invariant with respect to h* if and only if f is related to hf by $\sim_{G,m}$. Once again, the notion of invariance is isomorphism invariant. We will say that an equivalence class $C \in \widetilde{\mathcal{F}_m}(n)$ is invariant with respect to h if and only if its members are.

For every positive integer m and every permutation h of $\{1,\ldots,m\}$ we will use the notion of invariance to define an interesting sub-family of $\widetilde{\mathcal{F}_m}$ which we will call $\widetilde{\mathcal{F}_h}$. Suppose that m is a positive integer and that h is a permutation of $\{1,\ldots,m\}$. Suppose further that G is a group of permutations. We will define $\widetilde{\mathcal{F}_h}(G)$ to be the set of equivalence classes in $\widetilde{\mathcal{F}_m}(G)$ which are invariant with respect to h.

Let m be 2 and consider the permutation $(1\,2)$ of $\{1,2\}$. It is easy to use the definitions that we have provided to show that each equivalence class in $\widetilde{\mathcal{F}_{(1\,2)}}(S_p^2)$ contains the (encoded) members of a self-complementary isomorphism class in $\widetilde{\widetilde{\mathcal{G}}}(p)$. Therefore, the problem of designing an efficient listing algorithm for self-complementary unlabeled graphs can be viewed as a special case of the problem of designing an efficient listing algorithm for $\widetilde{\mathcal{F}_{(1\,2)}}$.

Suppose that m is a positive integer and that id_m is the identity permutation acting on the set $\{1,\ldots,m\}$. It is easy to see that the family $\widetilde{\mathcal{F}_m}$ is identical to the family $\widetilde{\mathcal{F}_{id_m}}$. Therefore the generalized framework that we have just described subsumes the original framework.

We have already shown that by choosing the permutation h appropriately we can use an efficient listing algorithm for $\widetilde{\mathcal{F}_h}$ as an efficient listing algorithm for unlabeled graphs and as an efficient listing algorithm for self-complementary unlabeled graphs. There are many other interesting combinatorial families that can be described in this framework. See, for example, the papers by De Bruijn [DeB 63,DeB 64], the translation of Pólya's paper, and the accompanying paper by Read in [PR 87]. The examples described in these papers will convince the reader that it would be extremely useful to have an efficient listing algorithm for $\widetilde{\mathcal{F}_h}$ (or a method for designing such an algorithm given a positive integer m and a permutation h of $\{1,\ldots,m\}$).

As a first step, it would be useful to have a method for designing an efficient listing algorithm for $\widetilde{\mathcal{F}_m}$ given a positive integer m. Following Pólya's work in 1937 there have been various published listing algorithms for $\widetilde{\mathcal{F}_m}$ (see the references in [PR 87]). Most of these algorithms have been designed and used by chemists in their efforts to list chemical compounds. However, none of these methods seems to be computationally efficient, except in special cases. In [BFP 89] Brown, Finkelstein, and Purdom have combined various heuristics to obtain a general backtracking listing algorithm for $\widetilde{\mathcal{F}_m}$. They state that their algorithm is useful in practice, although it does not have polynomial delay.

Brown, Finkelstein, and Purdom point out that the problem of designing an efficient listing algorithm for $\widetilde{\mathcal{F}_m}$ is made easier if we restrict the inputs of the algorithm to the set of *p-groups*. They point out that in this restricted case Luks's methods from [Luk 82] can be used to perform the symmetry testing in their algorithm.

Thus, if we want to design a polynomial delay listing algorithm for $\widetilde{\mathcal{F}_m}$ a good starting point might be to restrict the parameter values of $\widetilde{\mathcal{F}_m}$ to the set of *p*-groups and to consider ways of combining the methods of [BFP 89] and the methods of [Luk 82].

An alternative approach (which may also work well in the restricted case) is to attempt to use the random sampling methods from subsections 2.1.2 and 2.3.1. Designing an efficient random sampling algorithm for $\widetilde{\mathcal{F}_m}$ could, however, turn out to be a difficult problem. The interested reader should start by consulting [DW 83] and [Wor 87].

5. Related Results

The two sections in this chapter contain work which is related to the work described in chapters 1–4. In section 5.1 we compare the computational difficulty of the listing problem with the difficulty of other computational problems involving combinatorial structures. In section 5.2 we consider a particular computational counting problem which is related to a listing problem described in chapter 4.

5.1. Comparing Listing with other Computational Problems

In this section we compare the listing problem with other computational problems involving combinatorial structures. The problems that we consider are described in [JVV 86]. For completeness, we provide a description of the problems here. Suppose that S is a family of combinatorial structures. We consider five computational problems associated with S. In each case the input is a parameter value p of S:

Problem 1 — The *Existence* Problem

Determine whether or not $S(p) = \varnothing$.

Problem 2 — The *Construction* Problem

If $S(p)$ is non-empty then output a member of an equivalence class in $S(p)$. Otherwise, halt without output.

Problem 3 — The *Listing* Problem

If $S(p)$ is non-empty then output one representative from each equivalence class in $S(p)$. Otherwise, halt without output.

Problem 4 — The *Random Sampling* Problem

If $S(p)$ is non-empty then "randomly" choose an equivalence class in $S(p)$ and output a member of that equivalence class. Otherwise, halt without output.

Problem 5 — The *Counting* Problem

Output the size of $S(p)$.

In order to compare the computational difficulty of the listing problem with the difficulty of the other four problems we must establish criteria by which we can evaluate algorithms which *solve* the problems. The existence, construction, and counting problems which we described here have already been studied extensively from the perspective of computational complexity [Sim 77, GJ 79, Val 79]. We will use the standard criterion for efficiency, saying that an algorithm that solves one of these problems is efficient if and only if its running time is bounded from above by a polynomial in the size of the input.

We discussed the notion of an efficient *random sampling* algorithm in chapter 2. In that chapter, we defined the *bias factor* of a random sampling algorithm. The bias factor measures the extent to which the probability distribution from which the algorithm samples equivalence classes deviates from the uniform distribution. We said that a random sampling algorithm is *efficient* if and only if its expected running time and its bias factor are bounded from above by polynomials in the size of the input.

Throughout this thesis we have said that a *listing* algorithm is efficient if and only if it has cumulative polynomial delay. We maintain that criterion in this section. However, we will sometimes get stronger results by considering a weaker criterion. In particular, we will sometimes consider the notion of *polynomial total time*. This notion was defined in the bibliographic note at the end of chapter one. Quite simply, a listing algorithm for a family of combinatorial structures is said to run in *polynomial total time* if and only if its running time is bounded from above by a polynomial in the size of the input and in the number of outputs.

Having established these criteria for efficiency we can now compare the computational difficulty of the listing problem with the difficulty of the other problems that we have described. We start by comparing the difficulty of the listing problem with the difficulty of the existence and construction problems.

Let Ex denote the set of families of combinatorial structures whose existence problems can be solved in polynomial time. Let Con denote the set of families whose construction problems can be solved in polynomial time. Let PTT denote the set of families with polynomial total time listing algorithms and let CPD denote the set of families with cumulative polynomial delay listing algorithms. The following diagram illustrates the relationship between these sets.

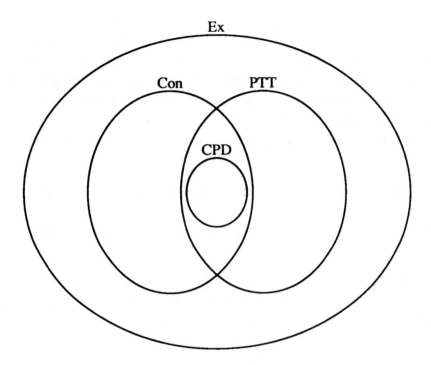

The relationships indicated in the diagram are established in the following observations:

Observation 15.   CPD $\subseteq$ Con, CPD $\subseteq$ PTT, Con $\subseteq$ Ex, and PTT $\subseteq$ Ex.

Proof: All of the inclusions are straightforward except the last. Suppose that $\mathcal{A}$ is a polynomial total time listing algorithm for a family S. By the definition of polynomial total time there is a polynomial q such that whenever $\mathcal{A}$ is run with an input p such that $S(p) = \varnothing$ the number of machine instructions that it executes is bounded from above by $q(|p|)$. Given this fact it is clear that $\mathcal{A}$ could be modified to obtain a polynomial time algorithm for solving the existence problem that is associated with S. $\square$

Observation 16.   There is a family which is a member of Ex but is not a member of Con or PTT.

Proof: Consider the family CHECKERS$_1$ which was defined in the bibliographic note at the end of chapter one. $\square$

Observation 17.   There is a family which is a member of Con but is not a member of PTT.

Proof: To obtain an example of such a family we need only make a slight modification to the family $CHECKERS_1$. Let $CHECKERS_3$ be the family with the following definition. Every parameter value of $CHECKERS_3$ is a square checkers board with some arrangement of black and white pieces. The board B is associated with the set $CHECKERS_3(B) = \{1\} \cup CHECKERS_1(B)$. □

Observation 18.   There is a family which is a member of PTT but is not a member of Con.

Proof: Consider the family $CHECKERS_2$ which was defined in the bibliographic note at the end of chapter one. □

Observation 19.   There is a family which is a member of Con ∩ PTT but is not a member of CPD.

Proof: To obtain an example of such a family we need only make a slight modification to $CHECKERS_2$. In particular, let $CHECKERS_4$ be the family with the following definition. Every parameter value of $CHECKERS_4$ is a square checkers board with some arrangement of black and white pieces. The $n \times n$ board B is associated with the set $CHECKERS_4(B) = \{1\} \cup CHECKERS_2(B)$. □

Observation 20.   There is a family which is a member of CPD.

Proof: We have seen lots of examples of members of CPD in this thesis. Take, for example, the family $\tilde{\tilde{\mathcal{G}}}$. □

Now that we have compared the difficulty of the listing problem with the difficulty of the existence and construction problems we proceed to compare the difficulty of the listing problem with the difficulty of the random sampling problem. Let RS denote the set of families which have efficient random sampling algorithms. Let PPD denote the set of families with probabilistic listing algorithms which have polynomial delay and exponentially small failure probability. The following diagram illustrates the relationship between these sets, assuming that RP $\neq$ NP.

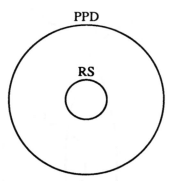

We established in chapter 2 (theorem 2) that RS ⊆ PPD. Therefore, the claim follows from the following observation.

Observation 21. If RP ≠ NP then there is a family which is a member of PPD and is not a member of RS.

Proof: Let *Cycles* be the family with the following definition. Every parameter value of *Cycles* is a directed graph. The value G is associated with the set *Cycles*(G) which contains all simple cycles in G. Johnson's paper [Joh 75] contains a polynomial delay listing algorithm for *Cycles*. However [JVV 86] shows that there is no efficient random sampling algorithm for *Cycles* unless RP = NP. □

Now that we have compared the difficulty of the listing problem with the difficulty of the existence, construction, and random sampling problems we proceed to compare the difficulty of the listing problem with the difficulty of the counting problem. Let C denote the set of families whose counting problems can be solved in polynomial time. The following diagram illustrates the relationship between C, CPD, and PTT.

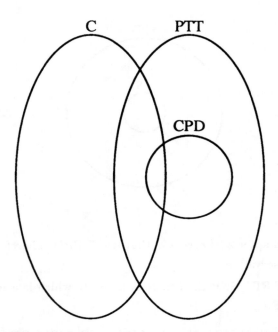

The relationships indicated in the diagrams are established in the following observations.

Observation 22. There is a family which is a member of C and is not a member of PTT.

Proof: Consider the family CHECKERS$_1$, which was defined in the bibliographic note at the end of chapter one. □

Observation 23. There is a family which is a member of C ∩ PTT and not a member of CPD.

Proof: Consider the family CHECKERS$_2$, which was defined in the bibliographic note at the end of chapter one. □

Observation 24. There is a family which is a member of CPD ∩ C.

Proof: Consider the family $\mathcal{G}$. □

Observation 25. There is a family which is a member of CPD but not a member of C.

Proof: Consider the family CHECKERS₅ which is defined as follows. Every parameter value of CHECKERS₅ is a square checkers board with some arrangement of black and white pieces. The $n \times n$ board B is associated with the set

$$\text{CHECKERS}_5(B) = \begin{cases} \{1, \dots, 5^{n^2}\} \cup \{\text{"yes"}\} & \text{if white can force a win on } B \\ \{1, \dots, 5^{n^2}\} & \text{otherwise } \square \end{cases}$$

Observation 26. There is a family which is a member of PTT but not a member of CPD ∪ C.

Proof: Consider the family CHECKERS₆ which is defined as follows. Every parameter value of CHECKERS₆ is a square checkers board with some arrangement of black and white pieces. The $n \times n$ board B is associated with the set

$$\text{CHECKERS}_6(B) = \begin{cases} \text{CHECKERS}_2(F) \cup \{\text{"yes"}\} & \text{if white can force a win on } B \\ \text{CHECKERS}_2(F) & \text{otherwise } \square \end{cases}$$

We have now compared the difficulty of the listing problem with the difficulty of each of the problems described in [JVV 86]. While our results are conclusive, the constructions used in this section have been rather artificial. It would be interesting to find examples of *natural* combinatorial families which separate the complexity classes that we have separated in this section. We conclude the section by describing one natural candidate for the class Con − PTT.

In order to define the candidate we need some definitions. A *monotone boolean formula* is a boolean formula in which the negation symbol does not appear. An *implicant* of such formula is a subset I of its variables, such that, whenever each of the variables in I is set to **true**, the value of the formula is **true**. A *prime implicant* is an implicant that does not contain any other implicant as a proper subset. The family PI is defined as follows. Every parameter value of PI is a monotone boolean formula. The value F is associated with the set PI(F) which contains the prime implicants of F.

It is easy to design a polynomial time algorithm which solves the construction problem that is associated with PI. (For example, there is a simple algorithm which uses the greedy heuristic to solve this problem.)

However, there is no polynomial total time listing algorithm for PI unless P = NP. We demonstrate this fact by reduction from SAT. Suppose that F is a boolean formula (a parameter value of SAT) with variables $x_1, \dots, x_n$. Let F_m denote the monotone boolean formula that is formed by replacing each unnegated variable x_i by t_i and each negated variable $\overline{x_i}$ by f_i. Let F'_m be the formula $t_1 f_1 \vee \ldots \vee t_n f_n \vee F_m$. The claim is established by observing that F is unsatisfiable if and only if $\text{PI}(F'_m) = \{t_1 f_1, \ldots, t_n f_n\}$†.

We have now shown that PI is a member of Con but that it is not a member of PTT unless $\text{P} = \text{NP}$. This fact explains the inefficiency of the many published listing algorithms for PI [Bre 72, Obe 83]. It also demonstrates the fact that PI is not likely to be self-reducible since self-reducible families with easy existence problems have polynomial delay listing algorithms (see chapter 2).

5.2. Evaluating the Cycle Index Polynomial

In this section, we will investigate the computational difficulty of evaluating and approximately evaluating Pólya's *cycle index polynomial*. The results that we obtain will have corollaries concerning the difficulty of solving the counting problems that are associated with the families $\widetilde{\mathcal{F}_m}$ and $\widetilde{\mathcal{F}_h}$.

Before describing the computational problems that we study in this section, we provide the necessary definitions. Suppose that G is a group of permutations of $\{1, \ldots, n\}$. We will use the notation $|G|$ to denote the number of permutations in G. It is well known that each permutation $g \in G$ decomposes the set $\{1, \ldots, n\}$ into a collection of *cycles*, which we will call the cycles of g. We will use the notation $c(g)$ to denote the number of cycles in this decomposition and the notation $c_i(g)$ to denote the number of cycles of length i. The *cycle index polynomial* of G is the n-variable polynomial $P_G(x_1, \ldots, x_n) = \frac{1}{|G|} \sum_{g \in G} x_1^{c_1(g)} \cdots x_n^{c_n(g)}$.

The first computational problem that we discuss is the generic cycle index evaluation problem:

Generic Cycle Index Evaluation

  Input: A set of generators for a degree n permutation group G

         n non-negative rational numbers $y_1, \ldots, y_n$

  Output: $P_G(y_1, \ldots, y_n)$.

It is easy to see that we could implement an algorithm that solves the generic cycle index evaluation problem by summing over the permutations in the group G. However, the size of a permutation group can be exponential in the size of its smallest generating

---

† The idea behind this construction is taken from [LLR 80] where it is presented in terms of maximal independent sets.

set†, so this method is infeasible computationally. In fact, no feasible method for solving this problem is known to exist. Furthermore, the construction from Lubiw's #P-hardness proof for *#Fixed-Point-Free Automorphism* [Lub 81] can be used to show that the generic cycle index evaluation problem is #P-hard.

Although the cycle index polynomial can be used to solve the counting problems that are associated with $\widetilde{\mathcal{F}_m}$ and $\widetilde{\mathcal{F}_h}$, a proof that the generic cycle index evaluation problem is #P-hard does not necessarily imply that the counting problems are #P-hard. On the contrary, the counting problems that are associated with $\widetilde{\mathcal{F}_m}$ and $\widetilde{\mathcal{F}_h}$ correspond to *special cases* of the generic cycle index evaluation problem. In particular, each positive integer m and each permutation h of $\{1, \ldots, m\}$ can be associated with a specific sequence $y_1, y_2, \ldots$ of non-negative rational numbers in such a way that counting the equivalence classes in $\widetilde{\mathcal{F}_h}(G)$ for a degree n permutation group G is equivalent to evaluating the cycle index polynomial of G at the point $(y_1, \ldots, y_n)$.

In order to obtain interesting results about the difficulty of solving the counting problems associated with $\widetilde{\mathcal{F}_m}$ and $\widetilde{\mathcal{F}_h}$ and in order to obtain the strongest possible results about the difficulty of evaluating the cycle index polynomial we will let $y_1, y_2, \ldots$ stand for an arbitrary fixed sequence of non-negative rational numbers and we will study the computational difficulty of the following cycle index evaluation problem:

Cycle Index Evaluation$(y_1, y_2, \ldots)$

    Input: A set of generators for a degree n permutation group G.

    Output: $P_G(y_1, \ldots, y_n)$.

In order to show that the cycle index evaluation problem is #P-hard we will consider the difficulty of determining a particular coefficient of the cycle index polynomial. In particular, we will consider the following problem in which i is taken to be a fixed positive integer.

Cycle Index Coefficient(i)

    Input: A set of generators for a permutation group G whose degree, n,
           is a multiple of i.

    Output: The coefficient of $x_i^{n/i}$ in the cycle index polynomial of G.

We will obtain the following result:

---

† A degree n permutation group can contain up to $n!$ permutations. However, every degree n permutation group has a generating set of size at most $n-1$, as [Jer 86] demonstrates.

Theorem 21. Let $i > 1$ be a fixed positive integer. *Cycle Index Coefficient*(i) is #P-hard.

The coefficient of $x_i^{n/i}$ in P_G is $1/|G|$ times the number of permutations in G that have n/i cycles of length i. Therefore theorem 21 implies that it is #P-hard to determine how many permutations in a group have a given cycle structure.

As well as being interesting in its own right, theorem 21 is the main tool which we use to establish the computational difficulty of cycle index evaluation. Using theorem 21 we obtain the following result:

Theorem 22. If $y_1, y_2, \ldots$ is a sequence of non-negative rational numbers and there exists an i such that $y_i \neq y_1^i$ and $y_i \neq 0$ then *Cycle Index Evaluation*$(y_1, y_2, \ldots)$ is #P-hard.

Theorem 22 has some interesting corollaries which describe the computational difficulty of solving the counting problems that are associated with $\widetilde{\mathcal{F}_m}$ and $\widetilde{\mathcal{F}_h}$. The corollaries will be discussed in subsection 5.2.1.

It would be interesting to determine the computational difficulty of *Cycle Index Evaluation*$(y_1, y_2, \ldots)$ when $y_1, y_2, \ldots$ is a sequence for which the condition in theorem 22 is false. We have not solved this problem in this work, although we make the following observations:

Observation 27. Let $y_1, y_2, \ldots$ be a fixed sequence of non-negative rational numbers such that for every positive integer j we have $y_j = y_1^j$. Then *Cycle Index Evaluation*$(y_1, y_2, \ldots)$ can be solved in polynomial time.

Observation 28. Let $y_1, y_2, \ldots$ be a fixed sequence of non-negative rational numbers such that for every integer $j > 1$ we have $y_j = 0$. Then *Cycle Index Evaluation*$(y_1, y_2, \ldots)$ can be solved in polynomial time.

We conjecture that *Cycle Index Evaluation*$(y_1, y_2, \ldots)$ is #P-hard for every sequence $y_1, y_2, \ldots$ which fails to satisfy the conditions in observation 27 and observation 28. The techniques which we use to prove theorem 24 can be adapted to establish the #P-hardness of *Cycle Index Evaluation*$(y_1, y_2, \ldots)$ for many such sequences.

Since *Cycle Index Evaluation*$(y_1, y_2, \ldots)$ is almost always #P-hard we will be interested in determining the computational difficulty of *approximately* solving the cycle index evaluation problem. In particular, suppose that q is a function from $\mathbf{N}$ to $\mathbf{N}$ and consider the following approximation problem:

Cycle Index Approximation$(q, y_1, y_2, \ldots)$

Input: A set of generators for a degree n permutation group G.

Output: A rational number z such that

$$\frac{1}{q(n)} P_G(y_1, \ldots, y_n) \leq z \leq q(n) P_G(y_1, \ldots, y_n).$$

We will obtain the following result concerning the computational difficulty of *Cycle Index Approximation*$(q, y_1, y_2, \ldots)$.

Theorem 23. If $y_1, y_2, \ldots$ is a sequence of non-negative rational numbers and there exists an i such that $y_i > y_1^i$ then *Cycle Index Approximation*$(q, y_1, y_2, \ldots)$ is NP-hard for every polynomial q.

As one would expect, we will be able to use theorem 23 to derive corollaries about the computational difficulty of approximately solving the counting problems.

It seems to be difficult to determine the computational complexity of *Cycle Index Approximation*$(q, y_1, y_2, \ldots)$ when $y_1, y_2, \ldots$ is a fixed sequence such that the conditions in observation 27, observation 28, and theorem 23 are false.

We consider the special case in which $y_1 = y_2 = \cdots = y$ for some positive rational number y and we obtain the following theorem.

Theorem 24. [Goldberg, Jerrum] If y is a positive rational number that is not an integer then *Cycle Index Approximation*$(q, y, y, \ldots)$ is NP-hard for every polynomial q.

It will be clear from the proof of theorem 24 that our technique does not say anything about the difficulty of *Cycle Index Approximation*$(q, y, y, \ldots)$ when y is an integer. The condition that y be a non-integer seems rather odd at first but we will see in subsection 5.2.1 that it is precisely the *integer* values of y for which $P_G(y, y, \ldots)$ has a combinatorial meaning. Therefore, our theorem leaves open the possibility that the combinatorial interpretation of $P_G(y, \ldots, y)$ in the integer case could be exploited to provide a fast algorithm.

The structure of this section is the following: Subsection 5.2.1 describes the relationship between the counting problems that are associated with $\widetilde{\mathcal{F}_m}$ and $\widetilde{\mathcal{F}_h}$ and the problems *Cycle Index Evaluation*$(y_1, y_2, \ldots)$ and *Cycle Index Approximation*$(q, y_1, y_2, \ldots)$. In subsection 5.2.1 we derive some corollaries of theorems 22 and 23 which relate to the difficulty of counting equivalence classes. Subsection 5.2.2 discusses the computational difficulty of evaluating the cycle index polynomial. It contains a proof of theorems 21 and 22. Finally, subsection 5.2.3 discusses the difficulty of approximately evaluating the cycle index polynomial. It contains the proofs of theorems 23 and 24.

Before considering the relationship between the counting problems and the cycle index evaluation problems, we state two definitions which will be used throughout the section.

1. The *cycle bound* of a permutation group is the length of the longest cycle of a permutation in the group. That is, the cycle bound of G is the maximum over all permutations $g \in G$ of the maximum i such that $c_i(g) > 0$.

2. Let ID_j denote the trivial group of permutations of $\{1, \ldots, j\}$. (That is, let ID_j consist of the identity permutation on $\{1, \ldots, j\}$.) Let G be any group of permutations of $\{1, \ldots, n\}$. The *Kranz Group* $G[ID_j]$ [DeB 64] is the group of permutations of $\{\langle a, b \rangle \mid 1 \le a \le n, 1 \le b \le j\}$ with the following description. Each permutation $g \in G$ corresponds to exactly one permutation $g[ID_j] \in G[ID_j]$. If g maps the object o_1 to o_2 then $g[ID_j]$ maps $\langle o_1, l \rangle$ to $\langle o_2, l \rangle$ for $1 \le l \le j$. We will use the fact that $P_G(y_1{}^j, \ldots, y_n{}^j) = P_{G[ID_j]}(y_1, \ldots, y_n)$.

Having stated these definitions, we proceed to consider the relationship between the counting problems and the cycle index evaluation problems.

5.2.1. Evaluating and Counting Equivalence Classes

The relationships between the counting problems that are associated with $\widetilde{\mathcal{F}_m}$ and $\widetilde{\mathcal{F}_h}$ and the problems *Cycle Index Evaluation*$(y_1, y_2, \ldots)$ and *Cycle Index Approximation*$(q, y_1, y_2, \ldots)$ are captured in the following theorems. The proofs of the theorems can be found in [DeB 63] and [DeB 64].

Theorem 25. (Pólya) Suppose that m is a positive integer and that G is a group of permutations. The number of equivalence classes in $\widetilde{\mathcal{F}_m}(G)$ is $P_G(m, \ldots, m)$.

Theorem 26. (De Bruijn) Suppose that n and m are positive integers, that h is a permutation of $\{1, \ldots, m\}$, and that G is a group of permutations of $\{1, \ldots, n\}$. The number of equivalence classes in $\widetilde{\mathcal{F}_h}(G)$ is $P_G(y_1, \ldots, y_n)$ where y_j denotes the number of objects $k \in \{1, \ldots, m\}$ such that $h^j(k) = k$.

Using theorem 25 we can immediately derive the following corollary of theorem 22.

Corollary 10. Let $m > 1$ be a fixed integer. The counting problem that is associated with $\widetilde{\mathcal{F}_m}$ is #P-hard.

We can also derive the following corollary, which is a generalization of corollary 10.

Corollary 11. Let $m > 1$ be a fixed integer and let h be any fixed permutation of $\{1, \ldots, m\}$. The counting problem associated with $\widetilde{\mathcal{F}_h}$ is #P-hard.

Proof: Let y_j denote the number of objects $k \in \{1, \ldots, m\}$ such that $h^j(k) = k$. By De Bruijn's theorem, the number of equivalence classes in $\widetilde{\mathcal{F}_h}(G)$ is $P_G(y_1, \ldots, y_n)$. Suppose that y_1 is zero or one. Let i be the order of h (note that $i > 1$). Then $y_i = m$ so $y_i \neq y_1^i$ and $y_i \neq 0$. The corollary follows from theorem 22. So, suppose that $y_1 > 1$. Let p be a prime number that is larger than m. It is easy to see that $y_p = y_1$. We conclude that $y_p \neq y_1^p$ and that $y_p \neq 0$. The corollary follows from theorem 22. □

In addition, we can derive a corollary of theorem 23.

Corollary 12. Let $m > 1$ be a fixed integer and let h be any fixed permutation of $\{1, \ldots, m\}$. Let y_j denote the number of elements in $\{1, \ldots, m\}$ that are fixed by h^j. If there exists some i such that $y_i > y_1^i$ then the following problem is NP-hard for any polynomial q:

Input: A set of generators for a degree n permutation group G

Output: A quantity z that is within a factor of $q(n)$ of the number of equivalence classes in $\widetilde{\mathcal{F}_h}(G)$.

The condition that there exists an i such that $y_i > y_1^i$ restricts the values of m and h to which the NP-hardness result applies. This restriction makes corollary 12 more difficult to appreciate than corollaries 10 and 11, so it is worth considering a special case. Suppose that G is a group of permutations of $\{1, \ldots, n\}$ and that f is a function from $\{1, \ldots, n\}$ to $\{1, 2\}$. We will say that f is *self-complementary* if and only if f is equivalent to $(1\,2)f$ under the equivalence relation $\sim_{G,2}$. We will say that an equivalence class in $\widetilde{\mathcal{F}_2}(G)$ is self-complementary whenever its members are. We can apply theorem 23 directly to the problem of counting self-complementary equivalence classes, obtaining the following corollary:

Corollary 13. The following problem is NP-hard for any polynomial q:

Input: A set of generators for a degree n permutation group G

Output: A quantity z that is within a factor of $q(n)$ of the number of self-complementary equivalence classes in $\widetilde{\mathcal{F}_2}(G)$.

Proof: By De Bruijn's theorem, the number of self-complementary equivalence classes in $\widetilde{\mathcal{F}_2}(G)$ is equal to $P_G(y_1, y_2, \ldots)$ where y_j is the number of objects $k \in \{1, 2\}$ that are fixed by $(1\,2)^j$. It is easy to see that $y_j = 0$ if j is an odd number and that $y_j = 2$ otherwise. Therefore, the number of self-complementary equivalence classes is $P_G(0, 2, 0, 2, \ldots)$. □

Corollaries 10— 13 relate the problem of evaluating the cycle index polynomial to the counting problems that are associated with $\widetilde{\mathcal{F}_m}$ and $\widetilde{\mathcal{F}_h}$. In the remainder of this section we will leave aside the counting problems and we will focus on the problem of evaluating the cycle index polynomial.

5.2.2. The Difficulty of Evaluating the Cycle Index Polynomial

In this subsection we focus on the computational difficulty of the problem *Cycle Index Evaluation*$(y_1, y_2, \ldots)$. We start with some observations that place upper bounds on the difficulty of the problem.

Observation 27.   Let $y_1, y_2, \ldots$ be a fixed sequence of non-negative rational numbers such that for every positive integer j we have $y_j = y_1^j$. Then $P_G(y_1, \ldots, y_n) = y_1^n$. Therefore, *Cycle Index Evaluation*$(y_1, y_2, \ldots)$ can be solved in polynomial time.

Observation 28.   Let $y_1, y_2, \ldots$ be a fixed sequence of non-negative rational numbers such that for every integer $j > 1$ we have $y_j = 0$. Then $P_G(y_1, \ldots, y_n) = y_1^n / |G|$. Therefore, *Cycle Index Evaluation*$(y_1, y_2, \ldots)$ can be solved in polynomial time.

Observation 29.   Let $y_1, y_2, \ldots$ be a fixed sequence of non-negative integers. The following problem is in #P.

Input: A set of generators for a degree n permutation group G.

Output: $\sum_{g \in G} y_1^{c_1(g)} \cdots y_n^{c_n(g)}$.

The main results of this subsection are theorems 21 and 22. We begin our presentation of these results by setting up the framework for the proof of theorem 21. Then we prove a slightly stronger version of theorem 21 than the version stated in the introduction to this section. Finally, we use the strengthened version of the theorem to prove theorem 22.

Suppose that p is a prime number, that k is a positive integer, and that i is an integer such that $i \not\equiv 0 \pmod{p}$. We use the notation $\Upsilon(i, p, k)$ to stand for the size of the set

$$\{ m \mid (0 \leq m < pk) \quad \text{and} \quad (m \equiv i \pmod{p}) \quad \text{and} \quad (\gcd(m, pk) = 1) \}.$$

We will use the following fact in the proof of theorem 21.

Fact 1.   Let p be a prime number. Let k be a positive integer and let i and j be integers such that $i \not\equiv 0 \pmod{p}$ and $j \not\equiv 0 \pmod{p}$. Then $\Upsilon(i, p, k) = \Upsilon(j, p, k) \neq 0$†.

Proof:

Let k' be the positive integer such that $k = p^\alpha k'$ for some $\alpha \geq 0$ and $\gcd(p, k') = 1$. Since the integers mod p form a field, there is a non-negative integer λ such that $0 \leq \lambda < p$ and $i + \lambda k' \equiv j \pmod{p}$.

---

† The author is grateful to Paul Goldberg for helping to prove this fact.

We use the notation $S_{i,p,k}$ to represent the set $\{[lp + i] \bmod pk \mid l \in \mathbb{N}\}$. Using this notation, we see that $\Upsilon(i, p, k) = |\{m \in S_{i,p,k} \mid \gcd(m, pk) = 1\}|$. Furthermore, $S_{j,p,k} = \{[lp + i + \lambda k'] \bmod pk \mid l \in \mathbb{N}\}$.

The equality of $\Upsilon(i, p, k)$ and $\Upsilon(j, p, k)$ follows from the fact that
$\gcd([lp + i] \bmod pk, pk) = \gcd(lp + i, pk) = \gcd(lp + i, k') = \gcd(lp + i + \lambda k', k') = \gcd([lp + i + \lambda k'] \bmod pk, pk)$.

The fact that $\Upsilon(i, p, k) \neq 0$ follows from the fact that $\Upsilon(1, p, k) \neq 0$. $\square$

We have now established the fact that the value of $\Upsilon(i, p, k)$ does not depend upon i (so long as $i \not\equiv 0 \pmod{p}$). Therefore, we will drop the parameter "i", and we will refer to $\Upsilon(p, k)$. Using fact 1, we can now prove theorem 21:

Theorem 21. Let $i > 1$ be a fixed positive integer. The following problem is #P-hard:

Cycle-Bounded Cycle Index Coefficient(i)

    Input: A set of generators for a permutation group G whose cycle bound is i, and whose degree, n, is a multiple of i.

    Output: The coefficient of $x_i^{n/i}$ in the cycle index polynomial of G.

As we pointed out in the introduction, the coefficient of $x_i^{n/i}$ in P_G is $1/|G|$ times the number of permutations in G that have n/i cycles of length i. Therefore, *Cycle-Bounded Cycle Index Coefficient(i)* is polynomially equivalent to the following problem:

    Input: A set of generators for a permutation group G whose cycle bound is i, and whose degree, n, is a multiple of i.

    Output: The number of permutations in G that have n/i cycles of length i.

The #P-hardness of this problem is established by considering three cases. Let p be a prime number and k be a positive integer such that $i = pk$. Lemma 22 establishes the #P-hardness of *Cycle-Bounded Cycle Index Coefficient(i)* for $p > 3$. Lemma 23 establishes the result for $p = 3$ and lemma 24 establishes the result for $p = 2$.

Lemma 22. Let $p > 3$ be a fixed prime and let k be any fixed positive integer. The following problem is #P-hard:

    Input: A set of generators for a permutation group G whose cycle bound is pk, and whose degree, n, is a multiple of pk.

    Output: The number of permutations in G that have n/pk cycles of length pk.

Proof: For any integer $l \geq 3$ the following problem is #P-hard [Edw 86]:

#Graph l-Colorability

Input: An undirected graph Γ

Output: The number of l-colorings† of Γ.

We will proceed by reduction from *#Graph $(p-1)$-Colorability*. Suppose that we have a graph Γ with vertex set $\{v_1, \ldots, v_\nu\}$ and edge set $\{e_1, \ldots, e_\mu\}$. We construct a permutation group G by using the following method.

1. For each vertex v_i, we introduce a set V_i of pk objects and a permutation g_{v_i} that cycles them.

2. For each edge e_j, we introduce a set E_j of pk objects and a permutation g_{e_j} that cycles them.

3. Let G be the group generated by the following three sets:

   i. $\bigcup_i \{g_{v_i}^p\}$

   ii. $\bigcup_j \{g_{e_j}^p\}$

   iii. $\{g_i \mid g_i = g_{v_i} g_{e_\alpha} g_{e_\beta} \cdots g_{e_a}^{-1} g_{e_b}^{-1}\}$

   where v_i is a vertex of Γ and it is the vertex of smaller index in edges $e_\alpha, e_\beta, \ldots$ and the vertex of larger index in edges $e_a, e_b, \ldots$

We claim that each $(p-1)$-coloring of Γ corresponds to a set of $\Upsilon(p,k)^{\nu+\mu}$ permutations in G, each of which has n/pk cycles of length pk. Furthermore, we claim that G has no other permutations that have n/pk cycles of length pk. We prove the claim in two steps.

1. Suppose that we have a $(p-1)$-coloring of Γ and let c_i denote the color of vertex v_i. Since $c_i \not\equiv 0 \pmod{p}$, we can use fact 1 to show that there are $\Upsilon(p,k)$ members of the set $\{[c_i + pl] \bmod pk \mid l \in \mathbb{N}\}$ that are relatively prime to pk. Therefore, the set $\{g_{v_i}^{c_i} g_{v_i}^{pl} \mid l \in \mathbb{N}\}$ contains $\Upsilon(p,k)$ permutations that are cycles of length pk.

Suppose that e_j is an edge in Γ whose smaller endpoint is colored with color c and whose larger endpoint is colored with a different color, d. The restriction of the permutation $g_1^{c_1} \cdots g_\nu^{c_\nu}$ to the objects in E_j is $g_{e_j}^{c-d}$. Since $c-d \not\equiv 0 \pmod{p}$ we can use fact 1 to show that the set $\{g_{e_j}^{c-d} g_{e_j}^{pl} \mid l \in \mathbb{N}\}$ contains $\Upsilon(p,k)$ permutations that are cycles of length pk.

Finally, we conclude that the set $\{\, g_1^{c_1} \cdots g_\nu^{c_\nu} g_{v_1}^{pl_1} \cdots g_{v_\nu}^{pl_\nu} g_{e_1}^{pl_1'} \cdots g_{e_\mu}^{pl_\mu'} \mid l_i, l_i' \in \mathbb{N} \,\}$ contains $\Upsilon(p,k)^{\nu+\mu}$ permutations which have n/pk cycles of length pk.

---

† An l-coloring of a graph is an assignment of a color from the set $\{1, \ldots, l\}$ to each vertex in the graph in such a way that no two adjacent vertices receive the same color.

2. Suppose that g is a permutation in G which has n/pk cycles of length pk. It is easy to see that we can rewrite g as $g_1^{c_1} \cdots g_\nu^{c_\nu} g_{v_1}^{pl_1} \cdots g_{v_\nu}^{pl_\nu} g_{e_1}^{pl'_1} \cdots g_{e_\mu}^{pl'_\mu}$ where $0 \le c_1, \ldots, c_\nu < p$ and $l_i, l_i' \in \mathbb{N}$. Since the restriction of g to the objects in V_i is a cycle of length pk, it must be the case that $c_i \ne 0$ for all i. Consider the function that assigns color c_i to vertex v_i for each i. We must show that this function is a coloring of Γ.

Suppose that there is an edge e_j whose vertices are both assigned the same color. Then the restriction of g to the objects in E_j is $g_{e_j}^{pl'_j}$. Now $\gcd(pl'_j, pk) \ne 1$. Therefore, the restriction of g to the objects in E_j is not a cycle of length pk, which is a contradiction. $\square$

Lemma 23. Let k be any fixed positive integer. The following problem is #P-hard:

Input: A set of generators for a permutation group G whose cycle bound is $3k$, and whose degree, n, is a multiple of $3k$.

Output: The number of permutations in G that have $n/3k$ cycles of length $3k$.

Proof:

This proof is very similar to the proof of lemma 22. We start by observing that the following problem is #P-hard: *#Not-All-Equal 3Sat*

Input: A Set U of Boolean variables and a collection C of clauses over U, each of which contains three literals.

Output: The number of assignments of truth values to the variables that have the property that the number of "true" literals in any given clause is either one or two.

To see that *#Not-All-Equal 3Sat* is #P-hard, recall that the following problem is #P-hard [Val 79].
#Monotone 2Sat

Input: A Set U of Boolean variables and a collection C of clauses over U, each of which contains two variables.

Output: The number of assignments of truth values to the variables that have the property that the number of "true" literals in any given clause is either one or two.

Let $\langle U, C \rangle$ be an input to *#Monotone 2Sat*. Let $U' = U \cup \{x\}$ for some variable x that is not in U and let $C' = \{c \cup \{x\} \mid c \in C\}$. The assignments of truth values to the variables in U that are counted in the output *#Monotone 2Sat(U, C)* are in one-to-one correspondence with the assignments of truth values to the variables in U' that are counted in *#Not-All-Equal 3Sat(U', C')* and have $x =$ "false". The result follows from the fact that $x =$ "false" in exactly half of the assignments that are counted in

#Not-All-Equal 3Sat(U', C'), which follows from the fact that the definition of the problem *#Not-All-Equal 3Sat* does not change if we substitute "false" for "true".

Now that we have established the #P-hardness of *#Not-All-Equal 3Sat*, we proceed by reduction from this problem. Suppose that we have a set $U = \{u_1, \ldots, u_\nu\}$ of variables and a collection $\{c_1, \ldots, c_\mu\}$ of clauses over U. We construct a permutation group G by using the following method.

1. For each variable u_i, we introduce a set U_i of $3k$ objects and a permutation g_{u_i} that cycles them.

2. For each clause c_j, we introduce a set C_j of $3k$ objects and a permutation g_{c_j} that cycles them.

3. Let G be the group generated by the following three sets:

   i. $\bigcup_i \{g_{u_i}^3\}$

   ii. $\bigcup_j \{g_{c_j}^3\}$

   iii. $\{g_i \mid g_i = g_{u_i} g_{c_\alpha} g_{c_\beta} \cdots g_{c_a}^{-1} g_{c_b}^{-1}\}$

   where u_i is a variable in U that occurs positively in clauses $c_\alpha, c_\beta, \ldots$ and negatively in clauses $c_a, c_b, \ldots$

We claim that each assignment of truth values to the variables in U that has the property that the number of "true" literals in any given clause in C is either one or two corresponds to a set of $\Upsilon(3, k)^{\nu+\mu}$ permutations in G, each of which has $n/3k$ cycles of length $3k$. Furthermore, we claim that G has no other permutations that have $n/3k$ cycles of length $3k$. We prove the claim in two steps.

1. Suppose that we have an assignment of truth values to the variables in U. Let t_i be 1 if the variable u_i is assigned the value "true" and -1 otherwise. Since $t_i \not\equiv 0 \pmod 3$ we can use fact 1 to show that the set $\{g_{u_i}^{t_i} g_{u_i}^{3l} \mid l \in \mathbb{N}\}$ contains $\Upsilon(3, k)$ permutations that are cycles of length $3k$.

Consider any clause c_j. If u_i or $\overline{u_i}$ is a "true" literal in c_j then the restriction of $g_i^{t_i}$ to the objects in C_j is g_{c_j}. If u_i or $\overline{u_i}$ is a "false" literal in c_j then the restriction of $g_i^{t_i}$ to the objects in C_j is $g_{c_j}^{-1}$.

Now, suppose that exactly one of the literals in c_j is "true". In this case the restriction of $g_1^{t_1} \cdots g_\nu^{t_\nu}$ to the objects in C_j is $g_{c_j}^{-1}$. Since $-1 \not\equiv 0 \pmod 3$ we can use fact 1 to show that the set $\{g_{c_j}^{-1} g_{c_j}^{3l} \mid l \in \mathbb{N}\}$ contains $\Upsilon(3, k)$ permutations that are cycles of length $3k$. Alternatively, suppose that exactly two of the literals in c_j are "true". In this case the restriction of $g_1^{t_1} \cdots g_\nu^{t_\nu}$ to the objects in C_j is g_{c_j}. Since $1 \not\equiv 0 \pmod 3$ we can use fact 1 to show that the set $\{g_{c_j} g_{c_j}^{3l} \mid l \in \mathbb{N}\}$ contains $\Upsilon(3, k)$ permutations that are cycles of length $3k$.

Finally, we conclude that the set $\{ g_1^{t_1} \cdots g_\nu^{t_\nu} g_{u_1}^{3l_1} \cdots g_{u_\nu}^{3l_\nu} g_{c_1}^{3l_1'} \cdots g_{c_\mu}^{3l_\mu'} \mid l_i, l_i{'} \in \mathbb{N} \}$ contains $\Upsilon(3, k)^{\nu+\mu}$ permutations which have $n/3k$ cycles of length $3k$.

2. Suppose that g is a permutation in G which has $n/3k$ cycles of length $3k$. It is easy to see that we can rewrite g as $g_1^{t_1} \cdots g_\nu^{t_\nu} g_{u_1}^{3l_1} \cdots g_{u_\nu}^{3l_\nu} g_{c_1}^{3l_1'} \cdots g_{c_\mu}^{3l_\mu'}$ where $t_1, \ldots, t_\nu \in \{-1, 0, 1\}$ and $l_i, l_i{'} \in \mathbb{N}$. Since the restriction of g to the objects in U_i is a cycle of length $3k$, it must be the case that $t_i \neq 0$ for all i. Consider the truth assignment that gives u_i the value "true" if t_i is 1 and "false" otherwise. We must show that one or two literals are "true" in any given clause.

Suppose that c_j is a clause with three "true" literals. Then the restriction of g to the objects in C_j is $g_{c_j}^{3+3l_j'}$. Since $\gcd(3+3l_j', 3k) \neq 1$, the restriction of g to the objects in C_j is not a cycle of length $3k$, which is a contradiction. Similarly, if C_j has three "false" literals then the restriction of g to the objects in C_j is $g_{c_j}^{-3+3l_j'}$. Since $\gcd(-3 + 3l_j', 3k) \neq 1$, the restriction of g to the objects in C_j is not a cycle of length $3k$. Once again, we get a contradiction. $\square$

Lemma 24. Let k be any fixed positive integer. The following problem is #P-hard:

Input: A set of generators for a permutation group G whose cycle bound is $2k$, and whose degree, n, is a multiple of $2k$.

Output: The number of permutations in G that have $n/2k$ cycles of length $2k$.

Proof: Lubiw's proof that *#Fixed-Point-Free Automorphism* is #P-hard† [Lub 81] establishes the lemma for the case $k = 1$. Following Lubiw, we proceed by reduction from the following #P-hard problem [Val 79]:

#Satisfiability

Input: A Set U of Boolean variables and a collection C of clauses over U, each of which contains three literals.

Output: The number of assignments of truth values to the variables that have the property that each clause has at least one "true" literal.

Our clause checker will be a generalization of Lubiw's, so we use the following gadget (which was used in her paper).

---

† Since every permutation in Lubiw's group has cycle bound 2, her proof actually shows that *Cycle Index Evaluation*$(y_1, y_2, \ldots)$ is #P-hard whenever $y_1 = 0$ and $y_2 \neq 0$.

Gadget 1.   Let H be the group of permutations of $\{1, \ldots, 8\}$ that is generated by

$$h[1] = (1\ 2)(3\ 4)(5\ 6)(7\ 8)$$

$$h[2] = (1\ 3)(2\ 4)(5\ 7)(6\ 8)$$

$$h[3] = (1\ 5)(2\ 6)(3\ 7)(4\ 8)$$

This group is commutative.   Therefore, $H = \{h[1]^i h[2]^j h[3]^k \mid i, j, k \in \{0, 1\}\}$. Every member of H except the identity is the product of four transpositions $(i_1\ i_2)(i_3\ i_4)(i_5\ i_6)(i_7\ i_8)$ where $i_1, \ldots, i_8$ is a permutation of $1, \ldots, 8$.

In order to generalize to the case $k > 1$, we need an additional gadget.

Gadget 2.

Let S_l be a set of k objects $S_l[1], \ldots, S_l[k]$.

Let S_m be a set of k objects $S_m[1], \ldots, S_m[k]$.

Let $Swap(lm)$ represent the permutation $(S_l[1]\ S_m[1]) \cdots (S_l[k]\ S_m[k])$.

Let $Cycle(l)$ represent the permutation $(S_l[1] \cdots S_l[k])$.

It is easy to prove the following identity†.

$$Cycle(m)Swap(lm) = Swap(lm)Cycle(l) = (S_m[1]\ S_l[1] \cdots S_m[k]\ S_l[k]).$$

Let J' be the group $\langle Cycle(l), Cycle(m)\rangle$‡ and let $J = \langle Swap(lm), Cycle(l), Cycle(m)\rangle$. Using the identity, it is easy to see that $J = J' \cup \{Swap(lm)\lambda \mid \lambda \in J'\}$. Clearly, J' has no cycle of length $2k$. We know from the identity that at least one member of J is a cycle of length $2k$, however. Let $\Upsilon(k)$ denote the number of members of J that are cycles of length $2k$.

We are now ready to proceed. Suppose that we have a set $U = \{u_1, \ldots, u_\nu\}$ of variables and a collection $\{c_1, \ldots, c_\mu\}$ of clauses over U. We construct a permutation group G by using the following method.

1. For each variable u_i, we introduce a set U_i of $2k$ objects and a permutation g_{u_i} that cycles them.

2. For each clause c_j, we introduce eight sets of objects, $C_{j1}, \ldots, C_{j8}$.   Each set C_{jl} contains k objects, $C_{jl}[1], \ldots, C_{jl}[k]$. Using the notation that we defined in our description of gadget 2, we let $Swap_j(lm)$ represent the permutation $(C_{jl}[1]\ C_{jm}[1]) \cdots (C_{jl}[k]\ C_{jm}[k])$ and we let $Cycle_j(l)$ represent the permutation $(C_{jl}[1] \cdots C_{jl}[k])$. We introduce three permutations:

---

† Note that permutations are being composed from right to left.

‡ Recall that the notation $\langle g_1, g_2, \ldots \rangle$ represents the group generated by $g_1, g_2, \ldots$

$$h_j[1] = Swap_j(12)Swap_j(34)Swap_j(56)Swap_j(78)$$
$$h_j[2] = Swap_j(13)Swap_j(24)Swap_j(57)Swap_j(68)$$
$$h_j[3] = Swap_j(15)Swap_j(26)Swap_j(37)Swap_j(48)$$

3. Let G' be the group generated by $\bigcup_j \{Cycle_j(1), \ldots, Cycle_j(8)\}$.

4. Let G be the group generated by the following four sets:

   i. $\bigcup_i \{g_{u_i}^2\}$

   ii. $\{\lambda \mid \lambda \in G'\}$

   iii. $\{\pi_i \mid \pi_i = g_{u_i} h_j[1] h_k[1] \cdots h_l[2] h_m[2] \cdots h_y[3] h_z[3] \cdots\}$

   where u_i occurs in position 1 in clauses $c_j, c_k, \ldots$ and in position 2 in clauses $c_l, c_m, \ldots$ and in position 3 in clauses $c_y, c_z, \ldots$

   iv. $\{\rho_i \mid \rho_i = g_{u_i} h_j[1] h_k[1] \cdots h_l[2] h_m[2] \cdots h_y[3] h_z[3] \cdots\}$

   where $\overline{u_i}$ occurs in position 1 in clauses $c_j, c_k, \ldots$ and in position 2 in clauses $c_l, c_m, \ldots$ and in position 3 in clauses $c_y, c_z, \ldots$

We claim that each assignment of truth values to the variables in U which has the property that each clause has at least one "true" literal corresponds to a set of $\Upsilon(2, k)^\nu \Upsilon(k)^{4\mu}$ permutations in G, each of which has $n/2k$ cycles of length $2k$. Furthermore, we claim that G has no other permutations that have $n/2k$ cycles of length $2k$. We prove the claim in two steps.

1. Suppose that we have an assignment of truth values to the variables in U. Let g_i denote π_i if the variable u_i is assigned the value "true" and let g_i denote ρ_i otherwise. The restriction of g_i to the objects in U_i is g_{u_i}. Since $1 \not\equiv 0 \pmod 2$ we can use fact 1 to show that the set $\{g_{u_i} g_{u_i}^{2l} \mid l \in \mathbb{N}\}$ contains $\Upsilon(2, k)$ permutations that are cycles of length $2k$.

Let g be $g_1 \cdots g_\nu$. Consider any clause c_j and let g_j' denote the restriction of g to the objects associated with c_j. By construction, $h_j[t]$ is a factor of g_j' if and only if the tth literal in c_j has been assigned the value "true". Suppose that at least one of the literals in c_j is "true". Our consideration of gadget 1 shows that $g_j' = Swap_j(i_1, i_2)Swap_j(i_3, i_4)Swap_j(i_5, i_6)Swap_j(i_7, i_8)$ where $i_1, \ldots, i_8$ is a permutation of $1, \ldots, 8$. If we consider one of the four factors $Swap_j(i_l, i_m)$ and the permutations $Cycle_j(i_l)$ and $Cycle_j(i_m)$ then we can use our analysis of gadget 2 to show that the set $\{Swap_j(i_l, i_m)\lambda \mid \lambda \in \langle Cycle_j(i_l), Cycle_j(i_m)\rangle\}$ has $\Upsilon(k)$ permutations which are cycles of length $2k$. Therefore, the set $\{g_j'\lambda \mid \lambda \in \langle Cycle_j(1), \ldots, Cycle_j(8)\rangle\}$ has $\Upsilon(k)^4$ permutations which are cycles of length $2k$.

Finally, we conclude that the set $\{\, g_1 \cdots g_\nu g_{u_1}^{2l_1} \cdots g_{u_\nu}^{2l_\nu} \lambda \mid l_i \in \mathbb{N},\, \lambda \in G' \,\}$ contains $\Upsilon(2,k)^\nu \Upsilon(k)^{4\mu}$ permutations which have $n/2k$ cycles of length $2k$.

2. Suppose that g is a permutation in G with cycles of length $2k$. It is easy to see that we can re-write g as $\pi_1^{t_1} \rho_1^{f_1} \cdots \pi_\nu^{t_\nu} \rho_\nu^{f_\nu} g_{u_1}^{2l_1} \cdots g_{u_\nu}^{2l_\nu} \lambda$ where $t_i, f_i \in \{0,1\}$, $l_i \in \mathbb{N}$, and $\lambda \in G'$. Since the restriction of g to the objects in U_i is a cycle of length $2k$, it must be the case that one of t_i, f_i is 1 and the other is 0 for each i. Consider the truth assignment that gives u_i the value "true" if t_i is 1 and "false" otherwise. We must show that each clause contains at least one "true" literal.

Suppose that c_j is a clause with no "true" literals. Then none of $h_j[1], \ldots, h_j[3]$ is a factor of g. Therefore, the restriction of g to the objects associated with c_j is not a cycle of length $2k$, which is a contradiction. □

Having completed the proof of theorem 21, we use it to prove the following theorem.

Theorem 22. If $y_1, y_2, \ldots$ is a sequence of non-negative rational numbers and there exists an i such that $y_i \neq y_1^i$ and $y_i \neq 0$ then *Cycle Index Evaluation*$(y_1, y_2, \ldots)$ is #P-hard†.

Proof: First, suppose that $y_1 = 0$. Choose the index i such that for all $j < i$ we have $y_j = 0$ and $y_i \neq 0$. If G is a permutation group whose cycle bound is i and whose degree, n, is a multiple of i then the coefficient of $x_i^{n/i}$ in P_G is $|G|\, y_i^{-n/i} P_G(y_1, \ldots, y_n)$ so the result follows from theorem 21.

Otherwise, choose the index i such that for every $j < i$ either $y_j = 0$ or $y_j = y_1^j$ but $y_i \neq 0$ and $y_i \neq y_1^i$. Let $\widehat{G}$ stand for the set

$$\widehat{G} = \{g \in G \mid g \text{ has no cycle whose length is a member of } \{j \mid y_j = 0\}\}.$$

Let $P'_{G,i}$ be the single-variable polynomial defined by $P'_{G,i}(z) = \frac{1}{|G|} \sum_{g \in \widehat{G}} z^{c_i(g)}$. If G is a permutation group whose degree, n, is a multiple of i then the coefficient of $z^{n/i}$ in $P'_{G,i}$ is the same as the coefficient of $x_i^{n/i}$ in P_G. Furthermore, we claim that if G has cycle bound i then $P_G(y_1, \ldots, y_n) = y_1{}^n P'_{G,i}(y_i/y_1{}^i)$.

Suppose that the claim is true. Suppose further that we could compute the values $P_{G[ID_l]}(y_1, \ldots, y_n) = P_G(y_1^l, \ldots, y_n^l)$ for $1 \leq l \leq n+1$. Then we would be able to evaluate $P'_{G,i}$ at the $n+1$ points $z = (y_i/y_1{}^i)^l$ for $1 \leq l \leq n+1$. (Note that $y_i/y_1{}^i \neq 1$ and that $y_i/y_1{}^i \neq 0$.) We could interpolate to get the coefficient of $z^{n/i}$ in $P'_{G,i}$ which is the

---

† The author is grateful to an anonymous referee for finding an error in the original proof of this theorem.

coefficient of $x_i^{n/i}$ in P_G. The theorem follows from the proof of the claim (which will be given below) and from the #P-hardness of *Cycle-Bounded Cycle Index Coefficient(i)*, which was established in theorem 21.

To prove the claim we must show that $P_G(y_1, \ldots, y_n) = y_1{}^n P'_{G,i}(y_i/y_1{}^i)$. Since the cycle bound of G is i the value of $P_G(y_1, \ldots, y_n)$ can be written as

$$P_G(y_1, \ldots, y_n) = \frac{1}{|G|} \sum_{g \in G} y_i{}^{c_i(g)} \prod_{1 \le j < i} y_j{}^{c_j(g)}.$$

Note that we can restrict the summation to permutations $g \in \widehat{G}$ since all of the terms which are eliminated by this restriction are equal to zero. Using the fact that $0^{c_j(g)} = y_1^{j c_j(g)}$ when $c_j(g) = 0$ we can replace the right hand side with

$$P_G(y_1, \ldots, y_n) = \frac{1}{|G|} \sum_{g \in \widehat{G}} y_i{}^{c_i(g)} \prod_{1 \le j < i} y_1{}^{j c_j(g)}.$$

Since $\sum_{j=1}^{i} j c_j(g) = n$ we get

$$P_G(y_1, \ldots, y_n) = \frac{1}{|G|} \sum_{g \in \widehat{G}} y_i{}^{c_i(g)} y_1{}^{n - i c_i(g)}.$$

Simplifying the right hand side we get

$$P_G(y_1, \ldots, y_n) = \frac{y_1^n}{|G|} \sum_{g \in \widehat{G}} \left(y_i/y_1{}^i\right)^{c_i(g)} = y_1{}^n P'_{G,i}(y_i/y_1{}^i) \;\; \square$$

5.2.3. The Difficulty of Approximately Evaluating the Cycle Index Polynomial

In this subsection we focus on the computational difficulty of *Cycle Index Approximation*$(q, y_1, y_2, \ldots)$. We start with the following lemma.

Lemma 25. Let $i > 1$ be a fixed positive integer. The following problem is NP-hard:

Cycles-of-Length(i)

> Input: A set of generators for a permutation group G whose cycle bound is i, and whose degree, n, is a multiple of i.

> Output: "Yes", if G has a permutation that has n/i cycles of length i. "No", otherwise.

Proof: It is known [GJ 79] that it is NP-hard to decide, given an input for *#Graph l-Colorability*, *#Not-All-Equal 3Sat*, or *#Satisfiability*, whether the corresponding output is zero. Therefore, the lemma follows from the proof of theorem 21. □

Using this lemma, it is easy to prove theorem 23.

Theorem 23. Let $y_1, y_2, \ldots$ be a fixed sequence of non-negative rational numbers. If there exists an i such that $y_i > y_1^i$ then *Cycle Index Approximation*$(q, y_1, y_2, \ldots)$ is NP-hard for every polynomial q.

Proof: Choose the index i such that $\forall j < i \,.\, y_j \leq y_1^j$ and $y_i > y_1^i$. Let G be any input to *Cycles-of-Length*(i) and let n be the degree of G. We make the following observations:

1. If G has a permutation that decomposes $\{1, \ldots, n\}$ into n/i cycles of length i then
$$P_G(y_1, \ldots, y_n) \geq |G|^{-1} y_i^{n/i}.$$

2. Otherwise, $P_G(y_1, \ldots, y_n) \leq y_i^{n/i-1} y_1^i$.

Let r be a polynomial and recall that $P_G(y_1^{r(n)}, \ldots, y_n^{r(n)}) = P_{G[ID_{r(n)}]}(y_1, \ldots, y_n)$. Using observations 1 and 2, we conclude:

1. If *Cycles-of-Length*$(i)(G)$ is "Yes", then $P_{G[ID_{r(n)}]}(y_1, \ldots, y_n) \geq |G|^{-1} y_i^{r(n) \times n/i}$.

2. Otherwise, $P_{G[ID_{r(n)}]}(y_1, \ldots, y_n) \leq |G|^{-1} y_i^{r(n) \times n/i} \times [y_1^i/y_i]^{r(n)} |G|$.

To establish the theorem, we need only choose the polynomial r in such a way that $[y_1^i/y_i]^{r(n)} |G|$ is exponentially small. □

We mentioned in the introduction to this section that it is difficult to determine the computational complexity of *Cycle Index Approximation*$(q, y_1, y_2, \ldots)$ when $y_1, y_2, \ldots$ is a fixed sequence such that $y_j \leq y_1^j$ for all j and for some i it is the case that $y_i < y_1^i$. We consider the special case in which $y_1 = y_2 = \cdots = y$ for some positive rational number y and we obtain the following theorem.

Theorem 24. [Goldberg, Jerrum] If y is a positive rational number that is not an integer then *Cycle Index Approximation*$(q, y, y, \ldots)$ is NP-hard for every polynomial q.

Before proving theorem 24, we set up the framework for the proof. Let S_l stand for the symmetric group of degree l and let A_l stand for the alternating group of degree l. Define the polynomials $f_{C,l}$ and $f_{A,l}$ as follows: $f_{C,l}(x) = \sum_{g \in S_l - A_l} x^{c(g)}$ and $f_{A,l}(x) = \sum_{g \in A_l} x^{c(g)}$. We will use the following fact:

Fact 2. Suppose that y is a positive rational number that is not an integer and that $l = \lceil y \rceil + 1$. Then $f_{C,l}(y) > f_{A,l}(y)$.

Proof: Let $f_l(x) = f_{A,l}(x) - f_{C,l}(x)$. It is easy to see that the coefficient of x^l in $f_{A,l}$ is 1 and that the degree of $f_{A,l}$ is l. The degree of $f_{C,l}$ is less than l. Therefore, f_l is a degree l polynomial and for big enough values of i, $f_l(i)$ is positive. Suppose that i is an integer such that $0 \leq i < l$. We claim that $f_l(i) = 0$. (To see that the claim is correct, use Pólya's theorem to show that $P_{S_l}(i) = P_{A_l}(i)$ for every integer i such that $0 \leq i < l$. Then use the definition of the cycle index polynomial, observing that $|S_l| = 2 \times |A_l|$.) Since a degree l polynomial has at most l zeros, we conclude that $f_l(i)$ is negative in the range $l-2 < i < l-1$, which establishes the fact. □

Using fact 2, it is not hard to prove theorem 24.

Proof of Theorem 24: Suppose that y is a positive rational number that is not an integer and let $l = \lceil y \rceil + 1$. Fact 2 shows that $f_{C,l}(y) > f_{A,l}(y)$. Let r be a polynomial such that $[f_{A,l}(y)/f_{C,l}(y)]^{r(\nu)} 2^{\nu}$ is exponentially small (as a function of ν). We proceed by reduction from the following NP-hard problem [GJ 79]:

Simple Max Cut

Input: A connected graph Γ and a positive integer k.

Output: "Yes", if Γ has a cut-set† whose size is at least k. "No", otherwise.

Suppose that we have a graph Γ with vertex set $\{v_1, \ldots, v_\nu\}$ and edge set $\{e_1, \ldots, e_\mu\}$. We construct a permutation group G using the following method:

1. For each edge e_j, we introduce $r(\nu)$ sets of objects, $E_j[1], \ldots, E_j[r(\nu)]$. Each set $E_j[\kappa]$ contains l objects. We use the notation $A_j[\kappa]$ to stand for the alternating group of degree l acting on the objects in $E_j[\kappa]$.

2. For each vertex v_i, we let g_{v_i} be the permutation which transposes the first two objects in each set $E_j[\kappa]$ such that e_j is incident on v_i and $1 \leq \kappa \leq r(\nu)$.

3. Let G' be the group generated by $\{\lambda \in A_j[\kappa] \mid 1 \leq j \leq \mu, 1 \leq \kappa \leq r(\nu)\}$.

4. Let G be the group generated by $\{g_{v_i} \mid 1 \leq i \leq \nu\} \cup \{\lambda \mid \lambda \in G'\}$.

Each permutation $g \in G$ corresponds to exactly one (unordered) partition (S, T) of the vertices in Γ and to one permutation $\lambda \in G'$. g can be written as $\prod_{v_i \in S} g_{v_i} \lambda$ and as $\prod_{v_i \in T} g_{v_i} \lambda$. We associate g with the cut-set (S, T). Consider an edge e_j with endpoints v_α and v_β and let $g_{j,\kappa}$ be the restriction of g to the objects in $E_j[\kappa]$. It is easy to see that $g_{j,\kappa} \in S_l - A_l$ if exactly one of v_α, v_β is in S and that $g_{j,\kappa} \in A_l$ otherwise. That is, $g_{j,\kappa} \in S_l - A_l$ if e_j spans the two subsets of the cut-set that is associated with g and $g_{j,\kappa} \in A_l$ otherwise.

---

† A size k cut-set of Γ is a partition of the vertices of Γ into two disjoint (and indistinguishable) subsets such that the number of edges which span the two subsets is k.

Let (S, T) be a cut-set of Γ and let $G(S, T)$ stand for the set of permutations in G that are associated with the cut-set (S, T). Suppose that the size of the cut-set (S, T) is k. It is not difficult to see that $\sum_{g \in G(S,T)} x^{c(g)} = f_{C,l}(x)^{r(\nu)k} f_{A,l}(x)^{r(\nu)(\mu-k)}$.

We make the following observations:

1. If Γ has a cut-set (S, T) whose size, k', is at least k, then

$$P_G(y, \ldots, y) \geq |G|^{-1} f_{C,l}(y)^{r(\nu)k'} f_{A,l}(y)^{r(\nu)(\mu-k')}.$$

Fact 2 shows that $f_{C,l}(y) > f_{A,l}(y)$. Therefore,

$$P_G(y, \ldots, y) \geq |G|^{-1} f_{C,l}(y)^{r(\nu)k} f_{A,l}(y)^{r(\nu)(\mu-k)}.$$

2. If Γ does not have a cut-set whose size is at least k, then

$$P_G(y, \ldots, y) \leq 2^{\nu} |G|^{-1} f_{C,l}(y)^{r(\nu)(k-1)} f_{A,l}(y)^{r(\nu)(\mu-k+1)}$$
$$= |G|^{-1} f_{C,l}(y)^{r(\nu)k} f_{A,l}(y)^{r(\nu)(\mu-k)} \times [f_{A,l}(y)/f_{C,l}(y)]^{r(\nu)} 2^{\nu}.$$

The proof is concluded by observing that we have chosen the polynomial r in such a way that $[f_{A,l}(y)/f_{C,l}(y)]^{r(\nu)} 2^{\nu}$ is exponentially small. (We chose r so that the relevant quantity was exponentially small as a function of ν. By construction, it is also exponentially small as a function of the degree of G.) □

As we pointed out in the introduction to this section, our proof of theorem 24 says nothing about the difficulty of *Cycle Index Approximation*$(q, y, y, \ldots)$ when y is an *integer*. Furthermore, it is the *integer* values of y for which $P_G(y, \ldots, y)$ has a combinatorial meaning. It is an interesting open problem to determine the computational difficulty of *Cycle Index Approximation*$(q, y_1, y_2, \ldots)$ when $y_j \leq y_1^{j}$ for all j and there exists an i such that $y_i < y_1^{i}$. It would also be interesting to determine the difficulty of *Cycle Index Approximation*$(q, y, y, \ldots)$ for integer values of y.

6. Bibliography

[AHU 74]   A. V. Aho, J. E. Hopcroft, and J. D. Ullman, *The Design and Analysis of Computer Algorithms* (Addison-Wesley, 1974).

[BK 79]   L. Babai and L. Kučera, Canonical Labelling of Graphs in Linear Average Time, *Proc. IEEE Symp. on Foundations of Computer Science* **20** (1979) 39–46.

[BH 80]   T. Beyer and S. M. Hedetniemi, Constant Time Generation of Rooted Trees, *SIAM Journal of Computing* **9(4)** (1980) 706–712.

[BvL 87]   G. J. Bezem and J. van Leeuwen, Enumeration in Graphs, Technical Report RU-CS-87-7 Rijksuniversiteit Utrecht, The Netherlands, 1987.

[BW 79]   N. L. Biggs and A. T. White *Permutation Groups and Combinatorial Structures* (Cambridge University Press, 1979).

[BH 79]   A. Blass and F. Harary, Properties of Almost all Graphs and Complexes, *Journal of Graph Theory* **3** (1979) 225–240.

[Bol 85]   B. Bollobás, *Random Graphs* (Academic Press, 1985).

[Bol 88]   B. Bollobás, The Chromatic Number of Random Graphs, *Combinatorica* **8(1)** (1988) 49–55.

[BFF 85]   B. Bollobás, T. I. Fenner, and A. M. Frieze, An Algorithm for Finding Hamilton Cycles in a Random Graph, *Proc. ACM Symp. On Theory of Computing* **17** (1985) 430–439.

[BFP 89]   C. A. Brown, L. Finkelstein, and P. W. Purdom Jr., Backtrack Searching in the Presence of Symmetry, Pre-print (1989) Submitted to *Journal of the ACM*.

[Bre 72]   M. A. Breuer, *Design Automation of Digital Systems — Theory and Techniques,* Volume 1, Chapter 2 (Prentice-Hall, 1972).

[Chr 75]   N. Christofides, *Graph Theory: An Algorithmic Approach* (Academic Press, 1975).

[CDN 89]   C. J. Colbourn, R. P. J. Day, and L. D. Nel, Unranking and Ranking Spanning Trees of a Graph, *Journal of Algorithms* **10** (1989) 271–286.

[CR1 79]   C. J. Colbourn and R. C. Read, Orderly Algorithms for Generating Restricted Classes of Graphs, *Journal of Graph Theory* **3** (1979) 187–195.

[CR2 79]   C. J. Colbourn and R. C. Read, Orderly Algorithms for Graph Genera-
           tion, *International Journal of Computer Mathematics, Section A* **7** (1979)
           167–172.

[CLR 90]   T. H. Cormen, C. E. Leiserson, and R. L. Rivest, *Introduction to Algorithms*
           (MIT Press, 1990).

[DeB 63]   N. G. De Bruijn, Enumerative Combinatorial Problems Concerning Struc-
           tures, *Nieuw Archief voor Wiskunde* **3, XI** (1963) 142–161.

[DeB 64]   N. G. De Bruijn, Pólya's Theory of Counting, *Applied Combinatorial Math-
           ematics* (Beckenbach, E. F., Ed.), (John Wiley and Sons, Inc. 1964).

[DW 83]   J. D. Dixon and H. S. Wilf, The Random Selection of Unlabeled Graphs,
           Journal of Algorithms **4** (1983) 205–213.

[DF 89]   M. E. Dyer and A. M. Frieze, The Solution of Some Random NP-Hard
           Problems in Polynomial Expected Time, *Journal of Algorithms* **10** (1989)
           451–489.

[Edw 86]   K. Edwards, The Complexity of Colouring Problems on Dense Graphs,
           Theoretical Computer Science **43** (1986) 337–343.

[Fag 76]   R. Fagin, Probabilities on Finite Models, *Journal of Symbolic Logic* **41(1)**
           (1976) 50–58.

[FGJS 89] R. J. Faudree, R. J. Gould, M. S. Jacobson, and R. H. Schelp, Neighborhood
           Unions and Hamiltonian Properties in Graphs, *Journal of Combinatorial
           Theory, Series B* **47** (1989) 1–9.

[Fel 68]   W. Feller, *An Introduction to Probability Theory and its Applications* Third
           Edition, Volume **1** (John Wiley and Sons, 1968).

[FHL 80]   M. Furst, J. Hopcroft, and E. Luks, Polynomial-Time Algorithms for Per-
           mutation Groups, *Proc. IEEE Symp. on Foundations of Computer Science*
           21 (1980) 36–41.

[GJ 79]   M. R. Garey and D. S. Johnson, *Computers and Intractability: A Guide to
           the Theory of NP-Completeness*, (W. H. Freedman and Company, 1979).

[Gib 85]   A. Gibbons, *Algorithmic Graph Theory* (Cambridge University Press,
           1985).

[Gil 77]   J. Gill, Computational Complexity of Probabilistic Turing Machines, *SIAM
           Journal of Computing* **6** (1977) 675–695.

[Gol1 90]   L. A. Goldberg, Efficient Algorithms for Listing Unlabeled Graphs, Internal Report CSR-7-90 Department of Computer Science, University of Edinburgh, May 1990, to appear, *Journal of Algorithms*.

[Gol2 90]   L. A. Goldberg, Automating Pólya Theory: The Computational Complexity of the Cycle Index Polynomial, Internal Report CSR-8-90 Department of Computer Science, University of Edinburgh, October 1990, to appear, *Information and Computation*.

[GM 75]   G. R. Grimmett and C. J. H. McDiarmid, On Colouring Random Graphs, *Math. Proc. Camb. Phil. Soc.* **77** (1975) 313–324.

[HR 90]   T. Hagerup and C. Rüb, A Guided Tour of Chernoff Bounds, *Information Processing Letters* **33** (February 1990) 305–308.

[HP 73]   F. Harary and E. M. Palmer, *Graphical Enumeration*, (Academic Press, 1973).

[HY 84]   J. Hartmanis and Y. Yesha, Computation Times of NP Sets of Different Densities, *Theoretical Computer Science* **34** (1984) 17–32.

[HHSY 91]   L. A. Hemachandra, A. Hoene, D. Siefkes, and P. Young, On Sets Polynomially Enumerable by Iteration, *Theoretical Computer Science* **80** (1991) 203–225.

[Hof 82]   C. M. Hoffmann, *Group-Theoretic Algorithms and Graph Isomorphism* Lecture Notes in Computer Science **136** (Springer-Verlag, 1982).

[HU 79]   J. E. Hopcroft and J. D. Ullman, *Introduction to Automata Theory, Languages, and Computation* (Addison-Wesley, 1979).

[Imm 87]   N. Immerman, Languages that Capture Complexity Classes, *SIAM Journal of Computing* **16(4)** (1987) 760–778.

[Jer 86]   M. R. Jerrum, A Compact Representation for Permutation Groups, *Journal of Algorithms* **7** (1986) 60–78.

[Jer 90]   M. R. Jerrum, The Elusiveness of Large Cliques in a Random Graph, Internal Report CSR-9-90 University of Edinburgh Department of Computer Science 1990.

[JMS 89]   M. R. Jerrum, B. D. McKay, and A. J. Sinclair, When is a Graphical Sequence Stable?, Internal Report CSR-309-89 University of Edinburgh Department of Computer Science 1989. (To Appear in the Proceedings of *Random Graphs* 1989.)

[JS 90]   M. R. Jerrum and A. J. Sinclair, Fast Uniform Generation of Regular Graphs, *Theoretical Computer Science* **73** (1990) 91–100.

[JVV 86]   M. R. Jerrum, L. G. Valiant, and V. V. Vazirani, Random Generation of Combinatorial Structures From a Uniform Distribution, *Theoretical Computer Science* **43** (1986) 169–188.

[Joh 75]   D. B. Johnson, Finding All the Elementary Circuits of a Directed Graph, *SIAM Journal of Computing* **4(1)** (1975) 77–84.

[JYP 88]   D. S. Johnson, M. Yannakakis, and C. H. Papadimitriou, On Generating all Maximal Independent Sets, *Information Processing Letters* **27** (March 1988) 119–123.

[Knu 73]   D. E. Knuth, *Fundamental Algorithms* The Art of Computer Programming Volume 1 Second Edition (Addison-Wesley, 1973).

[Kuč 89]   L. Kučera, Graphs with Small Chromatic Numbers are Easy to Color, *Information Processing Letters* **30** (1989) 233–236.

[Law 76]   E. L. Lawler, A Note on the Complexity of the Chromatic Number Problem, *Information Processing Letters* **5(3)** (1976) 66–67.

[LLR 80]   E. L. Lawler, J. K. Lenstra, and A. H. G. Rinnooy Kan, Generating all Maximal Independent Sets: NP-Hardness and Polynomial-Time Algorithms, *SIAM Journal of Computing* **9(3)** (1980) 558–565.

[Led 73]   W. Ledermann, *Introduction to Group Theory*, (Oliver & Boyd, 1973).

[Lub 81]   A. Lubiw, Some NP-Complete Problems Similar to Graph Isomorphism, *SIAM Journal of Computing* **10(1)** (1981) 11–21.

[Luk 82]   E. M. Luks, Isomorphism of Graphs of Bounded Valence can be Tested in Polynomial Time, *Journal of Computer and System Sciences* **25** (1982) 42–65.

[McD 79]   C. McDiarmid, Colouring Random Graphs Badly, *Graph Theory and Combinatorics* (Wilson, R. J., Ed.), Pitman Research Notes in Mathematics 34 (1979) 76–86.

[MR 86]   B. D. McKay and G. F. Royle, Constructing the Cubic Graphs on Up to 20 Vertices, *ARS Combinatoria* **21-A** (1986) 129–140.

[NW 78]   A. Nijenhuis and H. S. Wilf, *Combinatorial Algorithms for Computers and Calculators, Second Ed.* (Academic Press, 1978).

[Obe 83]   W. Oberschelp, Fast Parallel Algorithms for Finding All Prime Implicants
            for Discrete Functions, In E. Börger, G. Hasenjaeger, and D. Rödding, edit-
            ors, *Logic and Machines: Decision Problems and Complexity* (Proceedings
            of the Symposium "Recursive Kombinatorik") Lecture Notes in Computer
            Science **171** (Springer-Verlag, 1983) 408–420.

[Pal 70]   E. M. Palmer, Asymptotic Formulas For the Number of Self-Complementary
            Graphs and Digraphs, *Mathematika* **17** (1970) 85–90.

[PR 87]   G. Pólya and R. C. Read, *Combinatorial Enumeration of Groups, Graphs,
            and Chemical Compounds* (Springer-Verlag, 1987).

[Rag 88]   P. Raghavan, Probabilistic Construction of Deterministic Algorithms: Ap-
            proximate Packing Integer Programs, *Journal of Computer and System
            Sciences* **37** (1988) 130–143.

[Rea 63]   R. C. Read, On the Number of Self-Complementary Graphs and Digraphs,
            Journal of the London Mathematical Society **38** (1963) 99–104.

[Rea 78]   R. C. Read, Everyone a Winner or How to Avoid Isomorphism When Cata-
            loguing Combinatorial Configurations, *Annals of Discrete Mathematics* **2**
            (1978) 107–120.

[Rea 81]   R. C. Read, A Survey of Graph Generation Techniques, *Combinatorial
            Mathematics, VIII* Lecture Notes in Mathematics **884** (Springer, 1981)
            77–89.

[RT 75]   R. C. Read and R. E. Tarjan, Bounds on Backtrack Algorithms for Listing
            Cycles, Paths, and Spanning Trees, *Networks* **5** (1975) 237–252.

[Rob 84]   J. M. Robson, N By N Checkers is EXPTIME Complete, *SIAM Journal
            of Computing* **13(2)** (1984) 252–267.

[Ruc 87]   A. Ruciński, Induced Subgraphs in a Random Graph, *Annals of Discrete
            Mathematics* **33** (1987) 275–296.

[RH 77]   F. Ruskey and T. C. Hu, Generating Binary Trees Lexicographically, *SIAM
            Journal of Computing* **6(4)** (1977) 745–758.

[Sch 76]   C. P. Schnorr, Optimal Algorithms for Self-Reducible Problems, *Proc. In-
            ternational Colloquium on Automata Theory, Languages, and Programming*
            3 (1976) 322–337.

[Sim 77]   J. Simon, On the Difference Between One and Many, *Proc. International
            Colloquium on Automata Theory, Languages, and Programming* **4** Lecture
            Notes in Computer Science **52** (Springer-Verlag, 1977) 480–491.

[Sin 88]   A. J. Sinclair, Randomized Algorithms for Counting and Generating Combinatorial Structures, PhD Thesis CST–58–88, Department of Computer Science, University of Edinburgh, November 1988.

[Spe 87]   J. Spencer, *Ten Lectures on the Probabilistic Method* (SIAM, 1987).

[SW 86]   D. Stanton and D. White, *Constructive Combinatorics* Undergraduate Texts in Mathematics (Springer-Verlag, 1986).

[Tar 73]   R. Tarjan, Enumeration of the Elementary Circuits of a Directed Graph, *SIAM Journal of Computing* **2(3)** (1973) 211–216.

[TIAS 77]   S. Tsukiyama, M. Ide, H. Ariyoshi, and I. Shirakawa, A New Algorithm for Generating all the Maximal Independent Sets, *SIAM Journal of Computing* **6(3)** (1977) 505–517.

[TSOA 80]   S. Tsukiyama, I. Shirakawa, H. Ozaki, and H. Ariyoshi, An Algorithm to Enumerate all Cutsets of a Graph in Linear Time per Cutset, *Journal of the ACM* **27(4)** (1980) 619–632.

[Tur 88]   J. S. Turner, Almost all k-Colorable Graphs are Easy to Color, *Journal of Algorithms* **9** (1988) 63–82.

[Val 79]   L. G. Valiant, The Complexity of Enumeration and Reliability Problems, *SIAM Journal of Computing* **8(3)** (1979) 410–421.

[Wil 89]   H. S. Wilf, *Combinatorial Algorithms: An Update* (SIAM, 1989).

[Wor 87]   N. C. Wormald, Generating Random Unlabelled Graphs, *SIAM Journal of Computing* **16(4)** (1987) 717–727.

[Wri 61]   E. M. Wright, Counting Coloured Graphs, *Canada Journal of Mathematics* **13** (1961) 683–693. (See also R. C. Read and E. M. Wright, Coloured Graphs: A Correction and Extension, *Canada Journal of Mathematics* **22(3)** (1970) 594–596.)

[Wri 64]   E. M. Wright, Counting Coloured Graphs II, *Canada Journal of Mathematics* **16** (1964) 128–135.

[WROM 86]   R. A. Wright, B. Richmond, A. Odlyzko, and B. D. McKay, Constant Time Generation of Free Trees, *SIAM Journal of Computing* **15(2)** (1986) 540–548.

[You 69]   P. R. Young, Toward a Theory of Enumerations, *Journal of the ACM* **16(2)** (1969) 328–348.

Lightning Source UK Ltd.
Milton Keynes UK
22 March 2010

151716UK00001B/19/P